A Political Economy of the United States, China, and India

The precipitous rise in global and national economic inequality, which the inexorable force of globalization promised to address with affluence and abundance for all, has returned with a vengeance. The problem of worsening socioeconomic inequality and how best to ameliorate this pernicious resurgence occupies center stage of national and international politics. This study investigates the coexistence of high rates of economic growth and unparalleled prosperity (including a review of the decline in poverty levels in China and India and many other developing countries) with rises in income and wealth inequality in the United States, China, and India. The author examines the overall effectiveness of the measures taken by these three countries to address such anomalies and what they should do to tackle the problem of widening inequality. This study breaks new ground by providing an original comparative analysis of the challenges facing the world's three major economies.

Shalendra D. Sharma is a professor in the Department of Politics at the University of San Francisco as well as the Lee Shau Kee Foundation Chair Professor of Political Science at Lingnan University, Hong Kong.

A Political Economy of the United States, China, and India

Prosperity with Inequality

SHALENDRA D. SHARMA

Lingnan University, Hong Kong

CAMBRIDGE
UNIVERSITY PRESS

CAMBRIDGE
UNIVERSITY PRESS

University Printing House, Cambridge CB2 8BS, United Kingdom

One Liberty Plaza, 20th Floor, New York, NY 10006, USA

477 Williamstown Road, Port Melbourne, VIC 3207, Australia

314–321, 3rd Floor, Plot 3, Splendor Forum, Jasola District Centre, New Delhi – 110025, India

79 Anson Road, #06–04/06, Singapore 079906

Cambridge University Press is part of the University of Cambridge.

It furthers the University's mission by disseminating knowledge in the pursuit of education, learning, and research at the highest international levels of excellence.

www.cambridge.org
Information on this title: www.cambridge.org/9781107183582
DOI: 10.1017/9781316871997

© Shalendra D. Sharma 2018

First published 2018

Printed in the United States of America by Sheridan Books, Inc.

A catalogue record for this publication is available from the British Library.

Library of Congress Cataloging-in-Publication Data
Names: Sharma, Shalendra D., author.
Title: A political economy of the United States, China, and India : prosperity
with inequality / Shalendra D. Sharma, University of San Francisco.
Description: Cambridge, United Kingdom ; New York, NY : Cambridge University
Press, 2018. | Includes bibliographical references and index.
Identifiers: LCCN 2017054572 | ISBN 9781107183582 (hbk : alk. paper)
Subjects: LCSH: Income distribution – United States. | Income distribution – China. | Income
distribution – India. | Equality – United States. | Equality – China. | Equality – India. | United
States – Economic policy. | China – Economic policy. | India – Economic policy.
Classification: LCC HC79.I5 S436 2018 | DDC 339.2–dc23
LC record available at https://lccn.loc.gov/2017054572

ISBN 978-1-107-18358-2 Hardback
ISBN 978-1-316-63500-1 Paperback

Contents

Figures

Tables

Preface

Even as global poverty levels have sharply declined, economic inequality has risen around the world, especially in the United States, China, and India. This study provides an authoritative account of a counterintuitive and paradoxical trend: growing prosperity and dramatic improvements in standards of living coupled with rapid rise in income and wealth inequality with reference to the world's three large economies: the United States, China, and India. Contextualized within a broad, comparative political economy framework, the study provides detailed and nuanced insights into the roots, nature, and extent of the inequality problem in the three countries as well as what these countries can do to ameliorate this serious problem. Among the highlights, the study provides a corrective to the Piketty thesis and explores the reasons why both democratic and authoritarian forms of governance have failed to promote more equitable development.

Acknowledgments

In writing this book I have incurred enormous debts, both professional and personal, to many colleagues and friends from around the world that are simply too extensive to adequately acknowledge. The extensive bibliography confirms my intellectual debt to numerous individuals and organizations – albeit, all such sources should be absolved of responsibility for any errors that remain in this text.

Nonetheless, it is with great pleasure that I extend my appreciation to some of them – with apologies to those I have inadvertently left out. At the University of San Francisco, I thank Elliot Neaman, Hartmut Fischer, Tony Fels, Michael Lehmann, Max Neiman, Sunny Wong, Horacio Camblong, Jay Gonzales, Steve Roddy, James Taylor, and Xiaohua Yang for their friendship and support. For proficient administrative assistance and unwavering support for all things big and small, I extend my thanks to Spencer Rangitsch, whose always-incisive comments and deep and critical insights were of great help to me. I owe a huge debt of gratitude to Lingnan University for providing a supporting intellectual environment indispensable for research and writing. Indeed, my affiliation with Lingnan has been my good fortune, for without Lingnan's steadfast support this book would not have come to fruition. For their wise counsel and consistent encouragement, I thank my colleagues, in particular, Leonard Cheng, Yiu-chung Wong, Jesus Seade, Baohui Zhang, Che-po Chan, Ka Ho Mok, Ersu Ding, Marcus Chu Pok, Wai-Keung Tam, Tommy Yeung, Kenneth Law, Simon Fan, Richard Davis, Koon-hung Chan, Lin Ping, Zong-qi Cai, Wendy Lai, Sharon Tam, and Charles Kwong. I also extend my appreciation to Lingnan's Council and Court members, in particular, Bernard Charnwut Chan, Rex Pk-kuen Auyeung, Simon Ip, Loretta Shuen, Albert Ip, and Dr. Frank Sai-Kit Law, for their heartfelt support, good advice, and inspiration.

This is my third book with Cambridge University Press. I have nothing but the highest praise for the Press and my editors. One could not ask for more thoughtful and meticulous editors than Robert Dreesen and Meera Seth. I am deeply indebted to both for their interest in this project and for their sound advice, professional guidance, and extraordinary forbearance. It has been a great pleasure working with both of them. I am deeply indebted to the reviewers for Cambridge University Press who provided thoughtful, detailed, and trenchant criticisms and suggestions that have significantly improved this book. I have tried my best to incorporate their critique, suggestions, and recommendations in the following pages. However, I take full responsibility for the remaining flaws and omissions.

My greatest debt, however, is to my wife Vivian and our son Krishan. They have been a pillar of support from the beginning to end. For their unconditional love and support, I humbly dedicate this book to Vivian with gratitude and affection. Without her, this book could not have been written.

Introduction: Prosperity with Inequality in the Age of Globalization

The precipitous rise in global and national economic inequalities which the inexorable and transformative power of globalization promised to relegate to the dustbin of history with rising affluence and abundance has come back to haunt the world with a vengeance. A chorus of voices representing a wide spectrum of viewpoints has placed the problem of worsening socioeconomic inequalities – with a small percentage of households accumulating a disproportionate share of income and wealth and the majority experiencing falling or stagnating incomes – and how best to ameliorate this pernicious resurgence back to the center stage of national and international politics.

Deep resentment, indeed visceral anger, against the fast-widening income and wealth gap between the alleged "1 percent" hedonistic and pretentious "haves" and the "99 percent" disenfranchised and dispensable "have-nots" has served as a lightning rod for popular discontent and a rallying cry for the "Occupy Wall Street" movement in the United States – which began symbolically in Manhattan's Zuccotti Park. Seeing it as their inalienable right to end such inequalities by whatever means possible, the occupiers, often with unrestrained vehemence, have called for the destruction of the "new Gilded Age" with both punitive and compensatory redistribution of wealth and power to the dispossessed majority.[1] Although eschewing the incendiary language and methods of the "occupiers," Pope Francis nevertheless preaches and chastises with equal measure at every opportunity that vicarious "inequality is the root of social ills" which can only be cured by "rejecting the idolatry of money and the absolute autonomy of markets and financial speculation." Admittedly finding inspiration in the Pope's words, President Barak Obama called "inequality the defining issue of our times." In his 2014 State of the Union address, Obama was unapologetic when he noted that "after four years of economic growth, corporate profits and stock prices have rarely been higher, and those at the top have never done better. But average wages have barely budged. Inequality has deepened. Upward mobility has stalled." The President promised to use his "executive order privilege" to correct this "unfairness" – beginning with raising

American workers' minimum wage from $7.25 to $10 an hour. This, the President claimed, would combat the twin evils of widening inequality and poverty.

The multitude of voices has precipitated a seismic shift in attitudes towards the problem of rising inequality. Even the world's premier financial institution, the International Monetary Fund (IMF), long accused of representing the interests of the "1 percent," seems chastened. In recent months the IMF addressed the problem of rising worldwide inequality head-on (an issue that, in the past, it left to its sister-organization, the World Bank) by acknowledging that "there is growing evidence that high income inequality can be detrimental to achieving macroeconomic stability and growth" and that "reform of expenditure and tax policies" can "help achieve distributive objectives ... " (IMF 2014, 2–3). The Fund's conclusion was based on an internal "Staff Discussion Paper" (see Ostry, Berg, and Tsangarides 2014), which, after exhaustive analysis of a large dataset covering some 150 countries over 40 years, found a negative correlation between income inequality and future economic growth – showing that societies with more unequal income distributions grow at a slower pace, and that a more equitable distribution of income does not have a negative effect on economic growth. Perhaps this explains why Christine Lagarde, the head of the IMF, broke with the organization's usual cautious reticence to solicitously warn that "rising inequality and economic exclusion can have pernicious effects ... in the years ahead, it will no longer be enough to look simply at economic growth ... we will need to ask if this growth is inclusive."

Apparently, even those most oblivious and disconnected from the objective reality of human want and anguish – whom Freeland (2012) has called the world's "super-rich" – billionaires, corporate CEOs, heads of state, celebrities, and the nouveau-riche who make the annual pilgrimage to the very exclusive World Economic Forum in Davos, have become decidedly uncomfortable with the growing economic divide. During the 2014 Davos, these cloistered elites found inspiration in an exaggerated, if not alarmist, 2013 Oxfam report that with zealous certitude asserts that the world's 85 richest people have more wealth than the poorest 3.5 billion – the vast majority of whom exist on less than a dollar a day. It seems that the Davos elites were so moved by the plight of the have-nots, not to mention the many risks associated with such capricious inequalities, that they departed from their usual issuance of standard press briefings to release a lengthy programmatic action plan on how best to narrow the widening economic divide (WEF 2014). Beyond their usual exhortation of the innate superiority of the market system as best antidote to sustained economic growth and poverty reduction, they did acknowledge that free-market capitalism could do with some fine tuning. In the end, the Davos participants endorsed a benevolently paternalist form of wealth redistribution, including strengthening of social safety nets to ameliorate the suffering of those precariously trapped in poverty and destitution and to substantively narrow the gap between haves and have-nots. For good measure, they rhetorically warned that failure to heed their words could trigger a tsunami of violence and instability the likes of which the world has not seen.

The release of Thomas Piketty's (2014) *Capital in the Twenty-First Century* in early 2014 with its trenchant indictment of the growing income inequality both nationally and globally gave intellectual legitimacy to the widespread perception that economic inequalities had grown to such disproportionately ostentatious levels that dichotomy of "1 percent" versus the "99 percent" was no exaggeration. Moreover, punitive expropriation of income and wealth of the so-called conspicuous and pretentious nouveau-riche (who lack the traditional bourgeois restraint and propriety) via increased taxes – that Piketty unflinchingly advocates – as entirely justified. Hailed in near-reverential terms as the new "Marx," Piketty soon acquired the mantle of a new "progressive" hero, and his dense, 700-page academic tome became an international bestseller. Drawing meticulously on a prodigious data base, Piketty provides a scrupulous assessment of how and why since the latter part of the 1970s income and wealth inequality have risen to astronomical levels in the OECD or the advanced industrial economies, and in particular in the United States and the United Kingdom. Specifically, Piketty rigorously documents that not only the share of the richest 1 percent in total pre-tax income increased in most OECD countries over the past three decades, overall, the pre-tax/pre-transfer "market" inequality as well as inequality in disposable incomes has risen in most rich countries over the last three decades. Moreover, although the top 1 percent in the United States and the United Kingdom captured a disproportionate share of overall income growth, countries that traditionally have enjoyed a more equal income and wealth distribution, including Finland, the Netherlands, Canada, Norway, Sweden, and other Nordic countries have also seen a sharp increase in the share of income going to the most affluent, in particular, the top 1 percent. Indeed, the old distinction between "Social Europe versus Liberal America" is increasingly a misnomer, as even the traditionally egalitarian Scandinavian economies are faced with rising inequality (Kvist et al. 2012).

According to Piketty, the widening income and wealth inequalities in the advanced industrial economies (indeed, the widening inequalities worldwide) is fundamentally rooted in the pathology of the capitalist system. Specifically, capitalism operates according to inexorable laws – in Piketty's inimitable formulation as $r>g$. That is, "r" is the rate of return on capital whereas "g" is the rate of economic growth. The "central contradiction of capitalism" is that the rate of return on capital (r) will always exceed the rate of economic growth (g). Because the rate of return on capital is higher than the economy's overall rate of growth, widening income and wealth inequality is intrinsic to capitalism. Drawing on Marx's famous critique that the impersonal and dehumanizing calculus of the capitalist system ensures that the returns on capital (which to Piketty are mainly wealth in the form of financial assets and equity) tend to be far greater than the growth rate of the economy, Piketty concludes that the owners of equity will always see their wealth grow much faster than those depended on earning income from labor. And since capital tends to be concentrated in very few hands while income generated from labor is more widely dispersed, it is hardly surprising that the relatively small capital-owning class have seen their incomes and overall wealth grow at an exponential rate, whereas the vast majority who sell their labor for a living have become pauperized as their incomes have either stagnated or declined in real purchasing terms.

Again, in step with Marx's pessimistic *Zeitgeist*, Piketty argues with almost missionary certitude that capitalism's fundamental nature – indeed, its irreducible essence – means that income and wealth inequality are not only transmitted over time, they also worsen over time. Drawing assiduously from an enormous volume of comparative data, Piketty notes that although advanced capitalist economies have grown at a rate of 1 to 1.5 percent per year, the average return on capital has been between 4 to 5 percent per year. He argues that the sharp rise in income inequality in the OECD economies, and in particular in the United States and the United Kingdom, has been driven mainly by steep increases in "wage inequality." Moreover, since income and wealth inequality increase as the economy's long-run rate of economic growth slows (as it has in the aftermath of the Great Recession and the ensuing slow recovery), Piketty warns that the trend towards slower growth in the advanced economies in years ahead will make inequalities in income and wealth even more pronounced and irrevocable. In fact, Piketty predicts a sustained increase in economic inequality because, as he argues, the distribution of wealth is mainly the outcome of the after-tax rate of return on capital minus the growth rate of GDP (i.e., r – g). Since wealth grows irrevocably along with the after-tax return on capital (r), while wages grow along with GDP growth (g), and because wealth will inevitably become more important than earned income, inequality will also sharply increase.

Just as it was for Marx, to Piketty the capitalist system characterized by impersonal, hierarchical, and exploitative market relations is the principal determinant of socioeconomic inequalities. In sharp contrast to the Nobel prize-winning economists Paul Krugman's impassioned *The Conscience of a Liberal* (2007) and *End This Depression Now* (2012) and Joseph Stiglitz's iconoclastic riposte, *The Price of Inequality: How Today's Divided Society Endangers Our Future* (2012), both of whom blame "market imperfections" for the widening wealth and income inequality, Piketty unequivocally argues that the rise in inequality "... has nothing to do with any market imperfection: the more perfect the capital market (in the economist's sense), the more likely r is to be greater than g" (Piketty 2014, 24). In other words, the higher the ratio, the wider the inequality gap. Given this, Piketty fatalistically concludes that inequality under capitalism is not some remediable contingent problem. Rather, even the well-intentioned reformist and redistributionist prerogatives of liberal democracies have failed and will continue to fail to meaningfully ameliorate income and wealth inequality.

THE NATURE OF ECONOMIC INEQUALITY

Although inequality can be deconstructed into separate categories based on "income," "wealth," "consumption," and "opportunity," income and wealth inequality usually receive the most attention. Income inequality (measured by the Gini coefficient, which takes values between 0 and 1, with 0 representing perfect equality) measures the distribution of income at a moment in time.[2]

Following Saez and Zucman (2014), wealth can be defined as "the stock of all the assets people own, including their homes, pension saving, and bank accounts, minus all debts. Wealth can be self-made out of work and saving, but it can also be inherited." Moreover, wealthier households are not necessarily high-income households. Thus, wealth is different from income – which measures the annual wages, interests, profits, and other sources of earnings. However, "income" is not always the best measure of inequality, and, contrary to conventional wisdom, neither is it easy to measure income inequality. Not only has income inequality historically fluctuated, the potentially several sources of income such as from wages, capital gains income, employer-provided health insurance, and other non-salaried compensation, not to mention that an individual's (and household's) income can vary significantly based on their access to credit, government welfare assistance, or family wealth, make measuring income inequality a challenge.[3] Yet, income is the most widely used indicator – with researchers and policy makers continuously refining the quantitative data by employing various metrics and definitions of income. For example, in many countries (including the United States), income inequality measures use income before taking into account taxes and transfer payments such as Social Security, food stamps, and unemployment benefits. Research confirms that "wealth" is more unevenly distributed than "income," while "consumption" tends to be less concentrated at the upper end than either wealth or income. Indeed, research often finds that consumption inequality is less than income inequality.[4] Adding further complexity, an individual's "net worth" (defined as household assets less liabilities) with assets that include both financial and non-financial (car, house) assets are not adequately factored in when measuring inequality.

It is well accepted that if an economy is to function relatively smoothly, individuals need incentives to work, innovate, consume, and save and be rewarded according to their intrinsic or marketable skills, intellect, and knowledge, as well as perseverance and grit. Certainly, the potential for a large economic reward plays an essential role in motivating innovators and entrepreneurs to take personal risks – their success benefiting not only themselves, but also the broader economy. Hence, conventional macroeconomic theory teaches that there is a "trade-off" between equality and growth – for example, since high-income individuals and households save more, greater inequality translates into more savings and investment – which, in turn, translates into higher output. Given this, the argument goes, some level of inequality is inevitable, if not desirable. Indeed, some degree of inequality in income and wealth is inevitable in a market-based economic system, even with completely equal opportunity, because variations in effort, skill, and luck will generate variations in outcomes.

The late economist Arthur Okun (1975) famously pointed out that some level of inequality may be necessary to generate economic growth because without the promise of economic gains, individual enterprise and innovation would suffer. Thus, Okun's apt warning that societies cannot have both perfect equality and perfect efficiency. Thus, the essential question is not whether inequality is "good" or "bad." Rather, as long as there is emphasis on "equal opportunity" (not "equal outcomes," as unequal outcomes may provide incentives for greater individual effort and determination), and as long as economic growth is broadly "lifting all boats," inequality may not be a problem.[5] Moreover, who could possibly object to the celebrated "Pareto criterion" – that is, if some people become better off without making anyone worse off, what is the problem? However, it is a problem if policies are designed to reduce income inequality by redistributing income from the productive to the less productive in the name of "fairness," or if inequality level keeps widening because of stagnant or declining income for the majority, or has reached the so-called "tipping point" and begins to act as a threat to economic growth and social and economic mobility, and in particular, intergenerational mobility.[6] As Panagariya (2010, 23) has succinctly noted, "inequality is certainly more tolerable in a growing economy. When everyone is moving up on an escalator, the fact that some manage to walk or run up on it is less bothersome than if the escalator is stuck, leaving some with no hope of reaching the top."

Although it is clichéd, it is important to reiterate that inequality is relative – influenced undoubtedly by the peculiarities of geography, politics, and level of economic development. Furthermore, inequality, and in particular wage inequality, has followed a broadly U-shaped pattern from its extreme in the early twentieth century to a period of more shared and equitable prosperity from the end of WWII to the mid-1970s (a period called the "Great Compression") and its sharp rise since. Hence, inequality is not only relative, the extent of measurable income gap varies, sometimes significantly, from country to country, and the levels of economic polarization depend on what evidence one looks at and how one interprets the data (Milanovic 2007; 2011; Radelet 2015). For example, the levels and extent of inequality can vary (sometimes sharply) depending how one puts controls for government taxes and transfers, household size, and the differences in the cost of living in the case for geographic comparisons. Also, in sharp contrast to Piketty, who views the self-perpetuating nature of income and wealth inequality as the natural equilibrium of capitalism (barring unprecedented events such as wars and economic crisis), or follows the "Kuznets curve" (the hypothesis developed by the Nobel Prize-winning economist Simon Kuznets), which claims that economic growth first increases income inequality within countries before reducing it – Milanovic (2016) proposes the idea of "Kuznets waves" to suggest that over time inequality rises, falls, and rises again in an endless cycle.

Even as income and wealth inequality has seen sharp increases in most countries, the absolute level of economic well-being has also improved, in many cases, immeasurably since the onset of the Industrial Revolution (Kenny 2011). In other words, although the fruits of economic growth (such as income) are not always evenly shared, overall all deciles of the income distribution have benefited from economic growth, even when inequality has increased. For example, although over the past two decades real household incomes in China have averaged annual growth of 10 percent and more, this growth has also been accompanied by an exponential rise in income inequality. Yet, this rise in inequality does not mean a stagnation of incomes for the poorer households or those in the lower income quintiles, but rather strong income growth among the richer households. According to the United Nations *Millennium Development Goals Report 2015* (United Nations 2015), the proportion of people living in extreme poverty in the developing countries declined by 50 percent over 1999 and 2011 – albeit, progress remained uneven, with sub-Saharan Africa making a modest reduction of just 21 percent, while in East Asia extreme poverty declined by 82 percent.[7] It is agreed that this reduction in global inequality has been driven by a convergence in average incomes across countries – propelled by rising incomes in large, populous countries such as China and India. This explains why global inequality has declined, but within-country inequality has increased. Indeed, in contrast to Piketty's rendition, Milanovic's (2016) *Global Inequality*, which focuses more on global than on national inequality, including more emphasis on income than wealth inequality, finds that while inequality is rising within most countries (in particular, the high-income countries), global income inequality has been steadily falling since 2000.[8] To Milanovic (2016) this is because global inequality or the sum of all national inequalities plus the sum of differences in mean incomes across countries (that is, the sum of intra- and inter-country inequality) has been declining due to the rise of emerging economies (especially in Asia) even as intra-country inequality is rising in many countries.

Similarly, Radelet (2016, 85–86) notes, "since the early 1990s, daily life in poor countries has been changing profoundly for the better: one million people have escaped extreme poverty, average incomes have doubled, infant death rates have plummeted, millions more girls have enrolled in school, chronic hunger has been cut almost in half, deaths from malaria and other diseases have declined dramatically ... This unprecedented progress goes way beyond China and India and has touched hundreds of millions of people in dozens of developing countries across the globe ... the number of extreme poor has fallen by more than 400 million. Since the 1980s, more than 60 countries have reduced

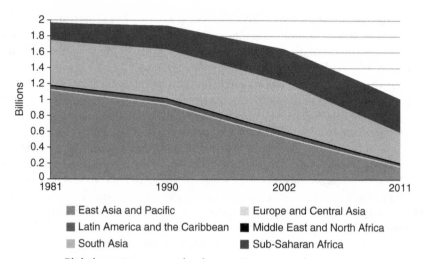

FIGURE 1.1 Global extreme poverty level
Source: World Bank, Our World in Data 2015.

the number of their citizens who are impoverished, even as their overall populations have grown." Thus, the growing income and wealth inequality does not necessarily mean a rise in poverty or declines in disposable income, purchasing power, and living standards for those at the lower end of the income distribution (Figure 1.1). Rather, it means that even as incomes have grown for most individuals and households, the rich are getting richer faster because the gains have been proportionally larger at the higher end of the income levels.

This explains the current trend of declining inequality among countries, but rising inequality within countries. As Bourguignon (2015) and Deaton (2013), among others, have noted this is partly because the "great divergence" in the average incomes that occurred during the nineteenth and early twentieth centuries was followed by a rather long period of postwar stability, including the unprecedented global economic integration of the past decades, which resulted in the "great convergence" of income and wealth. Specifically, as predicted by the "neoclassical convergence growth theory," technology spillovers, international capital flows, deepening trade links, and huge economies like China and India moving rapidly up the global income distribution have contributed substantially to income convergence across countries, including greater economic convergence between the developed and developing nations (Bourguignon 2015; Solow 1956). Indeed, according to Barro (2015), there is an "iron law of convergence" suggesting that both low-income (or the so-called "least developed countries") and developing nations can constantly reduce their income gap with the developed economies by half every 35 years. The extraordinarily rapid economic growth in China and India (which together make up about two-fifths of humanity), and the resultant meteoric rise in income and wealth (especially in China) that were simply unimaginable just a few decades earlier, explain the sharp decline in global household inequality, including changes in the distribution of relative average incomes of countries, weighted by population. This also explains why the proportion of the world's population living in extreme indigence has fallen from 32 percent in 1990 to about 16 percent in 2010.[9] Second, because economic growth is highly correlated with poverty reduction, growth matters. Therefore, even if the top 10, the top 1, or the top 0.1 percent of the population enjoy a disproportionately bigger share of the economic pie, the size of pie has also become bigger, enabling even the bottom or poorest percentile of the population to improve their overall economic well-being (Radelet 2015). Tyler Cowen (2011) cogently captures this paradox, noting that although income inequality is rising, the inequality of personal well-being has been declining:

the inequality of personal well-being is sharply down over the past hundred years and perhaps over the past twenty years as well. Bill Gates is much, much richer than I am, yet it is not obvious that he is much happier if, indeed, he is happier at all. I have access to penicillin, air travel, good cheap food, the Internet and virtually all of the technical innovations that Gates does. Like the vast majority of Americans, I have access to some important new pharmaceuticals, such as statins to protect against heart disease. To be sure, Gates receives the very best care from the world's top doctors, but our health outcomes are in the same ballpark. I don't have a private jet or take luxury vacations, and – I think it is fair to say – my house is much smaller than his. I can't meet with the world's elite on demand. Still, by broad historical standards, what I share with Bill Gates is far more significant than what I don't share with him.

Yet, this paradox – that of declining economic inequality among countries, but the widening of income and wealth disparities within countries alongside impressive gains in aggregate GDP growth and improvements in living standards of broad cross-sections of the populace – is not something one would glean from Piketty's rendition. Nevertheless, the empirical reality of the last several decades unequivocally confirms that in almost every country, including the poorest, even as the income and wealth gap has dramatically widened with the most affluent and the middle and upper-middle income groups capturing a disproportionately large share of the overall gains, sustained economic growth has also translated into higher incomes for the lower-middle, the working class, and the poor – for the latter, at least in terms of perceptible and measurable improvements in their purchasing power and ability to respond to the everyday adversities of life. In China and India (and many countries), sustained economic growth has not only created new classes of millionaires and billionaires, but also rapidly expanding middle classes who have seen an astronomical expansion in their incomes and wealth (Freund 2016). Similarly, as noted, growth has also translated into sharp reductions in crushing or "absolute" poverty – and in the process fundamentally transformed the lives of millions of people for the better.[10]

Thus, we are witnessing a counterintuitive and paradoxical phenomenon that can best be described as "growth with rising inequality, but declining poverty" – with many countries becoming less poor and more prosperous, but also more unequal in terms of income and wealth distribution. This trend is quite pervasive – confined not only to China, India, and the United States, but also the OECD countries like Denmark, Norway, and Finland with traditionally low levels of inequality.

Given this, how then to reconcile Piketty with the other face of "capital" and "capitalism": namely, that laissez-faire or "neoliberal" capitalism and the deepening global economic integration it has created in its wake has generated unprecedented levels of growth that is directly responsible for higher living standards in the advanced economies and for the dramatic reduction in worldwide poverty – lifting millions out of abject poverty in China, India, and elsewhere in the developing world. Economics Nobel laureate Angus Deaton's (2013) *The Great Escape* persuasively argues that worldwide "life is better now than at almost any time in history." What explains the startling divergence in Piketty and Deaton's renditions? In short, although at first glance these two narratives seem irreconcilable, in fact, they are both correct as each portrays a different aspect of a multifaceted reality. The evidence confirms that economic growth can generate simultaneous sharp increases in income inequality and equally sharp declines in poverty. Second, contrary to popular perception, Piketty's study is not about the trends in the global economy. Rather, his study provides an aggregate portrait of within-country inequality in the advanced OECD countries – most, if not all, of which have experienced modest growth rates (including sharp economic declines during the global financial crisis), yet an exponential widening of the income and wealth gap.

BRINGING POLITICS IN

Although the pivotal role market forces play in creating and distributing wealth and in the process shaping the fortunes of nations is undeniable, the dangers of single-minded and dogmatic focus on economic variables to explain such complex processes are also well known. Clearly, Piketty is cognizant of this as he notes that "one should be wary of any economic determinism in regard to inequalities of income and wealth. The history of the distribution of wealth has always been deeply political, and cannot be reduced to purely economic mechanisms" (Piketty 2014, 20). Yet, Piketty's account – which come perilously close to ignoring its own advice – remains unabashedly doctrinaire and monocausal.

Piketty not only views inequality as a natural outcome of capitalism, he is so fixated on "capital" that the non-economic exigencies of rising income and wealth inequality such as political influence and control are conspicuously absent in his analysis. In fact, Piketty's exclusive focus on "capital" leads him to present a rather rigid and starkly narrow picture of the sources, nature, and extent of income disparities, their socioeconomic and political implications, and how best to address this problem.

Certainly, economic transformations are constantly reshaping domestic and international politics. Yet, given that the market system is intricately and inextricably "embedded" in the political system, economic outcomes cannot just be the natural consequences of market forces (Polanyi 1944). In other words, politics plays a conspicuous role and can significantly shape and determine economic outcome – including the inequalities generated by public policies that distort market allocations of resources. In their acclaimed *Why Nations Fail: The Origins of Power, Prosperity, and Poverty*, Acemoglu and Robinson (2012) argue that economic development succeeds or fails depending on the "inclusiveness" of a nation's political and economic institutions. Nations blessed with inclusive political institutions have a well-functioning state and government, a "pluralistic" and representative distribution of political power, including limits on that power through the rule of law and regular open and fair elections. Inclusive economic institutions include secure property rights and competitive markets that allow ease of starting new businesses, and provide incentives for the citizenry to participate in their nation's economic life. On the other hand, nations fail when their institutions are "extractive" – that is, when political institutions serve and protect the interests of elites either through force or without imposing formal legal constraints on state power, and in the process allow the powerful privileged access to power and wealth. Of course, Acemoglu and Robinson's theory is too simple to elucidate the complexities of national development and social change. For example, although China is plagued with antediluvian extractive political and economic institutions – which should have suffocated growth – its turbocharged economic growth over the past three decades is the envy of the world. On the other hand, Acemoglu and Robinson claim that long-run growth under extractive regimes is unsustainable is persuasive – albeit, "long-run" can also mean that economic growth can continue in the foreseeable future under China's extractive regime. The case of India and the United States shows that democracies can have both inclusive as well as extractive institutions. A large body of scholarship underscores that the public policy preferences of the rich and powerful (rather than the masses) usually gets implemented in all types of political systems, including democracies like the United States and India. In fact, in democracies with wealthy individuals and groups exerting outsized influence in the political arena, the preferences of economically powerful have greater influence on the policy process than the preferences of ordinary citizens. The fact that in democracies, economic elites use their power and influence to shape and determine political outcomes is hardly a new revelation. In short, democracies can be just as extractive, and non-democracies or what the authors refer to as "autocracies" can have inclusive elements. As the following pages illustrate, such institutionalist insights can usefully shed light on the roots and nature of growth with inequality in the seemingly anomalous case of United States, China, and India.

Yet, open political systems can also act as a countervailing force against widening inequality. This is particularly true in "inclusive" representative political systems, not only because democracies give voice and representation to key stakeholders and "tame" markets with the establishment of legal and welfare protections, but also because the existence of checks and balances ("veto players") can act as a subtle constraint against unilateral and capricious policy actions. The classical theory of political economy (Meltzer and Richard 1981; Romer 1975; Roberts 1977) claims that high levels of economic inequality in a liberal democracy will ultimately force political elites to acquiesce to the "median voter" (voter at the median of the income distribution), to support higher taxes on the affluent and a more balanced and equitable distribution of income.[11] Similarly, research going back to Schumpeter (1942) has claimed that because democracies lower the "costs" of political participation for organized labor, unions are able to influence centralized wage bargaining and significantly mitigate income and wealth inequality (also Acemoglu 2008; Rodrik 1999). Stigler (1970) claims that since democracies transfer political power to the middle classes (instead of the majority working classes), redistribution can only take place if the middle classes support reformist and distributional policies. Finally, because gratuitous inequalities are incongruent with democratic and liberal ideals of social justice and equality and because democratic rule provides opportunities for vibrant civic and associational life that potentially empower the electorate to hold elected officials accountable, democratic governments are more inclined to adopt reformist and redistributive policies and programs such as more generous welfare and social safety-net spending and progressive taxation, including minimum wages and price subsidies to assist the widest possible sectors of society.[12] Given these, what explains why the world's richest democracy (the United States) and the largest (India) have defied expectations and failed to respond effectively to the problem of widening socioeconomic inequalities?[13] On the other hand, if insulation from powerful and obstinate societal and political pressures and longer time horizons give autocrats greater flexibility in policy decisions, what explains why the avowedly "pro-people" and "pro-masses" Communist leaders of China have failed to reconcile China's rapid and high economic growth with a fairer distribution of the fruits of growth?

FOCUS OF THIS STUDY

This study's central purpose is to investigate, elucidate, and provide more rigorous answers to a number of interrelated questions that have animated researchers, policy makers, and the general public in recent years. Specifically, what explains an anomaly, indeed a paradox: (a) the seeming coexistence of high rates of economic growth and unparalleled prosperity (including unprecedented declines in poverty levels in China and India and many other emerging market economies), (b) the coexistence of relatively low to moderate growth rates in the advanced economies over the period 1985–2015, and (c) in all settings – with particular reference to three sovereign states: the United States, China, and India – what explains why economic growth (either high, moderate, or low) have resulted in an equally ostentatious rise in income and wealth inequality? In addition, what accounts for the variations in the similarities and differences in outcomes in these three countries? And, third, how have these three sovereigns tried to address these anomalies and their overall effectiveness, and what should these countries do to ameliorate the problem of widening economic inequality?

More specifically, in the United States, although extreme poverty and destitution have been largely eliminated, the past three decades has also ushered in a "new gilded age," as incomes and wealth are now concentrated in fewer hands than at any time since the 1920s. In the case of post-reform China and India, even as sustained high rates of economic growth have emancipated millions of people from crushing poverty and abject deprivation and allowed the hitherto teeming masses to escape from the vicious cycle of poverty and indigence (albeit, illiberal China has been much more successful than democratic India), income and wealth disparities have also sharply increased, with a relatively small percentage of the population becomingly unimaginably rich and influential. In fact, the "socialist" Peoples Republic of China today also has the dubious distinction of being the most unequal country in the world in terms of income and wealth distribution, and democratic India is not too far behind in joining the ranks of the "most unequal."

These antinomies are explained through the prism of a broad political economy framework that deconstructs and untangles the ambiguities, contradictions, discrepancies, and countervailing tendencies of an exceedingly complex, prodigious, and amorphous process often arbitrarily (and impeccably) compartmentalized as "globalization," "capitalism," and "political systems" or "political order." In reality, globalization, capitalism, and a nation's political-institutional systems are deeply and intimately intertwined, their interstices and interactions blurring the distinctions between them, besides influencing and shaping each other indelibly and in multiplicity of ways. These forces also operate simultaneously at various levels – at the so-called "global," "regional," "national," and "local" levels – sometimes ebbing and flowing in synchronized tandem, and sometimes subversively pushing against each other. Given the strategic calculations as well as the conflicts and complicity inherent in asymmetrical interactions based on mutually beneficial cooperation as well as self-interested competition, it is not surprising that the outcomes often tend to be untidy and dissonant, making them both unpredictable and difficult to determine.

Economic Globalization

Beginning in the mid-1980s, the world economy entered a phase of rapid globalization. Falling trade barriers – in particular, lower tariffs negotiated as part of the Uruguay Round of multilateral trade negotiations – coupled with regional trade agreements such as the North American Free Trade Agreement (NAFTA), rapidly declining transportation costs, the revolution in information and communication technology which facilitated the dramatic increase in the tradability of services, the breaking-up of the production process across geographic regions and in stages, with value added at each stage, often in different countries and regions (i.e., "global value chains"), deepening financial globalization (or the integration of a country's financial system with international financial markets and institutions), and the integration of large emerging markets like India and China into the global economy have been the catalyst behind the rapid growth in global trade and dramatic socioeconomic and political convergence between nations.[14]

Thus, globalization has entailed worldwide "interconnectedness," "integration," and "interdependence" via the exchange of technology, goods, capital, services, and ideas, as well as freer movement of people. However, globalization's social, economic, and political impact and ramifications are fiercely contested. In particular, the debates on the distributional effects of globalization are highly polarized and formulaic, with opposing sides often caricaturing each other's viewpoints. Indeed, the various competing camps, often coming from different schools and pedagogical traditions and using starkly different vocabulary, rarely engage with the other. If to some, globalization has ushered in (or has the potential to bring) ostensible and incalculable benefits by effortlessly "lifting all boats," others see it as an irreversible and cataclysmically unrelenting "race to the bottom."

No doubt, globalization's unprecedented ability to interconnect and synchronize both time and space – or what Ogle (2015) has termed the prosaic stuff of modern life, such as production and business cycles, work schedules, and delivery timetables across the world – has not only enabled a deeper integration of the world economy, but as "pro-globalizers" claim, such integration into the global economy allows countries and individuals to benefit from access to a wider variety of goods and services, lower prices, greater employment opportunities, and higher living standards. The more unabashed champions of globalization enthusiastically argue that trade is a positive-sum game where the winners' gains exceed the losers' losses, and since there is irrefutable link between free trade and growth (because countries that have become integrated into the global economy have seen a sharp reduction in the percentage of people living in extreme poverty), further expanding trade is good – as growth is good for all, and in particular for the poor (Bhagwati 2004; Friedman 2005; Hufbauer and Suominen 2010; Mishkin 2006).

Predictably, in diametric opposition, skeptics and "anti-globalizers" usually apocalyptically claim that globalization's impact is profoundly destructive because the invasive, unpredictable, and volatile exogenous forces make nations (and societies) vulnerable to the vicissitudes of international trade and the vagaries of fickle and footloose capital, besides benefitting a small minority of so-called "winners" at the expense of a large and growing underclass of "losers" – further sharpening and perpetuating entrenched inequalities and poverty (Dreze and Sen 2013; Gray 1999; Milanovic 2007; Rodrik 2011; Stiglitz 2002; 2012). Some even dismiss the claim that global poverty has actually declined (or declined substantially), arguing that such claims are due to statistical distortion from China and India's rapid economic growth. To the contrary, they claim that unrestrained and unfettered globalization has created conditions for increasing both absolute and relative poverty in many countries.

Undeniably, globalization is as Janus-faced as it is ubiquitous. Hence, not only do economic theory and reality not always align, it is also not always easy to distinguish correlation from causation. Nevertheless, globalization's promises and potential are at the same time irresistible, bewildering, and frightening. For sure, the fruits of globalization have benefitted some far more than others and have not always been as bountiful as expected and not always broadly shared. In fact, both the oft-celebrated universalizing impulse of globalization and its inexorable ability to "lift all boats" as well as the charge that it induces "race to the bottom" are exaggerations. Rather, the contradictions inherent in such an all-encompassing process as globalization have produced its own asymmetries and unintended outcomes. For example, analysts have long recognized the benefits of free trade – in particular, its ability to achieve the most efficient allocation of resources and improving overall well-being. However, free trade also has distributional consequences, as various groups and constituencies are impacted differently. According to Rodrik (2011), among others, this is because globalization has been built on a faulty asymmetry – with the trade agreements and the global regulatory regimes designed to protect and advance the interests of capital. On the other hand, the interests of labor (such as good wages and employment security) are left to market forces, on the assumption that the gains to owners of capital will spill over or "trickle-down" in the form of higher-paying and better jobs and increases in tax revenues for support social welfare. Exacerbating this, the fact that capital and corporations are free to move relatively unhindered across national borders while labor faces numerous (and punitive) restrictions means that economic risk and uncertainty are borne disproportionately by the immobile factor: labor. This in turn explains why economic downturns and recessions have severely impacted workers, but owners of capital are partially protected by their global financial diversification. Milanovic's (2011; 2016) cogent cross-country comparisons (using the extensive data from the World Bank's household surveys covering some 120 countries from 1988 to 2008) show that although open trade is mostly an economic win, not everyone within an economy will be a winner – especially if there are no mechanisms in place to cushion the negative consequences of trade. Milanovic's study finds that the major beneficiaries of globalization have been the world's richest 1 percent and the emerging "global middle class," estimated to number some 400 million people in countries like China, India, Indonesia, and Brazil. Specifically, the top

1 percent saw their real incomes increase by more than 60 percent during the 20-year period. In absolute terms, this translated into about $23,000 per capita per year, compared with some $400 for those around the median. That is, the inflation-adjusted real income of the global middle class rose to 80 percent between 1988 and 2008. By contrast, the real incomes for the bottom and the second-lowest deciles only saw a modest increase, while the incomes of world's poorest 5 percent remained stagnant. Milanovic concludes that overall the lower-middle class in rich countries, including the world's poor or those "at the very bottom of the income ladder," have, on balance, lost out. On the other hand, the "great winners have been the Asian poor and middle classes," with China accounting for more than half of the decline in global inequality over the past three decades (Milanovic 2016, 20).

However, in regard to consumption, a recent study of 40 countries, including 12 developing economies, shows that the consumption benefits of international trade are much larger for the poor, since international prices of traded goods on average drop more than that of the non-traded, which tend to be consumed by the rich (Fajgelbaum and Khandelwal 2016). To add further complexity, Jaumotte, Lall, and Papageorgiou's (2013) exhaustive study based on data using a newly compiled panel of 51 countries over a 23-year period from 1981 to 2003, notes, "our analysis finds that increasing trade and financial globalization have had separately identifiable and opposite effects on income distribution. Trade liberalization and export growth are found to be associated with lower income inequality, while increased financial openness is associated with higher inequality. However, their combined contribution to rising inequality has been much lower than that of technological change, both at a global level and especially markedly in developing countries" (Jaumotte, Lall, and Papageorgiou 2013, 274).

According to Baldwin (2016), the current "new age" of globalization is drastically different from the "old," which lasted roughly between 1820 to 1990. In the 1800s, globalization powered with steam power sharply lowered the costs of trade, triggering "a self-fueling cycle of industrial agglomeration and growth that propelled today's rich nations to dominance." However, this "new globalization," driven by real-time information technology and high-tech manufacturing has revolutionized, indeed disrupted, the earlier cross-border movement of capital, production, and distribution. The new globalization is fundamentally different because the resultant fragmentation of manufacturing into highly complex cross-border supply chains has not only facilitated offshoring, but also the rapid movement of labor-intensive work out to lower-wage countries – as seemingly predicted by the famous Heckscher–Ohlin model, which claimed that as an economy opens up to trade, it will be associated with increasing demand for the less-skilled labor so abundant in developing and low-income economies. Although this combination of high tech with low wages has helped propel the rapid industrialization of a number of developing nations, including greater industrial deepening in some of the world's "least-developed countries," it has also simultaneously contributed to deindustrialization and "hollowing out" of jobs in the advanced economies – with adverse consequences for the working and middle classes, including rising inequality and unprecedented political pressures.

Undoubtedly, the dramatic advances in real-time information-processing technologies, reduced communication and transportation costs, and innovative production processes have made a wide range of goods and services (including, financial, engineering, medical, and legal) tradable. Similarly, the reorganization of production along "global supply chains" (meaning a product could be designed with high-value added in the advanced economies and the intermediate-value components used in the product sourced from several countries and assembled in China) has led to efficiency gains such as increased productivity and lower prices.[15] Hence, the scale of cross-border flows of goods, services, and capital is now unprecedented. Yet, a growing body of research also confirms that, although the globalization of trade provides access to wider markets and allows for greater specialization and in the process reduces costs and boosts incomes, the intense competition it generates can also eliminate jobs and depress wages – especially in industries and businesses exposed to cheap foreign (mostly Chinese) imports – while at the same time boosting corporate profits. Compounding this, the predicted rapid growth of higher-skilled, knowledge-based employment in the advanced economies to offset the loss of lower-skilled, labor-intensive jobs has, on balance, not materialized, while the often ad hoc and inadequate re-skilling and retraining of displaced workers via the various trade adjustment assistance programs has made it difficult for many to find productive employment. Not surprisingly, this has led some to conclude that the gains of globalization have accrued disproportionately to seemingly galvanized conglomerations of "winners" and "losers" (Rodrik 2011; Stiglitz 2012; 2002). According to the "Skill-Biased Technological Change" (SBTC) hypothesis, the introduction of advanced technology, in particular automation, even as it has increased the productivity and wages of skilled workers, has negatively impacted large numbers of workers engaged in routine work.[16] In the OECD economies (and in India), the winners or the beneficiaries overwhelmingly have been the better-educated or those with marketable skills, while "deindustrialization" and outsourcing have negatively impacted blue-collar and low-skilled workers – albeit, workers in the emerging markets such as China have benefitted from their comparative advantage in cheap labor (Krugman 1994; Stiglitz 2012).

Because financial assets are disproportionately held by wealthier households, the income earned from capital and financial assets has served to widen the income and wealth gap between top and bottom percentiles in the income and wealth distribution. Overall, as Piketty notes, the sharp growth in income from capital has exacerbated income inequality in the advanced economies.

Furthermore, even as deepening financial globalization via the integration of global capital markets allocates resources more efficiently than domestic ones and has helped to spread wealth and affluence more widely than ever before (and in the process enabled millions to better their lives), the growing intimacy and interconnections between individuals, households, governments, and national economies – in particular, the unprecedented level of integration between financial institutions, both within and across national borders – also mean that problems in one area are rapidly amplified across the entire gamut (Abdelal 2007; Greenspan 1998). With financial integration blurring distinctions and with the business cycles becoming increasingly synchronized across countries, there has been a simultaneous increase in the incidence of financial crises, including banking crises, currency crises, debt crises, and "sudden stops" – referred by some as the "crisis of financialization" (Freeman 2010; Galbraith 2012). For example, large volumes of financial flows can fuel macroeconomic and financial imbalances (including credit booms as well as currency, maturity, and liquidity mismatches) that can abruptly unwind with negative, indeed destructive, consequences for the economy. Similarly, increased trading between banks, especially the need to refinance in foreign currencies has dramatically increased the banking sector's balance sheet exposure to foreign currencies. Compounding this, the integration of inherently fragile and unstable financial markets has made the financial system more prone to excess and more vulnerable to cycles of boom and bust. Mishkin (2011; 2006) points out that financial globalization not only makes it easier for capital (especially inflows) to fuel excessive risk-taking by market participants, it also facilitates simultaneous and rapid buildup of systemic risks across national boundaries, and in the process enables financial shocks to spread more rapidly within and across countries.

In fact, Krugman (2008) has succinctly described the financial contagion as spreading like a chain reaction via what he calls an international version of the "financial multiplier process," where a fall in asset values in one country depresses the balance sheets of highly leveraged institutions. This in turn not only depresses the demand for financial assets in other countries, but also reduces asset prices, besides wreaking havoc on bank balance sheets, and so on. In other words, the deepening integration of global financial markets has meant more rapid and powerful spillover across economies through both traditional and newer types of "transmission channels." Although spillovers through the traditional trade channels remain a central transmission mechanism (even though global trade patterns have become more diversified), financial spillovers have become more pronounced as the rising correlation of global equity prices and the potential for sudden capital flow reversals mean that shocks in the core can be transmitted with great speed and force through the financial system. For example, during the global financial crisis of the period 2007 to 2009, as US financial institutions began to sell their assets to raise cash, that led to sharp drops in stock prices in Europe, Japan, and in emerging economies, including the relative increase in the value of the US dollar against other currencies, a sharp reversal in capital flows, and a shortage of liquid foreign reserves. Similarly, in the midst of the crisis, with the nominal interest rates already reduced to nearly zero (the so-called "zero-bound"), central banks in the advanced economies began to engage in unconventional monetary policies (the so-called "quantitative easing" program) such as asset purchases – which had the unintended and negative spillover effect in emerging economies of triggering a surge in capital inflows, rising asset prices, and corporate borrowing and build-up of credit bubbles. Thus, the overall impact of economic globalization (intended and unintended) remains circumspect and inconclusive because the impact has been uneven and experienced differently by the various countries, constituencies, communities, economic sectors, and individuals.

Although globalization has ushered in a neoliberal convergence – that is, the policies as well as the political and institutional arrangements of the world's economies have become increasingly oriented towards open markets, free trade, and deepening global economic integration – nation-states, nevertheless, are also zealously uncompromising when it comes to protecting their sovereignty and independence. As Rodrik (2011; 2007) has noted, deepening economic integration also requires greater harmonization of laws and regulations across countries – something nation-states have been generally reluctant to do. Nevertheless, cross-border economic integration and the resultant competition and tensions between national sovereignty and economic integration have constrained the autonomy of governments. Hence, states do what they can to retain policy autonomy (of course, some are more capable and successful than others) in order to mediate the inimical pressures emanating from deepening global economic integration. Of course, a state's capacity and elasticity to negotiate and effectively respond to the pressures emanating from globalization can have significant implications for the economy – in particular, economic growth and income and wealth distribution. Certainly, large and diverse economies such as the United States, China, and India are far better placed than most to navigate the rapidly shifting and turbulent waves triggered by globalization.

Yet, as the following pages elucidate, even these behemoths are not entirely immune to external economic pressures – hence, their adoption of a mix of sometimes surreptitious policy stratagems designed, on one hand, to maximize the gains of globalization, and on the other, to insulate themselves from its downsides. Not surprisingly, even as these countries accept the benefits of an open global economic system, they have also not hesitated in erecting barriers to "manage" globalization. For example, although the United States is the world's most open economy, including the largest importer of foreign goods, the United States' share of global exports has steadily fallen over the past few decades in the face of growing competition from emerging economies, most notably China. Not surprisingly, increasing volumes of imports coupled with declines in exports have led the United States to run large trade deficits since the mid-1970s.[17] However, advanced tradable services, including financial services and consulting, legal services, information technology, robotics, and engineering, where the American economy is most competitive, also make up the sector that faces intense protectionism – much to the chagrin of American policy makers. For their part, China and India continue to delay opening certain so-called key or strategic sectors of their economies to foreign trade, besides imposing capital controls to limit the destabilizing effects of capital flows. Moreover, in democracies, where those adversely impacted by changes emanating from globalization tend to oppose them vociferously, including engaging in mass protest and civil disobedience, incumbent regimes face tremendous pressures to acquiesce to their domestic constituencies. Of course, governments' responses do not always have the desired or intended outcome – either domestically or internationally.

This explains why, even as countries open their economies to international commerce and trade to reap benefits from economic globalization, they also adopt strategies and practices to insulate themselves from its downsides – for example, through various forms of protectionism to better manage and regulate cross-border exchange, including adjusting their monetary and fiscal policies to influence domestic inflation and employment. Indeed, despite deepening interdependence, the economic preferences and interests of countries (at least, the major players like the United States, China, and India) do not always align, often exacerbating differences and constraining both bilateral and multilateral cooperation. Not surprisingly, history shows that globalization is not irreversible, nor is it inevitable. The victory of "Leave" in the British referendum on European Union membership and the anti-globalization sentiment expressed by Donald Trump and populists and nationalists around the world confirm a growing backlash against deepening global integration. The following country case studies shed light into these complex and contradictory processes by elucidating how the world's three large economies have mediated the pressures of globalization, including why and how the demands of global economic integration both force a degree of de facto cooperation between them, as well as accentuating tensions and conflict, and of course, why on the one hand, globalization has helped boost per-capita incomes, including for even the poorest households (albeit, incomes of the rich have increased at a much faster rate), and on the other, sharply widened income and wealth inequality.

Capitalism

To Piketty, the fundamental problem with free-market capitalist system is that it has a natural tendency towards increasing the concentration of wealth because the rate of return on capital is consistently higher than the rate of economic growth. However, the essential question which remains contested (and unresolved) is whether the problem of rising inequality is the result of the natural workings of capitalism or due to the distortions in the market system that arise from political and monopoly power – which results in rent-seeking and undermines entrepreneurship and innovation. Indeed, if widening income and wealth inequality is endemic to capitalism, what then explains capitalism's remarkable stability during the six decades between 1914 and 1973 – the so-called "golden age" of capitalism – which, according to Piketty, is the only period in recorded history to experience a huge "leveling," when both the total wealth relative to income and wealth and income inequality actually declined, and prosperity and living standards improved across the board in the advanced capitalist economies?

Piketty claims that this period that saw the rate of economic growth exceed the after-tax rate of return on capital was an aberration – the result of the massive human and capital stock destruction due to the two World Wars (including the imposition of higher taxes on high incomes to finance the wars), which flattened income and wealth inequality, the establishment of an expansive "social state" following the Second World War (which imposed confiscatory taxation on high incomes, including high inheritance tax rates and state intervention to regulate capital and redistribute wealth), and the success of a mobilized and empowered labor movement in the advanced capitalist economies to garner concessions from the owners of capital.[18] However, as Piketty notes, this did not mean that the capitalist system had been "tamed" or reformed. To the contrary, the antagonistic laws of capitalism have remained fundamentally unaltered (that is, r always exceeds g), returning with a vengeance to its normal trajectory by the late 1970s under Reagan and Thatcher's unequivocally pro-capitalist, neoliberal agenda. Drawing on data from national accounts, Piketty shows that capital's share of income began to rapidly rise from 1975 to 2010, with particularly sharp increases in the United States, France, Germany, and the United Kingdom. He notes that even the recession of 2008–2009 did not result in a generalized fall in capital's share of income. To Piketty, this is because the neoliberal policies in the advanced economies promiscuously and systematically gutted the "social state" and facilitated the reemergence of an order marked by even greater disparity between capital and labor – with the wealthy capital-owning class deriving an increasingly larger share of their income and wealth through their control of capital.[19]

As Piketty reiterates, in a capitalist economy, the "means of production" or the capital and assets can be privately owned or controlled, labor is voluntarily purchased for wages on the basis of supply and demand, and the gains (capital) mostly accrue to private owners. Although the capitalist system is diverse and complex and not readily amenable to neat categorization, the system is nevertheless undergird by a set of institutional pillars such as respect for secure private property rights, legally enforceable and binding rules, and reliance on the market mechanism in the production and distribution of goods and services (Amable 2003; Frieden 2006; Shonfield 1965). This embedding, coupled with what Schumpeter (1942) described as the continuous "process of creative destruction," has endowed capitalism with a remarkable resilience and ability to adapt to changing circumstances by efficiently allocating and delivering goods and services regardless of scale, besides giving the system unprecedented resiliency and durability through downturns and crises. Gilpin (2000, 3) has succinctly noted that "Capitalism is the most successful wealth-creating economic system that the world has ever known," creating "wealth through advancing continuously to ever higher levels of productivity and technological sophistication; ... Although capitalism eventually distributes wealth more equally than any other known economic system, as it does tend to reward the most efficient and productive, it tends to concentrate wealth, power, and economic activities."

A useful and nuanced way to differentiate the capitalist system is on the level of its utilitarianism, the nature of its domestic institutional arrangements and how production, allocation, and distribution are organized. In the so-called *"liberal market economies"* such as the United States and the United Kingdom, a more decentralized, open and competitive market is prevalent, whereas in the so-called *"coordinated market economies"* such as Germany and Japan, non-market actors such as unions and business associations play a more significant role. Although the strength of liberal market economies lies in their particular ability to generate more robust growth and employment, their downside is that growth tends to be more inequitably distributed, with resultant higher levels of income inequality, higher poverty rates, and very modest social-welfare protection for the weak and vulnerable. On the other hand, although coordinated market economies provide more generous and stable welfare protection, their growth rates tend to be more modest vis-à-vis the liberal market economies (Crouch 2005; Hall and Soskice 2001; Pontusson 2005). The current trend of widening income and wealth inequality in the advanced capitalist economies underscores the inexorable spread and deepening of neoliberal convergence – namely, the privileging of markets (coupled with an instinctive resistant to statism), the gradual dismantling of welfare states, including neo-corporatism and related forms of state-market partnerships (for a good overview, see Panitch and Gindin 2012).

If the essential feature of a market economy is that key economic decisions are made predominantly by free individuals and independent firms and businesses, as its namesake implies, the government or the "state" is the lead actor under "state capitalism" as it controls, manages, and regulates the "commanding heights" of the economy. Bremmer (2010, 4) lucidly captures the essence of state capitalism defining it as "a system in which the state functions as the leading economic actor and uses markets primarily for political gain." Although it is difficult to know the precise nature of the relationship between the Chinese state (both the central government and the subnational units) and private firms, given the lack of transparency, there is broad agreement that the state's presence is large, if not dominant. The State Planning bodies still instruct enterprises and businesses on what to produce, the state continues to allocate goods, and prices and trade are not entirely market based. Leutert (2016, 86) notes that China's "central government currently owns 106 companies, out of which 47 firms ranked in the 2014 Fortune Global 500. These centrally owned firms … controlled more than $5.6 trillion in assets at the end of 2013, including more than $690 billion abroad." China's central government, through central planning and control and ownership of the country's key productive assets, including ownership of "… 113 very large monopolies and oligopolies … and an uncertain number of smaller SOEs owned by provincial and municipal governments" (Dobson 2017, 531), directs the economy, combining both statist and capitalist or market principles – this elasticity and hybridity is reflected in Beijing's self-proclamation that the Peoples Republic operates as a "socialist market economy." However, to Knight (2016, 138), China "has a semi-marketized economy involving much state intervention." McGregor (2012) claims that China's economic system can be best described as "authoritarian capitalism" because it is only partly a market economy, as a large part is still regulated and controlled by the party-state, while McNally (2012), notes that "Sino-capitalism" has a unique institutional structure, as it combines a top-down state-led development that plays "a leading role in fostering and guiding capitalist accumulation," with a bottom-up entrepreneurial and "networked" capitalism undergirded by *quanxi* – which "relies on informal business networks rather than on legal codes and transparent rules" (McNally 2012, 744).

These various characterizations of state capitalism are not mutually exclusive, as they all capture some important features of the system. In other words, the institutional underpinnings of China's post-reform economic order resonates all of these features and more. On the one hand, the Chinese state (or more aptly, party-state) sees itself as the sole legitimate authority and guardian of the national interest by directing, managing, and controlling all key levers of economic activity, while at the same time allowing for a private sector to flourish and operate under open-market competition. Yet, on the other hand, the state is deeply enmeshed in and an active participant in the global economic system through trade, capital flows, and foreign investments, besides adopting selected capitalist practices domestically, including the profit motive for state firms, performance incentives for managers, and internationally accepted best business practices. More specifically, reminiscent of pre-reform "state socialism," China's Communist Party elites who zealously control the party-state continue to assiduously regulate and direct industrial policy, shape and influence investment decisions, and function as the final arbiter when it comes to allocating resources to the state's expansive economic sectors via subsidies and concessionary finance, including exempting from competition the "strategically important sectors" the party-state hopes to promote and nurture.

What is different, however, is that, although the state still owns and controls the strategic economic sectors via state-owned enterprises (SOEs), it –breaking from its doctrinal past – has also nurtured a thriving private sector, including owning shares in private or non-state run companies, all the while maintaining strict control of non-state businesses by appointing party-approved bureaucrats to their boards.[20] Although SOEs involved in defense, telecommunications, and energy enjoy protected or favored status in terms of access to credit and markets, and with senior party members holding key positions, including as chairperson of the board, most state-run or state-managed and state-regulated firms have close relations with non-state and wholly private-sector business and commercial interests as patrons, investors, and shareholders. Moreover, as Kurlantzick (2016) notes, the new state capitalism (unlike the older and sclerotic, inward-oriented types) is very much compatible with economic globalization as the companies operate as private, market-oriented corporations. Indeed, Chinese SOEs and corporations operate freely in the global economy. They are deeply integrated into the global supply chains, welcome foreign investment and capital flows, are managed by professional technocrats (instead of party or government bureaucrats), and actively pursue commercial profitability. *The Economist* (2012) notes that "China's infrastructure companies win contracts the world over. The best national champions are outward-looking, acquiring skills by listing on foreign exchanges and taking over foreign companies."[21]

In fact, the majority of China's corporations are listed on the world's major stock exchanges, some have highly profitable corporate holdings, and the best of these, the so-called "national champions," operate globally as private conglomerates – some even earning a reputation for successfully taking over foreign companies and multinationals. Given this, although, to quote Lardy (2014), "markets" may have seemingly triumphed "over Mao," as many state-owned firms have been closed or privatized, the facts on the ground suggest that "state capitalism" remains as pervasive as ever. Not only are the remaining state-owned firms amongst the largest in China today, to quote Du (2014, 411), "Presently, SOEs constitute 80 percent of the value of the Chinese stock market and the Chinese government is the biggest shareholder in China's 150 largest companies. In 2013, 95 Chinese firms appeared on the list of Fortune Global 500, compared with 79 in 2012, 69 in 2011, 54 in 2010 and 13 in 2003, and 77 of the 95 firms on the list were SOEs. An OECD study, using data from 2006, estimated that SOEs account for 29.7 percent of GDP, 40 percent of fixed investment and employ 40 percent of the urban labour force in China." As Dobson (2017, 530) notes, "the 2000 largest companies on the *Forbes Global 2000* list in business year 2010–2011 included 204 [Chinese] SOEs" (see Table 1.1).

However, the defining feature of state capitalism – whether it takes the form of the authoritarian Chinese model or democratic state capitalism (like India), which combines economic statism with political freedoms and the welfare-based "coordinated market economies" in advanced western democracies, is that they share a deep and abiding distrust of markets, especially the way they

TABLE I.I *Top 30 non-financial Chinese enterprises by OFDI stock, 2012*

No.	Name of Enterprise	Industry	Ownership
1	China Petrochemical Corporation	Petroleum	SOE
2	China National Petroleum Corporation	Petroleum	SOE
3	China National Offshore Oil Corporation	Petroleum	SOE
4	China Mobile Communication Corporation	Telecommunication	SOE
5	China Resources (Holdings) Co., Ltd.	Cross-industry	SOE
6	China Ocean Shipping (Group) Company	Transportation	SOE
7	Aluminum Corporation of China	Metal	SOE
8	Sinochem Corporation	Chemical	SOE
9	China Merchants Group	Cross-industry	SOE
10	China State Construction Engineering Corporation	Construction	SOE
11	China Unicom Corporation	Telecommunication	SOE
12	China Minmetals Corporation	Metal	SOE
13	China National Chemical Corporation	Manufacturing	SOE
14	CITIC Group	Finance	SOE
15	China National Cereals, Oils & Foodstuffs Corporation	Food	SOE
16	China National Aviation Holding Corporation	Transportation	SOE
17	State Grid Corporation of China	Utility	SOE
18	SinoSteel Corporation	Metal	SOE
19	China Three Gorges Corporation	Utility	SOE
20	SINOTRANS Changjiang National Shipping (Group) Corporation	Logistics	SOE
21	China Shipping (Group) Company	Logistics	SOE
22	China Huaneng Group	Utility	SOE
23	HNA Group	Transportation	SOE
24	Huawei Technologies Co., Ltd.	Telecommunication	POE
25	China Nonferrous Metal Mining & Construction (Group) Co., Ltd.	Mining	POE
26	GDH Limited	Cross-industry	SOE
27	China North Industries Group Corporation	Manufacturing	SOE
28	China Communication Construction Company Ltd.	Construction	SOE
29	Shanghai Baosteel Group Corporation	Metal	SOE
30	Shanghai Geely ZhaoYuan Investments International Ltd.	Manufacturing	POE

Note: POE (privately owned enterprise); SOE (state-owned enterprise)
Source: Ministry of Commerce, People's Republic of China (2012), cited in Dobson (2017, S35).

operate under laissez-faire capitalism. Rather, to state capitalism, free and open markets are inherently unpredictable and increasingly volatile – especially in this age of global capitalism – and champions of state capitalism share Piketty's concern that such a system disproportionately benefits owners of capital or "capitalists." Moreover, in step with the Keynesian view that free-market economies go through regular bouts of cyclical instability and that "unregulated markets" cannot adequately meet society's needs, proponents of state capitalism argue not only that government intervention is necessary to correct market failure, but also that a pragmatically regulated and guided economy can promote balanced economic development. Not surprisingly, in the case of China, the state not only controls access to capital, its firms cannot access capital without political approval. In addition, private enterprises are not only credit-rationed by state banks but also face higher interest rates, and the state continues to influence, if not determine, key investment decisions. Milhaupt and Zheng (2016, 10) note that "Private ownership in China does not necessarily mean autonomy from the state ... the Chinese government exerts influence over private firms despite its lack of equity ownership interests."[22] Similarly, Kurlantzick (2016, 4) points out, "Beijing now appoints senior directors of many of the largest companies, who are expected to become Party members, if they are not already ... Working through these networks, the Beijing leadership sets state priorities, gives signals to companies, and determines corporate agendas, but does so without the direct hand of the state appearing in public." Liebman and Milhaupt (2015) sum it up well by noting that despite the rapid growth of a strong private sector, state control still permeates all levels of the Chinese economy – with the state increasingly finding itself in the conflicting roles of both "designer" of the economy and the "enforcer" of the rules that regulate it.

Yet, despite grandiose claims, statist economies, including its capitalist variants, suffer from capricious bureaucratic control, autarkic mismanagement, oligopolistic and inefficient allocation, production, and distribution of resources, and from the "laws of diminishing returns." Indeed, as Acemoglu and Robinson (2012) suggest, this is because state capitalism is inherently "extractive" – and although, state capitalism can generate high levels of growth in the early stages of economic development, over the long term it becomes a burden – producing diminishing and ultimately stagnant returns. Ljungqvist, Chen, Jiang, Lu, and Zhou's (2015) research on China's state business groups shows that state capitalism does a poor job of allocating capital, besides constraining private-sector growth and development. This is in large part due to the fact that the Chinese state has to constantly balance both the "economic" as well as "political" exigencies. The key objective of China's ruling Communist Party is unambiguous: it not only includes maximizing profits, but fundamentally protecting and strengthening the regime by creating a "harmonious society." Consistent with this, the career advancements for senior bureaucrats, including lower-level cadres, often depend on how consistently they disseminate and advance the policy goals of the party. Although, in the end, the Chinese model has a proven track record of generating high rates of growth, it also suffers from a pronounced inability to balance growth with more equitable distribution.

Since the early 1980s – or according to Piketty, the start of the "neoliberal era" – the capitalist system has undergone perhaps the most dramatic change with the ascendancy of "finance capitalism" – or what some have pejoratively labeled as "neoliberal capitalism" or "financialization" (Kotz 2015; Panitch and Gindin 2012). In basic terms, finance capitalism means a form of capitalism where finance plays a dominant role in the economy. As financial innovations have enabled national financial markets to become more globally intertwined, cross-border capital flows had risen from about $0.5 trillion in 1980 to roughly $12 trillion by the eve of global financial crisis in 2007. In many countries, the financial sector has not only grown both in terms of scale and complexity, it increasingly constitutes the largest part of the economy when measured as a share of GDP (Greenwood and Scharfstein 2013). According to Krippner (2005, 174), financialization can be best described as "a pattern of accumulation in which profits accrue primarily through financial channels rather than through trade and commodity production." To Kocka (2016), unlike earlier "productive" forms of finance, modern finance capitalism mainly consists of unproductive "locust" hedge funds that "cannibalize" good firms and stifle economic growth. Even more bluntly, the Occupy Movement blames untrammeled financialization for turning the "real economy" into a "giant casino" to benefit Wall Street at the expense of Main Street. Although exaggerated, there is no doubt that an array of financial intermediaries such as banks, hedge funds, asset management firms, insurance companies, and brokerage firms, among others, have seen an unprecedented growth in their earnings, both income and amassed wealth. Hence, Lapavitsas (2014), in *Profiting Without Producing*, argues that "financialization" is the most corrosive and promiscuous form of capitalism because "its most prominent feature is the rise of financial profit, in part extracted directly from households through financial expropriation," and that "financialized capitalism" is particularly prone to crises with the potential to destroy the real economy – something it came very close to doing during the global financial conflagration of 2007–2009 (also Kotz 2015; Panitch and Gindin 2012).

On the other hand, a large body of scholarship, notably William Goetzmann's (2016) aptly titled study, *Money Changes Everything: How Finance Made Civilization Possible*, persuasively illustrates how financial innovation throughout the span of recorded human history (from ancient Mesopotamia, classical Greece and Rome, medieval and Renaissance Europe, to twentieth-century America) has played a positive role not only in creating wealth but also in enriching human knowledge and civilization. Similarly, John Kay's (2015) succinct *Other People's Money: The Real Business of Finance* illustrates that while, on one hand, the extraordinary complexity of modern financial system, and in particular the development of markets in derivatives and swaps, has helped to dramatically boost productivity and profits, such complexity (and opacity) also generates vulnerabilities and greater potential for instability and crisis. Nobel-laureate Robert Shiller (2012) in his authoritative *Finance and the Good Society* notes that "this time in history will be remembered as a time financial capitalism took over the world ... A time when emerging countries became developed. The plan we're on is going to yield a remarkable world in the future. It's really about finance."[23] Although Shiller acknowledges that the financial sector bears a great deal of blame for the 2007 crisis, he also notes that economic development is impossible without countries having modern financial institutions. To Shiller, among others (Janeway 2012; Palmer 2015), there is no alternative to financial capitalism because finance plays a crucial role in promoting entrepreneurship and managing risk by providing valuable price signals and reducing informational asymmetries. According to Shiller, the Wall Street excesses that led to the "absurd concentrations of wealth" and eventually to the global financial meltdown happened in part because "people in the financial community lost their morality," creating a lapse in fiduciary responsibility. He claims that such egregious behaviors can be significantly mitigated with the imposition of an effective regulatory regime by both the government and the financial sector to protect consumers, promote the public interest and reduce economic inequality. Moreover, Shiller rejects the notion that finance capitalism is inherently exploitative and destructive, and inequality endemic to capitalism. Rather, far from an unholy creation designed to exploit, modern financial instruments are a deliberate creation of considerable genius. Shiller claims that "finance seems to breed inequality because it's such a powerful technology for wealth creation." The most effective way to overcome this is through the democratization of finance capitalism. For example, narrowing the information asymmetries between Wall Street and Main Street would enable "this powerful technology [to] accrue ... benefit of everyone, not just the minority."

In practice, however, countries are both blessed with specific advantages as well as cursed with debilitating disadvantages when responding to the complex of complementary and countervailing forces emanating from financial capitalism. While, in theory, financial globalization, by providing easier access to capital (both portfolio and foreign direct investment) and managerial skills, and by channeling capital more efficiently to the most productive areas, helps promote economic growth, the empirical evidence is mixed (see Rodrik 2011). Specifically, contrary to sanguine assumptions, we know that markets can produce less-than-optimal results, that market prices do not always reflect the true value of assets, that markets are not "frictionless," and people do not always make rational economic choices – or at least, individuals do not always optimize with perfect accuracy. Moreover, we now know that the advancements in financial innovations – in particular, the creation of the so-called sophisticated and "exotic" financial products – were not as benign, safe, and profitable as they were thought to be. Rather, the "democratization of credit" and the availability of easy credit made possible by dramatic advances in information technology and financial product innovations, and in particular, the securitization of debt and use of financial derivatives, came with many hidden and poorly understood risks. For example, subprime mortgages turned out to be both "attractive" and "toxic" at the same time because "securitization" made these highly risky products appear more secure and safe than they really were. The securitization of subprime mortgages not only allowed them to be traded directly as securities, these mortgages were also repackaged to create even more complex financial instruments (derivatives[24]) such as collateralized debt obligations (CDOs). The derivatives were again split and repackaged in various tranches several times over. However, each stage of the securitization process sharply increased the leverage or debt financial institutions were accumulating, as they were often purchasing these securities and derivatives with borrowed money. This greatly limited their ability to adequately value their holdings, raising uncertainty about the solvency of borrowers. Thus, the deeply woven and intricate web of connections that holds the globalized financial system together can also become a conduit for financial contagion and a source for debt problems as governments increasingly tap global capital markets to fund their budget deficits. Thus, global financial integration, and in particular, unfettered cross-border financial flows, can amplify economic vulnerabilities and increase macroeconomic volatility, especially in countries with weak and underdeveloped domestic financial infrastructure and poorly regulated administrative and supervisory frameworks.

For example, in the United States, the systematic deregulation of the financial sector over the past three decades has had a significant impact (both positive and negative) on the real economy – even as it has brought huge rewards for Wall Street. Indeed, politics contributed much to the vulnerability of the US financial system. The formal repeal of the Glass–Steagall Act in 1999 by Congress ended within the banking system the distinction between banking and trading, and created the conditions for speculative trading. Compounding this, the failure to regulate new financial instruments such as derivatives created the conditions for reckless risk-taking – ultimately resulting in the subprime crisis of 2007 (Sharma 2014a). Similarly, the economies of both China and India, even as they are major beneficiaries of global economic integration, have also been subjected to the contradictory forces of finance capitalism, in part because of their relatively shallow financial markets and weak regulatory and prudential systems. Although India's relatively closed economy is generally seen as less vulnerable to the vagaries of globalization, the reality is more complex. Certainly, India is less open to international trade (than China, and indeed, than most other emerging economies), and its exports are more diversified in terms of products and market destination. However, the Indian economy – in particular, the stock and financial markets – has become deeply linked to the global financial markets, making the country vulnerable to shifts in market sentiments, including cross-border financial contagion. China, despite the fact that its economy is now the second largest in the world, still remains incompletely integrated in the global financial system. In fact, China's financial system is more national than global, as foreign exchange controls remains in place, interest rates are still centrally determined, and SOEs rather than the private sector dominate the economy. Moreover, through deliberate intervention in the exchange rate markets, Beijing has kept the RMB undervalued, allowing China to accumulate the world's largest reserves of foreign exchange. Thus, China's high private sector saving and massive accumulation of US government debt is not simply due to the idiosyncrasies of China's financial system, but its incomplete integration in the world economy.

Political Systems, Public Policy, and Inequality

Arguably, at first glance, the experiences of the United States and India seem to belie the prevailing political-economy orthodoxy that democracies respond to socioeconomic inequalities better than non-democracies because an increase in inequality (reflected in median incomes falling relative to average incomes) eventually forces the median voter to demand redistribution, forcing politicians to limit after-tax and -transfer inequality. However, the fact that the world's two quintessential democracies, the wealthiest and the largest, and China, the contemporary exemplar of centralized authoritarianism, have similar outcomes in terms of income and wealth inequality seems to suggest prima-facie that there is little or no correlation between a country's political system – in particular, its "regime type" – and economic performance, at least in terms of its overall effectiveness when it comes to reconciling economic growth with more equitable distribution of the fruits of growth. Indeed, the fact that China's ruling Communist Party has long emancipated itself from the antediluvian ideological and policy straitjacket imposed during the Maoist era (1949–1975), and has effectively liberalized its control over the economy while simultaneously protecting its monopoly on political power, underscores that a Leninist political system is not necessarily incompatible with a functioning market-based economy.

Yet, as the following cases illustrate, a nation's political order, and in particular the institutional arrangements, state capacity vis-à-vis "autonomy" over influential state and societal actors, and the patterns of representation and contestation can provide valuable insights regarding the reasons for the widening socioeconomic inequalities and the challenges these countries face in checking and mitigating the growing income and wealth inequality.

The United States and India are pluralist representative democracies deriving their legitimacy from their citizens' consent. Both enjoy popular legitimacy and have established constitutional procedures and protocols with clearly defined separation of powers that constrain state power by maintaining oversight of the various administrative and bureaucratic institutions and checks on the executive and legislative branches of government. Both are also blessed with an independent judiciary, freedom of the press and assembly, and well-institutionalized and accountable electoral systems. Moreover, in both countries, fidelity to the rule of law and the principle of common citizenship based on individual rights and freedoms have helped erode, if not substantially weaken, the more egregious and entrenched social inequalities. For example, in India, not only are the quotidian forms of discrimination, oppression, and exclusion of lower castes and minorities now largely residues of the past, the practice of democratic politics has empowered the lower castes and other marginalized groups and communities to fight for their rights and better realize their hopes and aspirations. In fact, a 1992 constitutional amendment gave local governments new powers regarding oversight and implementation over many welfare-enhancing development projects, while the Right to Information Act of 2005 has given citizens sweeping rights to demand transparency and accountability from the government.[25] Similarly, in the United States, overt discrimination against racial, ethnic, sexual minorities, and women is no longer pervasive or acceptable. Although, in both democracies (parliamentary in India and presidential in the United States), citizens enjoy political equality (or at least are considered political equals, as the franchise is universal), and governments are avowedly committed to equal opportunity and reasonable and fairer distribution of the economic pie, income and wealth disparities have become progressively more unequal. What explains this incongruence?

The cases of the United States and India show that democratic governments have a varying capacity to act in the common interest when it comes to challenging the often-obstinate prerogatives of competing domestic interest groups and classes, especially organized lobbies and coalitions representing affluent and entrenched interests. Furthermore, in modern democratic politics, where money increasingly confers political voice and influence, responding effectively to the problem of widening economic inequalities is symptomatic of the broad political dysfunction and paralysis that has tilted economic outcomes in favor of the well-connected and high-income groups. As the political philosopher John Dunn (2014) has critically observed, modern democracies pretend to institutionalize the rule by the many, but in fact tend to reinforce the rule by the few. In the world's most powerful democracy, the United States, research underscores that the meteoric rise in both income and wealth inequality – in particular, skyrocketing incomes at the very top and stagnant incomes in the middle and lower-middle deciles – is because the affluent enjoy disproportionate influence over public policies that protect and advance their interests. According to Gilens and Page (2014, 576), in the US, public policies are responsive primarily to the preferences of the wealthy, and the preferences of average-income Americans are hardly factored when it comes to the formation of policy. Rather, "when a majority of citizens disagrees with economic elites or with organized interests, they generally lose." With the backing and support of both Democrat and Republican lawmakers, influential interests have been able to successfully push for "upwardly" redistributive policies such as reductions in income and estate tax (Bartels 2008; Carnes 2013; Gilens 2014; Hacker and Pierson 2010).

In the case of India, the gulf that has always existed between the normative aspects of democracy and its actual practice has become paradoxically wider. It is an increasingly chaotic polity where the corrosion and degeneration of public manners, the cynical politicization of systemic cleavages of caste and religion, the uncompromising zero-sum partisan politics, divided government, emasculation of representative institutions, and unchecked majoritarianism have created a conductive environment where politics seem to perpetually oscillate between universalism and particularism, while constantly making accommodation to circumstance. Such a permissive environment has also created protracted uncertainty around economic policies, including the adoption of policies and programs designed to placate plebiscitarian demands rather than deepen economic development. In fact, the resultant populist policies that cater to electoral cycles have enabled well-connected, "pro-business" interests to capture the "market" and reap a disproportionate share of the national wealth (Kohli 2012), the expedient privileging of costly but less-effective reformist and redistributive policies, and failure to fully reap the rewards offered by global economic integration.

In the case of China, the instrumental priority to significantly enlarge the economic pie via sustained growth in economic aggregates at the expense of a more equitable distribution of the fruits of growth has generated phenomenal GDP growth and sharp reductions in poverty, but also an exponential rise in income and wealth inequality. Arguably, such an outcome is partly intrinsic to China's developmental model (which is a replication of the putative East Asian export-oriented model), known for exacerbating income and wealth inequality in the initial stages of development. Reminiscent of the experience of the East Asian "tigers," China's singular focus on labor-intensive exports have created millions of jobs, lifted millions more out of poverty, and created a large and prosperous middle class, including growing numbers of overnight tycoons – many self-made.

Yet, unlike its erstwhile East Asian counterparts – who were able to significantly reduce economic inequality (and make the transition to democratic rule) – China has failed on both scores. A complex of factors explains China's failure to reconcile its hyper-growth with more equitable distribution. Specifically, the entrenchment and consolidation of state capitalism, even as it ostensibly helps to advance the political and economic prerogatives of ruling Communist Party elites and its array of supporters and cronies, has also inadvertently served to distort the workings of free markets. Through its tenacious control of the wealth generated by markets for the benefit of politically connected public sector companies (namely, the SOEs), including the party elite and their progeny (the princelings), and by creating opportunities for rent-seeking and corruption, state capitalism has distorted economic development, including exacerbating economic inequalities.

Compounding these problems are the vicissitudes of China's central-local relations.[26] Although the institutional structure undergirding the relationship has played a pivotal role in generating economic growth, it is also responsible for widening socioeconomic inequalities and social unrest (Fewsmith 2013; Montinola, Qian, and Weingast 1995). Specifically, even as political decentralization (which began in earnest in the 1980s) helped jump-start economic development, it has also served to distort economic and institutional incentives, exacerbating conflict between the central authorities (Beijing) and local governments. As Beijing's reach and capacity to enforce its writ has become constrained, so has the gap between central policy mandates and local policy implementation. Local governments more autonomous from and less accountable to the center have become havens for predatory rent-seeking, bureaucratism, and corruption as formal rules of governance have become replaced with opaque personal connections and "patronage networks." Furthermore, Beijing's punitive taxation policy (by underfunding local governments who are responsible for social welfare expenditures) has forced local governments to engage in a "winner-take-all," zero-sum approach towards the distribution of economic goods, such as the arbitrary expropriation of farmland (often in collusion with private developers), and simply jettisoning or turning a blind eye to the center's reformist and redistributive initiatives.

THE ORGANIZATION OF THIS BOOK

At the outset, it should be noted that this book is a work of synthetic interpretation that draws much from the labors of many researchers. The book is divided into five chapters. Chapters 2, 3 and 4 elucidate the conceptual framework with detailed reference to the three-country case studies. More specifically, Chapter 2 presents a comprehensive overview of the confluence of factors behind the widening income and wealth inequality in the United States. It underscores that market forces, including deepening global economic integration and greater international competition, as well as the structural changes in the domestic economy due to globalization and advances in technology have significantly determined economic outcomes in the United States. Yet politics has also played a major role in shaping and determining economic outcomes. Going beyond Manichean notions that the American political system and democracy are captured by elite interests, and are mostly responsive to the interests of a narrow oligarchy, the chapter illustrates how policies (both intentionally and unintentionally) over the past few decades have profoundly exacerbated the income and wealth divide in the United States by disproportionately benefiting the high-income groups.

Chapters 3 and 4 address why China's and India's phenomenal economic growth in the post-reform era has failed to effectively reconcile growth with redistribution – or more specifically, economic growth with a more equitable distribution of income and wealth, despite various programs ostensibly designed to promote greater socioeconomic equality. Both case studies illustrate that the standard explanation that widening income and wealth inequality is the result of an inevitable "trade-off" between rapid economic development and equity is only partly valid. In the case of China, although some rise in inequality was inevitable with the introduction of a market system and integration into the global economy of a hitherto centrally planned and closed economy, the sharp and rapid rise in inequality is driven also by the difficulties associated with China's post-socialist transition, the macroeconomic distortions due to the peculiarities of China's state capitalist model and by Beijing's policy choices – which have contributed (and not always intentionally) to the widening of economic inequalities.

In the case of India, rising inequality and the modest reduction in poverty levels are due to the country's singular failure to fully utilize the opportunities ushered in by economic globalization – namely, to create a wide range of basic and intermediate manufacturing jobs, which historically have served as a ladder out of low-income status. Unlike China's large, labor-intensive manufacturing sector, which has absorbed millions of workers, India's narrow dependence on just a few sectors such as services (banking, real estate, finance) and "IT," or information technology (which can mean everything from computer programming, software development and production, communication networks, call centers, and outsourcing services), relies on a small number of relatively well-educated and skilled workers. Unlike China's broad-based integration into the global economy, India's narrow and highly specialized comparative advantage in the skill-intensive services and technology sector rewards the "skill premium" – or individuals with advanced technical and communication skills. This explains the widening earning differentials among individuals and households and the rapidly growing income inequality in India. Compounding these problems, India's poor infrastructure, notorious for its delays and bottlenecks, coupled with the equally pernicious bureaucratic and regulatory red-tape have served to greatly limit the expansion of labor-intensive industrial and manufacturing sectors.

The Indian state's pronounced inability to expeditiously reorient public policies to benefit from the opportunities offered by globalization has much to do with the nature and practice of democracy in contemporary India. The pathologies associated with divided government, partisan polarization, plebiscitary politics, political brinkmanship, and the opportunistic use of identity politics to advance short-term, self-serving, and parochial goals have made political compromise and accommodation exceedingly difficult. As a result, the needed economic reforms either languish on the books, or the watered-down versions that do see the light of day are often ineffective to the challenges at hand. More perniciously, as Kohli (2012: 2) has argued, the Indian state since the 1980s has been "pro-business" rather than "pro-market." Because business enjoys "disproportionate control over economic resources," it "enables businessmen to 'buy' politicians" and shape policy. Kohli notes "the narrow nature of the ruling alliance in India that, in its newfound relationship with business, has prioritized economic growth above all other social and political considerations."

Why have India's voters (the vast majority of whom are poor and who regularly vote) in the world's largest democracy failed to hold their elected officials accountable for failing to deliver basic social services and providing more effective redistributive programs? In part, this discrepancy is the result of poor governance due to the state's limited institutional capacity as well as the fiercely partisan and divided nature of governance in India. In such an environment, despite the fact that both the central and state governments have increased expenditures for social services, including for programs explicitly aimed at redistribution and poverty alleviation, most tend to be short-term, populist palliative measures designed to get incumbents reelected, while others languish because of political gridlock, rent-seeking, and ineffective implementation.

Finally, according to Piketty, the solution to the widening economic inequality is rather simple: governments must reverse the advantages currently enjoyed by the owners of capital via imposition of a "progressive" (and punitive) income tax with rates of 50 to 60 percent on high incomes and a top marginal rate of 80 percent on very high incomes, including complete abolishment, if not drastic scaling back of a wide range of tax deductions and exemptions enjoyed by high income earners. Chapter 5 critically examines this prescription, including a general discussion of how best the three countries can promote economic growth with a more balanced and equitable distribution of the fruits of that growth.

2

Widening Income and Wealth Gap in the United States

In its October 2011 report of the distribution of household income both before and after government transfers and federal taxes, a Congressional Budget Office (CBO) study, "Trends in the Distribution of Household Income between 1979 and 2007," confirmed of a widening income gap in the United States since the late 1970s.[1] Specifically, the report finds that the average household income (adjusted for inflation) has grown across all the income groups during the 30-year period – with the real (inflation-adjusted) average household income in the United States increasing by 62 percent. However, the report also finds that the real incomes of households in the higher income brackets rose sharply and the main beneficiaries of the gains were the richest Americans or the "top 1 percent of US income earners," whose average real after-tax household income grew by a whopping 275 percent – albeit, the top 0.1 percent saw their real incomes rise more than 400 percent from 1979 to 2005. Overall, income for the top quintile (81st to 99th percentile) grew by 65 percent. In contrast, the average real after-tax household income grew by only 18 percent for the bottom 20 percent of wage earners, and by less than 40 percent for the middle class. Overall, between 1980 and 2005, more than 80 percent of the total increase in income went to the top 1 percent of American households. Not surprisingly, the study noted that the Gini Index grew from 0.479 to 0.590 between 1979 and 2007 – further suggesting prima facie that that the top income earners are getting richer relative to both the lower and the middle classes.[2]

More recent research confirms the disturbing trend noted by the CBO. The US Census Bureau, which publishes two measures of income inequality each year, noted in its September 2014 report that the top 5 percent of households received 21.8 percent of "equivalence-adjusted" aggregate income in 2014, while the bottom 60 percent received 27.1 percent (equivalence-adjusted estimates factor-in household size and composition; see DeNavas-Walt and Proctor, 2015).[3] Similarly, using an innovative "capitalization" approach (that estimates a family's wealth through the capital income declared to the Internal Revenue Service (IRS)), Saez and Zucman (2014) claim that inequality has followed a "U-shaped pattern." That is, while from the 1930s through the late 1970s there was significant "democratization of wealth," the trend then inverted, with the wealth shares growing fastest for those at the top of the income distribution and the share of total household wealth owned by the top 0.1 percent increasing to 22 percent in 2012.[4] Although this trend paused during the Great Recession of 2007–2009 (because of the wealth losses suffered by high-income earners due to sharp drop in stock prices), it has since resumed, because the weak labor market and sluggish wage growth negatively impacts middle- and working-class households, while the renewed gains in the stock market tend to benefit upper-income households. In fact, the inequality gap has not only continued to widen, with some 95 percent of all economic gains going to the top 1 percent of income earners, between 1974 and 2012 the share of the nation's wealth owned by the top 1 percent of families (ranked by wealth) rose from 25 percent to 42 percent. However, the top 0.1 percent saw their share jump from 8 percent to 22 percent, and for the top 0.01 percent (roughly 16,000 families) wealth quadrupled from 2.5 percent to 11.2 percent – confirming that even within the top 1 percent, wealth disparities have been growing. According to Piketty and Saez (2003; Atkinson, Piketty, and Saez (2011)), in the United States, the share of income, excluding capital gains, earned by the top 1 percent of earners jumped from 7.7 percent in 1973 to 17.4 percent in 2010. However, the top 0.01 percent (whose annual income is in excess of $5.9 million) saw their share of total income rise from 0.5 percent in 1973 to 3.3 percent in 2010. Indeed, the Federal Reserve's "Survey of Consumer Finance" (SCF) confirms that the top 3 percent of households have held over 50 percent of aggregate wealth since the mid-2000s. More specifically, the SCF shows that in 2013, while the top 3 percent of households with the most income received about 30 percent of all income, the wealthiest 3 percent of households held about 54 percent of all wealth (Bricker et al. 2016; 2014). Not surprisingly, Standard and Poor's has concluded that the United States may already have reached a "tipping point," where inequality is limiting socioeconomic mobility and constraining the country's ability to effectively compete in the global economy.[5]

Debacker et al. (2013), drawing on a "large, and confidential panel of tax returns," examines "the persistent-versus-transitory nature of rising inequality in male labor earnings and in total household income, both before and after taxes, in the United States over the period 1987–2009." By persistent inequality, the authors "mean long-run inequality, or the dispersion across the population in those components of income that are more or less stable over periods of more than a few years. By transitory inequality [they] mean the dispersion arising from short-run variability in incomes, as individuals move around within the income distribution at relatively short frequencies of one to a few years" (Debacker et al. 2013, 67–68). Their findings are troubling, as the increase reflects an increase in persistent inequality: "For male labor earnings, we find that the entire increase in cross-sectional inequality over our sample period was driven by an increase in the dispersion of the persistent component of earnings.

For total household income, we find that most of the increase in inequality reflects an increase in the dispersion of the persistent income component . . ." (Debacker et al. 2013, 67).

Although the data unequivocally reveals what Noah (2012) has termed "the great divergence" in income and wealth in the United States, it does not provide a complete picture of the causes of income inequality. As the following sections illustrate, Piketty's (2014) claim that because the return on capital is greater than the growth of the overall economy, the income of owners of capital will grow faster than those who earn income from labor, and because capital ownership is concentrated, income inequality inevitably grows over time in capitalist economies as a natural outcome of market forces, is just a part of a larger and complex puzzle. In other words, although an important driver of rising income inequality is the increase in the share of national income earned by "capital" (in the form of interest, dividends, and related investment returns) in relation to the share earned by "labor" (wages, pensions, and worker-benefits), the reasons for the rupture in balance between these two forms of income can be best understood by juxtaposing the dynamic relations between globalization, capitalism, and democratic politics, as this provides a more nuanced and textured understanding of the reasons behind the widening income and wealth inequality in the United States.

FIGURE 2.1 Wealth concentration in the United States.
Source: Saez and Zucman 2014.

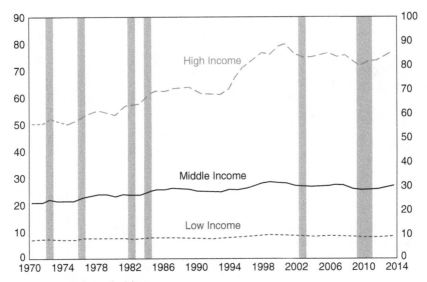

FIGURE 2.2 US household income.
Source: Alichi, Kantenga, and Sole 2016, 4.

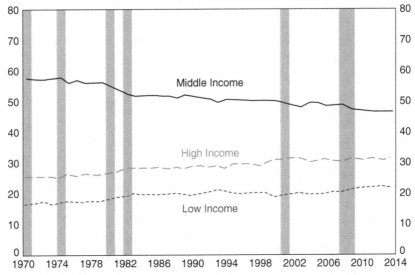

FIGURE 2.3 Number of households, 1970 to 2014.
Source: Alichi, Kantenga and Sole (2016, 5)

DOMESTIC FACTORS

In the past four decades, the US labor market has experienced dramatic change. In particular, the decline in unionization and the erosion in the bargaining

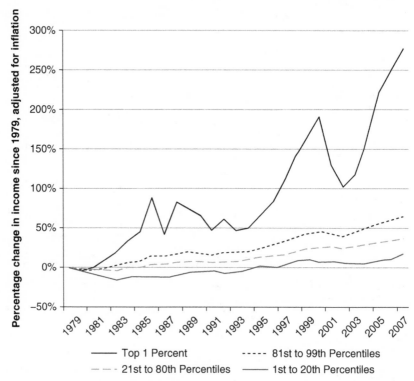

FIGURE 2.4 Distribution of household income.
Source: Congressional Budget Office 2011.

power of organized labor have translated into rising wage inequality – not only because of the fall in the real value of the minimum wage, but also because the equalizing effect of unions on the distribution of wages in both the union and non-union sectors has weakened.[6] Corporate restructuring due to the financialization of the economy and the resultant downsizing of the labor market through job cuts and the deterioration in working conditions via the use of non-standard employment practices have further exacerbated wage and income inequalities by widening the gap between Wall Street and Main Street (Kalleberg 2011; Lin and Tomaskovic-Devey 2013).

Thus, it is not surprising that the single major factor driving increase income inequality in the United States (and other OECD countries) has to do with the fact that wage gains have become appreciably unequal, with the top 10 percent experiencing the biggest increases. Although this trend began in the 1970s, in large measure the sharp rise in income inequality is due to the rise of a powerful financial sector, and their CEOs' ability to generate unprecedented increases in value has sharply driven up wage inequality between the top percentage of

TABLE 2.1 *Income and net worth in the US by percentile (2010 dollars, averages)*

Wealth or income class	Mean household income	Mean household net worth	Mean household financial (non-home) wealth
Top 1%	$1,318,200	$16,439,400	$15,171,600
80th to 99th%	107,000	1,295,600	1,010,800
60th to 80th%	72,000	216,900	100,700
40th to 60th%	41,700	61,000	12,200
Bottom 40%	17,300	(10,600)	(14,800)

Note: Only mean figures are available, not medians. Note that income and wealth are separate measures; so, for example, the top 1 percent of income-earners is not exactly the same group of people as the top 1 percent of wealth-holders, although there is considerable overlap.
Source: Piereson (2015, 8), original from Edward Wolff, "The Asset Price Meltdown and the Wealth of the Middle Class," August 26, 2012, Table 4, and Data source: Survey on Consumer Finances.

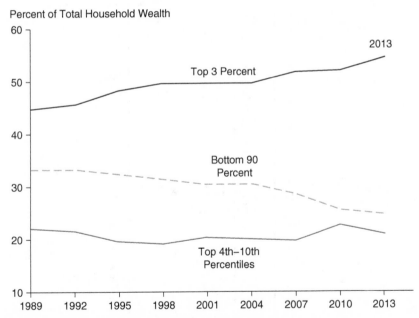

FIGURE 2.5 Share of total wealth held by wealth percentile, 1989 to 2013.
Source: Federal Reserve Board of Governors, "Survey of Consumer Finances," taken from Jason Furman (2016), "Norms and sources of inequality in the United States," March 17, http://voxeu.org/article/forms-and-sources-inequality-united-states (accessed November 30, 2016).

TABLE 2.2 *Average household income, transfers, and taxes by before-tax income groups, 2013*

	Lowest quintile	Second quintile	Middle quintile	Fourth quintile	Highest quintile	All households
			Dollars			
Market income	15,800	31,300	53,000	88,709	253,000	86,400
Government transfers	9,600	16,200	16,700	15,000	12,000	13,900
Before-tax income	25,400	47,400	69,700	103,700	265,000	100,200
Federal taxes	800	4,000	8,900	17,600	69,700	20,100
After-tax income	24,500	43,400	60,800	86,100	195,300	80,100

Source: Congressional Budget Office (2016, 2).

income earners and everyone else.[7] On the other hand, labor's ability to make commensurate gains from the rise in productivity has declined due to weakening of collective action via unions, globalization of capital, and innovations in labor-saving technologies. Not surprisingly, the nominal minimum wage has not increased in line with inflation. To the contrary, the real minimum wage has decreased in most OECD countries, including the United States. Tyson and Madgavkar (2016) note that "real income from wages and capital for households in the same part of the income distribution was lower in 2014 than in 2005 for about two-thirds of households in 25 advanced economies – more than 500 million people. From 1993 to 2005, by contrast, less than 2 percent of households in these countries had flat or falling incomes." In the United States, labor income (which includes wages, salaries, and work-related compensation) has not only declined because of the decline in average productivity growth, but also because it has declined relative to capital income such as rent, interest payments, dividends, and capital gains. In fact, not only have household median incomes stagnated (at least since the mid-1990s), the inflation-adjusted earnings of poorer households have also declined. Cumulatively, these have adversely impacted the income and wealth of the lower-middle- and working-class workers.[8]

Nevertheless, Piketty's claim that the level of income distribution in the United States is the "most unequal" among advanced industrial economies is misleading, as it is based on a rather selective reading of the data. As is well known, income can be measured in two ways: market income before taxes and transfer payments, or disposable income after taxes and transfer payments. As the data from the non-partisan Congressional Budget Office (CBO) shows, inequality of market income before taxes and transfer payments in the United States is actually slightly below that of most OECD countries, including the cradle-to-grave social-welfare states like Denmark, Sweden, and Norway. In fact, Germany has higher income inequality before taxes and transfers than the United States.

Undoubtedly, the systematic cuts in the top income tax rates over the past half-century have also played a big role in widening income inequality in the United States. For example, in the early 1960s the income tax applied to wages and savings interest was more than 90 percent. President Reagan cut this top rate from 70 percent in 1981 to 28 percent after 1986. Although increases under the first President Bush and President Clinton brought the top rate to 39.6 percent, the tax cuts under President George W. Bush and reauthorized by President Obama set it to 35 percent. Moreover, reduction in the tax rates on investment income in the form of capital gains taxes and dividends (the current rate of 15 percent is the lowest since 1933) has helped boost income for higher-income households. Similarly, corporate income tax has also declined both as a share of corporate profits and as a percentage of GDP over the past several decades. Clearly, the major beneficiaries have

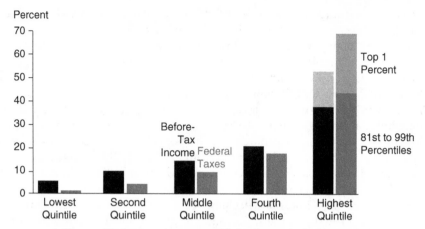

FIGURE 2.6 Shares of before-tax income and federal taxes by before-tax income group, 2013

*Before-tax income is market income plus government transfers. Market income consists of labor income, business income, capital gains (profits realized from the sale of assets), capital income excluding capital gains, income received in retirement for past services, and other sources of income.

* Government transfers are cash payments and in-kind benefits from social insurance and other government assistance programs. Those transfers include payments and benefits from federal, state, and local governments.

* Federal taxes include individual income taxes, payroll taxes, corporate income taxes, and excise taxes.

Source: Congressional Budget Office (2016, 3).

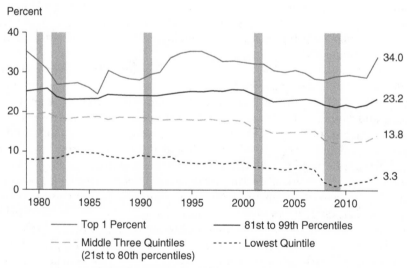

FIGURE 2.7 Average federal tax rates by before-tax income group, 1979 to 2013.
Source: Congressional Budget Office (2016, 4).

been those in the higher income brackets – further widening the income and wealth inequality.

Piketty is certainly correct to note that progressive taxation is one of the least distortionary policy tools for redistributing the fruits of growth. However, his claim that, compared to other advanced economies, the US taxation system is the "least progressive" because the distribution of disposable income after taxes and transfer payments is the most unequal in the United States needs to be qualified. Like many of its OECD counterparts, the US income tax code is progressive, with the average tax rates increasing up the income ladder.[9] As Martin (2016, 2) notes, "the differences in individual income tax collection at the extremes of the income distribution are striking. Filers earning less than $50,000 annually account for nearly two-thirds of all tax returns but contribute 7 percent of total revenue. Around half of the filers in this group report zero taxable income; for those with taxable income, the average income tax rate is 12 percent. In contrast, filers making at least $1 million annually account for 0.3 percent of all tax returns and contribute 27 percent of total revenue. Their average tax rate – 31 percent – is almost triple that of filers in the lowest income bracket." Overall, according to the CBO (2016; 2011), although the top 1 percent have seen a sharp rise in their incomes and wealth, they also pay an increasing share of the nation's taxes – about 40 percent of all federal taxes in 2007, compared to less than 20 percent in the 1970s.

In part, this anomaly has to do with the fact that, unlike most OECD countries, the United States does not use "consumption taxes" such as the VAT (value-added taxes) to collect revenue.[10] Of course, this does not mean that the VAT is progressive. The claim by supporters that VAT is progressive because the increases in generated revenue are used to fund welfare services and transfer programs and this has helped to keep inequality in check may be true in theory. However, in practice, the VAT can be just as regressive, as lower-income households spend a much higher percentage of their income on consumption. In other words, since poorer households consume a larger portion of their income, they bear a proportionally greater burden of the tax. Although a number of governments with VATs have exempted essentials such as food or medical care from the tax, this has had the effect of making the VAT more distortionary – which among other things discourages businesses from investing and creating jobs. Second, the US system is quite progressive for middle and low income earners. The "Earned Income Tax Credit" (EITC) helps to offset the federal income and payroll taxes of workers who earn below certain income levels. That is, households that fall within the middle to the bottom of the income distribution receive reductions in their tax liability in the form of a refund check from the Internal Revenue Service. About 80 percent of the tax credit goes to workers in the bottom 40 percent of the income distribution. In 2014, the EITC refunded "$66.7 billion in income tax credits to 27.5 million families … an average of about $2,400 per family" (Athreya 2016, 40). Complementing this is the Child Tax Credit, which reduces taxes of up to

$1000 for each dependent child under the age of seventeen. In fact, an estimated 40 percent of low-income US households do not pay any federal income tax. Finally, a number of nationwide programs for "income maintenance" such as food stamps, housing subsidies, and the Supplemental Security Income, among others, are available to individuals who fall under the officially designated "poverty" status.

Moreover, contrary to Piketty and the popular narrative, only a minority of the so-called "1 percenters" in the United States are products of the perverse compensation schemes of Wall Street. Rather, three factors are largely responsible for the widening income inequality between the so-called 1 percent and the rest. First is the increasing trend towards "assortative mating" – where individuals tend to marry others with the same educational background. Put bluntly, with the better educated marrying each other not only skews the distribution of household incomes in their favor, they are able to pass down their advantages to their offspring (Greenwood 2014). Second, as Reeves (2017) has argued, the fundamental problem with the widening economic stratification and inequality in the United States has hardly to do with the top 1 percent. Rather, the real problem lies with the "upper middle class" or the top 20 percent, whose household income is $112,000 and above. This overwhelmingly educated professional class has used a range of subtle (and not-so-subtle) strategies and "barriers" to keep the "bottom 80 percent" down. More specifically, Reeves accuses the upper middle class of "opportunity hoarding" by rigging the nation's educational system in such a way that it gives their children unfair advantages in getting into better schools and colleges – and ultimately, higher-paying jobs. Thus, to Reeves' view, opportunity hoarding, which leads to stifling the dreams of the bottom 80 percent (hence, the title of the book *Dream Hoarders*), has been a major factor in rising inequality in the United States. Third, the dramatic changes in family structure (such as the number of one-parent versus two-parent households) have served to act as a brake against upward mobility. And finally, significant numbers of the new rich and the growing affluent are both creators and products of the new economy. The vast majority is made up of highly educated and skilled professionals, including sport and entertainment super-stars. As Zingales (2009, 25) points out, "even before the internet boom created many young billionaires, in 1996, one in four billionaires in the United States could be described as self-made ... And the wealthiest self-made American billionaires – from Bill Gates and Michael Dell to Warren Buffet and Mark Zuckerberg – have made their fortunes in competitive businesses, with little or no government interference or help."[11]

Given this, Piketty's claim that intergenerational income mobility is lower in the United States than in most other advanced economies because the US has higher levels of income inequality can be misleading. After all, correlation between income inequality and economic mobility does not imply causality, as there are other factors that influence economic mobility such as investments in early childhood education and family structure. Indeed, research by Chetty et al. (2014a; 2014b) provides nuanced insights on the question: is relative mobility lower in the United States than in the other advanced countries? By compiling income data from millions of anonymous earnings records of all children in the United States born between 1980 and 1982, the authors measure their income in 2011–2012 – or when the cohort was approximately 30 years in age. Specifically, they calculate two measures of intergenerational mobility. First is "relative mobility," which measures the difference in the expected economic outcomes between children from high-income and low-income families, and second, "absolute upward mobility," which measures the expected economic outcomes of children born to a family earning an income of approximately $30,000 (or in the 25th percentile of the income distribution). Their findings show that there is substantial variation in intergenerational mobility across the United States – with mobility varying sometimes dramatically across the 741 geographical or "commuting zones" in the United States ("commuting zones are geographical aggregations of counties that are similar to metro areas but also cover rural areas"). Once the geographical differences are correlated with "segregation," "income inequality," "local school quality," "social capital," and family structure, the evidence reveals that some commuting zones have upward-income mobility comparable to the most upwardly mobile countries in the world, while others fall below that of any developed country. Overall, Chetty and his co-authors find that the probability of moving from the bottom quintile to the top quintile is 7.5 percent in the United States, as compared to 11.7 percent in Denmark and 13.5 percent in Canada – two countries with relatively high levels of intergenerational mobility. Nevertheless, because intergenerational mobility is a key indicator of equality of opportunity, there seems to be a striking correlation between the levels of inequality across countries and rates of intergenerational mobility. As research has confirmed that greater income inequality is associated with declines in intergenerational mobility, it has raised legitimate concerns that rising inequality is creating a "Great Gatsby curve" – or a sharp decline in intergenerational mobility in the United States and elsewhere (see Chetty et al. 2014a; 2014b; Davis and Mazumder 2017; Krueger 2012; Lee and Solon 2009). Indeed, the Great Gatsby curve does show that countries experiencing high inequality in one generation tend to experience lower intergenerational mobility in the next generation (Corak 2013). In the case of the United States, evidence shows that greater income inequality tends to generate less mobility for children from low-income families. Clearly, the consequences of being born to low- versus high-income parents are much larger now than in the past (Figure 2.8).

Yet evidence also indicates that there is strong cross-country relationship between intergenerational mobility and inequality in skills. That is, wide skill gaps seem to be behind both higher inequality and lower intergenerational mobility. Given the strong correlation between intergenerational mobility and

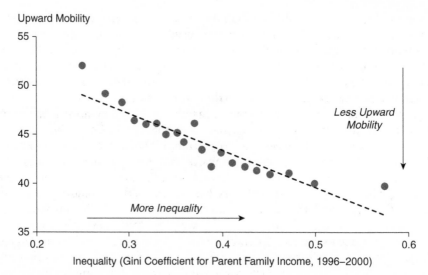

FIGURE 2.8 The "Great Gatsby Curve" within the United States.

Note: US commuting zones were ordered by Gini coefficient and divided into 20 equally sized bins. Each blue dot represents a single bin. Upward mobility reflects the mean percentile in the 2011–2012 national income distribution for those individuals in each bin whose parents were at the 25th percentile of the national income distribution between 1996 and 2000.

Source: Federal Reserve Board of Governors, "Survey of Consumer Finances," taken from Jason Furman (2016), "Norms and Sources of Inequality in the United States," March 17, http://voxeu.org/article/forms-and-sources-inequality-united-states (accessed November 30, 2016).

access to good education and stable family structure, the exploding cost of higher education and erosion of the family structure serve as significant constraints to upward mobility in the United States. In fact, Mettler (2014, 12) has compellingly shown that the American education system has changed "from one that provides access and opportunity to one that widens economic inequality and fosters social division." Coupled with the ineffectiveness of governmental retraining programs, including the Federal government's flagship "Trade Adjustment Assistance" program, the ranks of the underskilled and underemployed have mushroomed. The poor and the underclass suffer from all of the cruel pathologies as reported in the statistics on crime, drug use, broken single-parent families, and deepening humiliation and resignation – and are singularly unable to transfer the kinds of social norms and behaviors needed to effectively participate in the emerging twenty-first century economy (Vance 2016).

Finally, it is well known that median household incomes move up and down with the cycles of boom and bust in the macro economy. During 2007–2009, the

United States not only lost some nine million jobs (pushing the unemployment rate at its peak to about 10 percent), it also left millions precariously mired in debt, with many falling through the cracks and into the ranks of poor and the underclass. Piketty underestimates how the Great Recession of 2007–2009 and the resultant wealth destruction and painfully slow recovery (with high unemployment) have made income inequality far worse than it actually was before the recession. From 1947 to 2007, the American economy grew at roughly 3.4 percent annually.[12] This sustained growth translated to an average growth rate per capita of about 2.1 percent. Following the financial crisis and the Great Recession, growth from 2010 to 2017 has slowed to roughly 2.1 percent annually – which translates into an average growth rate per capita of about 1.3 percent. Over time, what may seem to be relatively small percentage differences do add up. A quick, back-of-the-envelope calculation shows that between 1950 to the mid-2000s, the 3.5 percent growth translated into real GDP growth per person from roughly $16,000 to $50,000 – while a 2.1 percent growth would have meant growth in income per person to around just $23,000. Clearly, such anemic growth has served to exacerbate income inequality and poverty. Moreover, even as unemployment has fallen from 9.5 percent in early 2009 to about 5.5 percent in May 2016, wage growth has remained flat. Industries that are susceptible to cyclical conditions such as manufacturing and construction have been particularly hard hit – with adverse impacts on the labor market.[13] Exacerbating this – arguably unintentionally – has been the Federal Reserve's decision in 2008 to slash long-term interest rates to near-zero, including buying large volumes of government bonds (under the "quantitative easing" program, ostensibly designed to stimulate the economy). Certainly, the Fed's policy raised asset prices (such as stocks), which are disproportionately held by richer households, while the "artificial" lowering of interest rates to near-zero negatively impacts retirees and those on fixed incomes.

Economists have long assumed that technological advances, by raising productivity (and therefore output per person), contribute to an overall higher standard of living. Some even argue that sustained productivity growth and rising standards of living also result in roughly stable unemployment and rising employment. However, evidence from the US manufacturing sector shows otherwise. That is, contrary to the conventional view, US manufacturing is not in decline. Rather, manufacturing growth remains robust in terms of output and overall share of the economy – it is declining in terms of job creation. As Francis Fukuyama (2012, 58) has noted, "… the real villain (behind rising inequality) is technology. In earlier phases of industrialization – the age of textiles, coal, steel, and the internal combustion engine – the benefits of technological changes almost always flowed down in significant ways to the rest of society in terms of employment. But this is not a law of nature. We are today living in what the scholar Shoshana Zuboff has labeled 'the age of the smart machine,' in which technology is increasingly able to substitute for more and higher human functions. Every great advance for Silicon Valley likely means a loss of low-skill jobs elsewhere in the economy, a trend that is unlikely to end anytime soon." In a similar vein, Brynjolfsson and McAfee (2014), Ford (2016), and Susskind and Susskind (2015) argue that the new information technologies are fundamentally different, as they have no historical precedent. That is, whereas earlier periods of technological advancements generated wealth and new types of employment (such as industrial work), the new information technologies are literally replacing human workers as they are turning into workers themselves. Thus, all types of workers (the unskilled, semi-skilled, and skilled) have been (or are at risk of being) replaced by intelligent machines. Brynjolfsson and McAfee (2014), in their provocative *The Second Machine Age*, point out that the quantum leap in technological progress, especially the expanding use of supercomputers, advanced digital automation, artificial intelligence, and robotics not only in manufacturing, clerical, and retail work, but also in professions such as legal services, financial services, education, and medicine, has been a major factor behind the displacement of labor, sluggish employment growth of the last two decades, and widening inequality in wages and overall incomes. They point out that, unlike the earlier periods when technological advancements both boosted productivity and created new jobs, the recent technological advancements, despite greatly improving productivity, have also been "destroying" jobs by making them obsolete much faster than they have created new jobs. The hardest hit have been workers with inadequate education and skills and those who skills have become redundant. Many of these workers, who have seen their jobs outsourced to other lower-wage countries, have either become unemployed or are employed in even-lower-paying jobs. These workers have experienced a prolonged period of wage stagnation.[14] Indeed, it is not only the lower-wage workers in the so-called "traded goods" sectors (or sectors in direct competition with imports) that have faced intense downward pressure on wages; smart machines have also negatively impacted jobs and wages of higher-skilled workers – contributing to the stagnation of median income levels and exacerbating inequality in the United States and other advanced economies. Compounding this, in the United States, the increased labor-market competition due to the huge influx of immigration (in particular, illegal immigration) has put tremendous downward pressure on wages for low-skilled and poorly educated workers, even as this has helped to greatly reduce the cost of living for those above the middle percentile of income distribution.

In an important study, David Autor (2010; also Acemoglu and Autor 2011; and Jaimovich and Siu 2012) provides new insights regarding the implications of the growing automation in the workplace. He persuasively argues that, contrary to conventional wisdom, the structural changes in the US national economy (instead of simply outsourcing and offshoring due to globalization) explain the profound shifts in employment patterns over the past three decades – in particular, the growing trend towards "job polarization" in the

United States. Specifically, Autor notes that although the growing sectoral mismatch between job openings and those qualified to fill them has contributed to the labor market's weak performance, it cannot account for the economy's jobless recovery and the problem of job polarization. Rather, Autor argues that the shift in US employment over the past three decades shows a clear trend towards (a) an increase in the demand for high-skilled and high-wage workers and for low-skilled and low-wage workers and (b) a sharp decline in employment growth for middle-skilled and middle-wage jobs, resulting in a "U-shaped employment distribution" or "job polarization."

To illustrate this "hollowing out" in employment growth, Autor examined changes in employment shares for different occupational skill levels by ranking occupations by their skill (wage) level and each skill level's change in employment share over the years 1979 to 2007. During the 1980s, occupations ranked below the median skill level lost employment share, while occupations above the median made gains. However, in the 1990s, polarization in employment patterns became visible, with the lowest-skilled and the highest-skilled occupations increasing their employment share (albeit, the growth was more significant among the highest-skill), but all of the middle-skilled occupations losing overall employment share. From 1999 to 2007, the low-skilled occupations experienced even larger gains in employment share and the high-skilled occupations experienced no change, but the middle-skilled again experienced employment loss. To better understand the roots and nature of job polarization – in particular, the reasons for the decline in demand for middle-skilled labor – Autor grouped "middle-educated and middle-paid occupations" into four job categories: (1) sales, (2) office and administrative, (3) production, craft and repair, and (4) operators, fabricators, and laborers. His findings confirm that the major contributor to job polarization in the United States has been the automation of "routine work" – which Autor defines as "procedural, rule-based activities" (that are widespread in many middle-skilled occupations) and that can be (and are) increasingly performed through the use of technological automation. On the other hand, the demand for both high-skilled and low-skilled "nonroutine" work has grown. Jaimovich and Siu (2012) persuasively show that, although manufacturing sector jobs tend to be more "routine-intensive," this does not mean that job polarization is largely the result of job losses in manufacturing through automation and off-shoring. In fact, they find that the manufacturing sector accounts for only 38 percent of job polarization. Hence, they note that job polarization is not simply a shift away from routine-intensive industries (such as manufacturing) and towards nonroutine-intensive industries, but also marks a shift across all industries from routine jobs and towards nonroutine jobs.

As Alichi, Kantenga, and Sole (2016) warn, the US middle class is shrinking. Specifically, the American "middle class" (or households with 50 to 150 percent of the national median pre-tax real income) has shrunk – with the middle-income households declining by 11 percentage points (from 58 to 47 percent) of the total US household population between 1970 and 2014. This hollowing of the US income distribution, which has made middle-income households poorer (that is, with more middle-income households falling into lower rather than higher income brackets), has had adverse implications for the American economy and society, as middle-class consumption is a major engine of US growth. The authors point out that from 1970 to 2000 this polarization was positive because more households moved into the ranks of the upper income (with real, or after-inflation, incomes higher than 150 percent of the median) than slipped down to real incomes less than 50 percent of the median. However, since 2000, more middle-income households have fallen into the ranks of lower-income households than have risen into higher-income ones. That is, while the majority of middle-income households moved up the income ladder between 1970 and 2000, since 2000 only 0.25 percent of households moved up to higher income. Rather, 3.25 percent of households fell from middle to low income. The authors note that, given that income share is a proxy for an income group's relative weight in the economy, the middle-income households' share of total national income has sharply declined, from about 47 percent of total US income in 1970 to about 35 percent in 2014, while the share for low-income households has remained flat at about 5 percent of total national income. This hollowing out has negatively impacted the economy by weakening consumption (the main engine of US growth) – which the authors estimate has led to the equivalent of about half a year of lost consumption growth between 1999 and 2013, or a cumulative 1¾-percentage-point loss over the period. It has also hurt families, as getting out of the lower-income trap is increasingly difficult because average real incomes have been stagnant (also see Danninger 2016). Recently, Acemoglu and Restrepo (2016) have warned that, although the decline in labor share and employment in the advanced economies due to automation, and in particular, advanced robotization, has been modest so far (between 360,000 and 670,000 jobs between 1999 and 2011), and they predict that further advances in industrial robotization have the potential not only to reduce wages (they estimate that one additional industrial robot per thousand workers reduces wages across the economy by 0.5 percent), but also to make many more jobs redundant.

THE POLITICS OF INEQUALITY

In their celebrated formulation in political economy, Meltzer and Richard (1981) point out that high levels of inequality in a democracy should ultimately force the political elites to acquiesce to the "median voter" (or the voter at the median of the income distribution) to support higher levels of taxes on the wealthy and greater redistribution of income. Similarly, according to Stigler (1970), since democracy tends to transfer political power to the middle classes rather than the poor, redistribution of wealth can only take place if the middle classes favor such redistribution. Thus, if electorates periodic hold governments accountable for their failure to deliver a more equitable distribution of economic goods, what explains the rise in inequality in the United States (and many other advanced democracies) over the past few decades – in particular, what explains why a disproportionate share of the national income has gone to the highest income earners in American society?

As noted earlier, in his many public statements, the former President Barack Obama called rising inequality "the defining challenge of our age," because it "distorts our democracy. It gives an outsized voice to the few who can afford high-priced lobbyists and unlimited campaign contributions, and it runs the risk of selling out our democracy to the highest bidder."[15] Others have raised similar concerns. Nobel-prize winning economist and New York Times columnist Paul Krugman has repeatedly warned that the United States is a "society in which money is increasingly concentrated in the hands of a few people, and in which that concentration of income and wealth threatens to make us a democracy in name only."[16] As the following sections illustrate, Obama's and Krugman's claims are supported by a large and growing body of research that has long claimed that despite the principle of one person-one-vote, in democracies power is generally proportional to wealth – with the wealthy exerting disproportionate influence on government policy, which they use to block policies that favor greater wealth equalization.

Mancur Olson (1982), in his brilliant *The Rise and Decline of Nations*, had lucidly described how narrowly based and well-organized interest groups (such as self-serving coalitions of business lobbies), in collusion with politicians and senior government officials and bureaucrats, had captured the key institutions of the post-war US government and were systematically using their privileged access to restructure the economy to their advantage – and in the process undermining entrepreneurial competition and economic growth. To Olson, this symbiotic relationship enabled these powerful interests to gain benefits and profits at the expense of the general public. On the other hand, the larger a coalition, the more difficult it is to organize and engage in "collective action." Thus, Olson reasoned, it is much harder for the bottom 50 percent to mobilize around a collective goal (such as demands for a more equitable redistribution of income and wealth) than it is for the top 10 percent. As Olson and the following more-recent studies show, it seems that despite their best efforts, the framers of the US Constitution failed to adequately protect the public interest from the machinations of the "faction."

Larry Bartels' (2008) provocative study *Unequal Democracy* provides some interesting answers. Drawing on a vast array of data spanning the past six decades, Bartels shows that the widening income gap in the United States is rooted in the country's political system. More specifically, both Republican and Democratic administrations have responded far more favorably to the interests of wealthy constituents, and as a result public policies have served to further the interests of these. Not surprisingly, Bartels shows that although the gap between the rich and poor has increased under Republican administrations, it has decreased only slightly under the Democrats – leaving America "grossly unequal." Yet, what explains the electorate's tolerance of rising inequality? Moving beyond conventional explanations that claim that working-class voters tend to vote against their own interests by voting Republican because they support conservative "values issues" such as gun rights, anti-abortion, and opposition to gay marriage, Bartels finds evidence of what he calls "class-biased economic voting." That is, rather perversely, American voters (including the middle- and lower-income populations) respond strongly and positively to growth at the very top (the richest 5 percent) of the income distribution – controlling for mean income growth. By not punishing administrations for their upwardly biased income distribution, middle- and low-income voters systematically undermine their own interests. Predictably, incumbents leverage their successes in generating income growth and prosperity for all during election time.

In a recent paper, Bonica, McCarty, Poole, and Rosenthal (2013, 1) ask why, "During the past two generations, democratic forms have coexisted with massive increases in economic inequality in the United States and many other advanced democracies. Moreover, these new inequalities have primarily benefited the top 1 percent, and even the top .01 percent. These groups seem sufficiently small that economic inequality could be held in check by political equality in the form of 'one person, one vote'." The authors provide "five possible reasons why the US political system has failed to counterbalance rising inequality. First, both Republicans and many Democrats have experienced an ideological shift toward acceptance of a form of free market capitalism that offers less support for government provision of transfers, lower marginal tax rates for those with high incomes, and deregulation of a number of industries. Second, immigration and low turnout of the poor have combined to make the distribution of voters more weighted to high incomes than is the distribution of households. Third, rising real income and wealth has made a larger fraction of the population less attracted to turning to government for social insurance. Fourth, the rich have been able to use their resources to influence electoral, legislative, and regulatory processes through campaign contributions, lobbying, and revolving door employment of politicians and bureaucrats. Fifth, the political process is distorted by institutions that reduce the accountability of elected officials to the majority and hampered by institutions that combine with political polarization to create policy gridlock."

In his path-breaking volume, *Political Order and Political Decay: From the Industrial Revolution to the Globalization of Democracy*, Francis Fukuyama (2014) cogently argues that the foundations of liberal democracies rest on three pillars: political accountability, an effective or strong state, and the impartial administration of the rule of law. In practice, this means no one person is above the rule of law, political leaders are accountable to their citizenry, among others, via regular and free elections, and the strong state (without which neither free markets nor democracy can survive) and its bureaucratic apparatus functions to provide public goods in a fair and equitable manner. Drawing on varied historical experiences, Fukuyama argues that these essential foundations have rarely emerged simultaneously. For example, although China developed a powerful state system (or at least a strong central state bureaucracy), its political order sorely lacked the rule of law and accountability. India and the Islamic world developed trappings of the rule of law, but have long suffered "a failure of the state" with their highly decentralized, fragmented, and weak political systems. It is only in late-eighteenth century Europe that these three pillars began to coalesce towards a more balanced equilibrium.

Fukuyama argues that throughout much of the nineteenth century, the United States was burdened with a corrupt and weak "patrimonial" state. However, beginning late in the nineteenth to the mid-twentieth century, the American state was gradually transformed into a strong activist actor, especially during the New Deal era. Yet, he cautions, "all political systems – past and present – are liable to decay." Over the past several decades, America's vibrant liberal democratic state has undergone a pronounced institutional decline – with both internal and external forces seemingly acting in tandem to systematically tear apart the liberal state and its representative institutions. Internally, the US political system with its many layers of checks-and-balances has spawned many more "veto players" than other parliamentary systems, and externally, sharp political and ideological polarization and the rise of powerful interest groups and lobbies with the ability to buy politicians and lawmakers with campaign contributions have created a "vetocracy" – which, on one hand, enables the various players to stifle and paralyze public policy formulation and implementation through gridlock, and more effectively manipulate the system to further protect and advance their interests, but on the other hand has few mechanisms and incentives to reach consensus for the common good. With the American political system seemingly "trapped in a bad equilibrium," government and governance have become less efficient, more corrupt, increasingly captured by vested special interests and the intractable and debilitating partisanship between Republicans and Democrats, resulting in wide oscillations in policy. Enjoying disproportionate influence, particularistic and unrepresentative interests ostensibly advance their special interests at the expense of the common good. The egregious concentration of wealth, stagnating incomes and widening economic inequality in the United States is the outcome of this larger political malaise and disfunction. Not surprisingly, to Fukuyama (2011) the emerging political order in the United States can best be described as a "plutocracy," or one based on the "rule by the rich and for the rich ... a state of affairs in which the rich influence government in such a way as to protect and expand their own wealth and influence, often at the expense of others." To Fukuyama, market forces alone are not responsible for the widening economic divide in the United States and elsewhere.

Indeed, Raghuram Rajan (2010) has persuasively argued that the growth of subprime lending was fueled by politicians' and policymakers' failure to address the root causes of rising income and wealth inequality in the United States. This failure forced them to make access to credit easier, especially for middle- and low-income households, in order to support their spending. Not only was the astronomical expansion of household debt as a share of household income the tragic result of this failure, the problem of widening income inequality was a direct cause of the housing boom and subsequent bust, which precipitated the financial crisis. Rajan (2010, 9) notes that "the political response to rising inequality – whether carefully planned or an unpremeditated reaction to constituent demands – was to expand lending to households, especially low income ones. The benefits – growing consumption and more jobs – were immediate, whereas paying the inevitable bill could be postponed into the future. Cynical as it may seem, easy credit has been used as a palliative throughout history by governments that are unable to address the deeper anxieties of the middle class directly." While one can quibble with Rajan's view as to why politicians, who are usually sensitive to high-income voters, should care about low-income ones, he lucidly argues that influential politicians and policymakers were only too happy to leave the mortgage markets alone as the expanding US housing market played a key role in stimulating the US economy after the 2001 dot-com crash. Not only did the easy lending practices bring in new buyers who had previously been shut out of the housing market to get that "starter house," besides allowing existing owners to move up to bigger houses (of course, with bigger mortgages), hundreds of thousands of construction and related jobs were at stake in the booming residential and commercial real estate sectors. Most important, the equity from the rapidly appreciating real estate yielded billions of dollars in cash for households to spend – leaving politicians and policymakers to postpone addressing the problem of rising income inequality for another day.

Jacob Hacker and Paul Pierson (2010), in their *Winner-Take-All Politics: How Washington Made the Rich Richer – and Turned Its Back on the Middle Class*, reject conventional economic explanations (globalization, technological changes, or educational levels) as the root cause of growing inequalities. Rather, they provocatively argue that the fundamental cause for rising inequality in the United States is "Washington," because the American government has been highjacked by powerful business and financial lobbyists to safeguard and serve the interests of the wealthy at the expense of the middle and lower classes – who have been systematically economically disenfranchised. This transformation in American politics began in the late 1970s under a Democratic president and a Democratic Congress, whose support for big-business interests led to the implementation of government policies that systematically weakened regulations that protected labor, the replacement of progressive tax policies (that had helped ensure a fairer distribution of income and wealth), and repeated tax cuts for the rich. The pro-business agenda continued under

Reagan, Bush 1, Clinton, Bush 2, and Obama, as the powerful business and financial lobbyists fund both Democrat and Republican politicians to safeguard and advance their interests. Pierson and Hacker underscore that income inequality in contemporary America fundamentally means that only a very tiny segment of the population (less than 1 percent), have made the real economic gains. Specifically, the "have-it-alls" or the top 1 percent of households captured some 40 percent of the nation's GDP growth since 1979, while the rest of the populace have barely seen their incomes grow in the last 30 years. The "winner-take-all economy" has benefited the rich at the expense of everyone because Democratic and Republican politicians and big business interests worked in tandem to undermine and gut the regulations and progressive tax policies that had earlier helped to provide a more fair economic distribution across all income groups. The end result is "winner-take-all gains," with a small minority benefiting, but a broad increase in inequality across income distributions, including a marked decline in economic security for the vast majority.

As the subtitle of Nicholas Carnes' (2013) *White Collar Government: The Hidden Role of Class in Economic Policy-Making* vividly states, the socioeconomic or "class" background of legislators profoundly influences and determines the content of policies the US political system generates. Specifically, Carnes argues that individuals from blue-collar or working-class backgrounds are woefully underrepresented in the American political system, while the overwhelming dominance of the white-collar or upper classes in America's legislatures gives the wealthy unprecedented political influence, in particular allowing them to skew policy that protects and advances elite economic interests. He notes that out of the 783 members of Congress who served between 1999 and 2008, only 13 had spent about a quarter of their prior careers engaged in blue-collar occupations, namely factory and retail. The overwhelming majority came from white-collar backgrounds, in particular, law and business.

To Carnes, a Congress member's socioeconomic or class background matters a great deal because class fundamentally shapes legislators' views on a host of important public policy issues such as taxation, corporate rights, labor, unemployment, welfare, anti-poverty policies and programs, health, and education, including the very role of government itself. However, even after controlling for differences in party affiliation, constituencies, campaign contributions, and changing demographic patterns, Carnes finds that legislators who have blue-collar or working-class roots are far more liberal on economic issues – in both their individual voting records and their favorable attitudes towards working-class concerns. Carnes notes that since individuals who come from working-class backgrounds or have held blue-collar occupations are conspicuously underrepresented in Congress, working-class voices are rarely heard – and that this neglect has only served to exacerbate income inequality. As he notes, "Policy makers from the working class bring a unique voice to the . . . legislative process, but in our white-collar government, they must shout to accomplish what other politicians can do with a whisper" (Carnes 2013, 60–61). Carnes concludes that if Congress's class composition were truly representative of the country as a whole, its policies would be more pro-labor and less pro-Wall Street. Specifically, Carnes conducts a simulation exercise on roll-call votes in Congress to find out how the last few Congresses would have voted on several key economic issues if it truly reflected the country's actual class makeup. He notes that a number of business-friendly policies, including the Bush tax cuts of 2001 and 2003 and the financial bailout following the subprime crisis, would have failed to pass. Even at the state and local levels (which have more variation among legislator backgrounds), a 10-percentage-point increase in the proportion of working-class legislators would translate into a 4- to 5-percentage-point increase in the share of budget expenditures earmarked for redistributive and welfare programs – even after controlling for the available resources, partisan divide, racial composition, and union density.

Martin Gilens' (2014) *Affluence and Influence* succinctly examines the relationship between public policy and public preferences to see if political influence and power has become more concentrated in the hands of the wealthy in the United States. To assess if mass or popular policy preferences were actually enacted into law, Gilens reviews almost two thousand survey questions conducted by different national polls between 1964 and 2006.[17] He concludes that "under most circumstances, the preferences of the vast majority of Americans appear to have essentially no impact on which policies the government does or doesn't adopt" (Gilens 2014, 1). Rather, the evidence shows that "higher-income respondents' views are more strongly related to government policy," and that "the strength of the relationship between preferences and policy outcomes not only increases with each step up the income ladder but does so at an increasing rate" (Gilens 2014, 76–77). Furthermore, the preferences of the majority or those in the middle and bottom income levels tend to translate into tangible outcomes when they happen to coincide with the preferences of influential interest groups (such as the protection of Social Security by the AARP) or the wealthy (such as the expansion of Medicare under President George W. Bush with strong backing of the pharmaceutical industry).[18] However, "when preferences between the well-off and the poor diverge, government policy bears absolutely no relationship to the degree of support or opposition among the poor" (Gilens 2014 81). Similarly, "median-income Americans fare no better than the poor when their preferences diverge from those of the well-off . . . when their views differ from those of more affluent Americans, government policy appears to be fairly responsive to the well-off and virtually unrelated to the desires of low-and middle-income citizens" (Gilens 2014, 81). Gilens concludes that if 80 percent of voters at the 90th income percentile support a change, it has a 50 percent chance of passing, versus a 32 percent chance when supported by 80 percent of voters at the 10th income percentile. Gilens also finds that, despite the Democrats' proclaimed identity as champions of the underclass, the Democrats are only slightly better at representing the interests of blue-collar and low-income constituencies than Republicans. Rather, the seemingly irreconcilable partisan considerations notwithstanding, both parties are far more responsive to the preferences of campaign contributors, interest groups, and wealthy members in their constituencies. To Gilens, this mismatch between policy preferences and actual policy outcomes lies at the root of the widening inequality in the United States.

Schlozman, Verba, and Brady's (2012) *The Unheavenly Chorus* authoritatively underscores the findings of Gilens. The authors draw on a voluminous compendium of some five decades of public opinion data to measure citizen political participation (or what they call "voice") across groups with different "socio-economic status" (SES). By combining income and education levels into an index of SES, the authors show that high-SES individuals tend to be conservative on economic matters and that their voices dominate economic policy-making in the United States. Not surprisingly, the authors conclude that "those who are not affluent and well educated are less likely to take part politically and are even less likely to be represented by the activity of organized interests" (Schlozman, Verba, and Brady 2012, 5). Specifically, the voices of lower-income groups are rarely heard, not only because of their very limited participation in the political system either as voters or volunteers for campaigns, but because the vast majority, either by choice or design, have become excluded from the system (as many are not registered voters), as they lack the resources for campaign contributions or have lobbyists and interest groups to promote their interests. Indeed, the authors argue that the Supreme Court and some other federal courts, in deregulating campaign finance have only served to further muzzle the voices of the less privileged.

Of course, the claim that the voices of the privileged and well-educated are over-represented in American politics is hardly new – indeed, the book's subtitle acknowledges E. E. Schattschneider's (1960, 35) famous observation that the "flaw in the pluralist heaven is that the heavenly chorus sings with a strong upper-class accent." However, what the authors convincingly show is that economic inequality significantly contributes to inequality in the citizenry involvement in politics and that unequal voices have become deeply institutionalized in the United States – noting that "Our analysis of the roots of political inequalities makes clear how deeply embedded they are in social, educational, and economic inequalities" (Schlozman, Verba, and Brady 2012, 539). As in Gilens study, the authors' research also raises questions regarding the long-established norm in political science: why politicians in the United States have generally ignored the "median voter." After all, classic political models show that the preferences of median voters tend to be more moderate and representative, and politicians gravitate to the middle in a two-party system because they ignore the median voter at their peril. The authors persuasively show that those active in politics (both Republicans and Democrats) have higher incomes than the median voter and generally share similar economic preferences. Hence, "there is no income confiscation in America. Political aspirants seeking the political support needed to be nominated by their parties and to run an effective campaign will be drawn away from the median voter, with clear consequences for policy outcomes" (Schlozman, Verba, and Brady 2012, 261).

In a vibrant representative democracy, all citizens (despite their economic standing) have their voices heard over the policies and programs their elected officials adopt. However, when the voices of the majority are marginalized and when influence and political power becomes disproportionately concentrated, then democracy is threatened. Clearly, as the preceding pages have shown, the growing income inequality is pushing that ideal aside and there is good reason to be worried about the current trajectory of American democracy. Yet, there is room for optimism. Democracies not only have the ability to correct course, we also know that key to reforming the current political order is reduction of the influence of money in politics. When the privileged and affluent learn that they cannot buy influence and access, policy can gradually shift into line with the preferences of all citizens. Meaningful campaign finance reforms, replacing gerrymandering with competitive districting, and registering voters is essential if we are ever to have a democracy that respects the aspirations and preferences of all its citizens.

GLOBALIZATION AND THE AMERICAN ECONOMY

The United States' extensive, intricate, and deep financial markets have not only enabled it to undergird and support international trade, but also facilitated the unparalleled expansion of global finance. Financial globalization or the integration of a country's financial system with international financial markets and institutions has served to dramatically expand and deepen cross-border financial interactions. In theory, financial liberalization, such as the removal of restrictions on capital import and export (or "capital account opening") and capital account liberalization (or the free entry and exit of capital flows to and from abroad), is expected to generate substantial macroeconomic benefits for both capital exporters and recipient countries. In addition, by promoting more efficient and productive allocation of capital, reduced borrowing costs through greater competition, and a transparent business environment through strengthening of corporate governance, financial globalization is expected to boost economic growth. Indeed, financial liberalization by more efficiently integrating global financial markets has facilitated robust economic growth and significantly contributed to the spectacular rise in the incomes of the top income earners in the United States and in other advanced economies – the vast majority of whom work for Wall Street or in the country's rapidly expanding financial sector.

However, along with these benefits, financial globalization also comes with risks. Specifically, even as global financial integration has enabled countries to boost economic growth, the deepening financial market interconnections mean that problems in one market have the potential to rapidly amplify and reverberate around the globe. These spillovers or contagion can quickly make countries succumb to market volatility, including prolonged and destructive financial crises. The resultant contractions can effectively undermine economic growth and erode gains in employment and savings – with the middle, the working classes, and the poor suffering the heaviest toll. The financial crisis of 2007–2009 triggered by speculative risk taking in the financial sector, including regulatory and supervisory failures, led to the great recession. In the US (and in other countries), the unprecedented wealth losses and the costs of adjustment have been borne disproportionately by tax payers – in particular, working- and middle-class households who suffered crippling losses from collapsing property prices, repossession of their homes, job losses, and crippling debt burdens. Furthermore, post-crisis recovery, often managed by imposing tough austerity measures such as wage and pension cuts, reductions in public health, education, and welfare spending, disproportionately hurts the middle- and low-income households.

Nineteenth-century British economist David Ricardo's classic formulation said that, if a country produces goods in accordance with its comparative advantage (in terms of resource endowments and human capital), it will gain through trade. To Ricardo, industry specialization and international trade – that is, if nations would concentrate solely on those industries in which they are more competitive relative to other nations, and trade with other countries for all other products, all countries would be better off. Drawing on this, proponents of globalization claim that global integration not only increases average income within countries, but also helps to reduce economic inequalities.

Yet, economic theory and reality do not always quite align. Certainly, in the aggregate, open trade promotes economic growth and generates overall gains for all parties. However, contrary to Ricardo's and his followers' seemingly sanguine assessments, it can also create winners and losers. Indeed, the integration of the American economy into the global economy has been a driver of both growing prosperity and rising income inequality. On one hand, the structural changes in the US economy as the result of deeper integration have disproportionately favored college-educated and skilled workers, who have seen a significant increase in their wages and overall incomes. On the other hand, rapid technological change and global connectedness also have unintended consequences. For example, addressing the question of whether foreign technological convergence is an important source of wage polarization in the United States, Cozzi and Impullitti (2016) answer in the affirmative by showing that technological globalization has been an important source of wage inequality as intense foreign technological competition has resulted in the erosion of the American industrial base. This has served to depress unskilled wages while raising the remuneration of skilled workers. Specifically, the reductions in trade barriers and the rapid diffusion of technologies across countries' borders have enabled multinational companies, especially those from Japan and Western Europe, to challenge and erode US technological leadership.[19] Their nuanced econometric model shows that foreign technological competition – which began to intensify beginning in the early 1980s – has contributed much to the polarization of the US labor market ... "to the advantage of the upper and lower tails of the skill distribution and the detriment of occupations performed by workers with intermediate levels of skills" (Cozzi and Impullitti 2016, 999–1000). Similarly, deepening linkages and integration have also resulted in the outsourcing and offshoring of work that has "hollowed-out" semi-skilled and unskilled jobs, worsening the stagnation of middle-class incomes. Nobel laureate Eric Maskin (2015) has insightfully captured this paradox by noting that, although average incomes have risen as a result of expanded trade and deeper global integration, so has inequality within countries. He notes that the inequality resulting from globalization takes two forms – one "less worse" than the other. The "less-worse" is when inequality is a necessary side-effect of increased economic growth within a country, while the "worse" is when incomes of a large segment of the workforce (usually low- and moderate-skilled workers) drop as a result of less demand for their skills, while the wages of higher-skilled workers increase.

More importantly, China's rapid integration into the global economy has had the most far-reaching impact on the American economy, indeed the global economy – in the process, turning the hallowed theory of comparative advantage upside down. The dissonance between economic models and the ground reality in US–China trade is largely due to China's unprecedented comparative advantage, given the very different levels of development and sharp differences in wages between the two countries. China's accession to the World Trade Organization (WTO) in 2001 was a huge boon, as membership in the WTO removed the risk that China would face tariff increases from the United States and China's other major trading partners.[20] This helped to further boost domestic and foreign investment in China's manufacturing sector – in the process making "Made in China" goods ubiquitous worldwide. Not surprisingly, the Chinese export juggernaut has accumulated huge trade surpluses with almost all of its major trading partners – in particular, the United States, which has the largest merchandise trade deficit with China, totaling approximately $365.7 billion in 2015.[21] In similar vein, China's current-account surplus has grown from an average of around 2 percent of GDP in the 1990s to over 5 percent in the following decade. China's unprecedented comparative advantage in low-cost manufacturing not only enabled it to capture about one-fifth of all manufacturing exports by 2013 (from a share of only 2 percent in 1991); the implications for manufacturing jobs in America have been negative. It is no coincidence that the downward pressures on the earnings of American factory workers and the sharp decline in US manufacturing employment began in 2000 – just as the Chinese imports took off.

Although the benefits of free and open trade have long been recognized, recent research is qualifying this conventional wisdom with the caveat, "in the long term" – because the short-term costs can be painful and traumatic. Autor, Dorn, and Hanson (2016) provide compelling evidence that sustained exposure to foreign competition, in particular, the intense competition from China (and other large emerging economies) can and has produced adverse effects such as a sharp contraction or elimination of jobs and depressed and stagnant wages for at least a decade in the advanced economies. This, the authors argue, is because during the post-war period (at least up to the 1980s), the rich OECD countries (with each having particular comparative advantages) mostly traded with each other, resulting in an overall win-win for all stakeholders. However, the rapid integration of China into the global economy and its transformation into a "global factory" (China's share of exports of manufactured goods skyrocketed from 2.3 percent to 18.8 percent between 1991 and 2013 and its share of world manufacturing value added increased by a factor of six, from 4.1 percent to 24 percent) overwhelmed the manufacturing and related sectors in the advanced economies. The sheer magnitude and range of Chinese exports – covering the primary, intermediate, and advanced manufactured goods, was simply too much to absorb – with adverse consequences for manufacturing employment and economic inequality. The authors bluntly note that "the advance of China … has also toppled much of the received empirical wisdom about the impact of trade on labor markets. The consensus that trade could be strongly redistributive in theory but was relatively benign in practice has not stood up well to these new developments" (Autor, Dorn, and Hanson 2016, 3). Autor, Dorn, and Hanson's study of manufacturing job losses in the United States finds that regions or industries with exposure to Chinese imports experienced sustained job losses. In fact, they conclude that Chinese imports directly eliminated nearly 1 million American manufacturing jobs between 1999 and 2011, and about 2.4 million jobs indirectly – if related industries and suppliers are included. Similarly, according to the Economic Policy Institute (EPI), a left-leaning think tank, between 2001 and 2013 the United States lost about 3.2 million manufacturing jobs to China via outsourcing and from Beijing's deliberate "mercantile policies" – and despite the US manufacturing sector's significant productivity growth, it could not overcome the huge trade advantage China has gained from having an undervalued currency (Scott 2014). Both agree that the unemployed workers have great difficulty in finding new jobs with similar salary levels. The small percentage fortunate to find new jobs are paid far less than in their previous jobs and are vulnerable to being laid-off or let go altogether, as they mostly found work in industries vulnerable to competition from imports or lower-paid service jobs.

Autor, Dorn, and Hanson's (2016) research provides an important corrective to the long-held assumptions that trade adjustment is mostly frictionless and that industry and labor can quickly and effortlessly adjust in the face of market changes. To the contrary, labor-market adjustment in the face of unprecedented trade with China has been difficult and protracted for American workers. Because US manufacturing is geographically concentrated (in the Midwest), the abrupt and the near total collapse of the manufacturing base in the American industrial "rust-belt" and the absence of a viable economic alternative triggered a veritable chain reaction that has not only weakened regional economies, but also grievously undermined the local service industries – thereby limiting their ability to absorb the displaced labor. Does this mean that trade with China has been a zero-sum game for the United States? Autor, Dorn, and Hanson (2016) note that whilst the United States' overall gains from trade with China have been quite modest, they also remind that some of these costs have been offset by consumers who have benefitted from "cheap" Chinese imports. Furthermore, the authors point out that workers in the United States and other advanced economies will benefit "over the long run" with trade with China, as firms and businesses become more competitive by reducing costs and reallocating labor and capital away from inefficient and uncompetitive manufacturing industries and into newer and more productive ones. Suffice it to note, this is hardly much comfort for the hundreds of thousands of displaced workers and businesses.

It is important to note that the Autor, Dorn, and Hanson study examines the impact of US–China trade on the US labor markets. The study does not evaluate the trade-off and "gains" from US–China trade. In other words, international trade includes more than goods and services – and to focus simply on the trade deficit (thereby primarily on goods and services) would mean to overlook the issues of balance of payments and national savings and investment. Specifically, investment in US assets allows US businesses to grow and expand, while the foreign purchase of US government bonds allows the United States to finance its growing national debt. Of course, if US consumers saved more (that is, spent less on foreign imports), the US trade deficit would be much smaller. Moreover, the division of production in global value chains makes it difficult to "accurately" measure the size of trade deficits between nations – a problem compounded by the fact that China is usually the final destination of assembly for the products of multinational companies, which source goods from several countries in an ever-expanding and complex supply chains. This partly explains the sharp discrepancy between the official trade statistics of China and the United States. For example, according to US figures, the 2014 bilateral trade deficit with China was $342.6 billion. However, China has long claimed that its actual trade surplus with the United States was $237.0 billion. The $105.6 billion gap can be explained by considering whether the trade surplus is measured in value-added terms or in gross exports terms. Given that the foreign content share of China's exports is around one-third (which is significantly above the levels of other large economies) this discrepancy is not surprising. Further, in the case of US–China bilateral trade, Martin (2015) points out that the discrepancies are also due to the differences in the "list value of shipments" when they leave China and when they enter the United States, including different attributions of both origin and destination of Chinese exports that are shipped through a third location (such as Hong Kong) before arriving in the United States. It should also be noted that the United States imports a large volume of goods from US companies based in China because of China's advantage in low-cost assembly. Yet once these goods are shipped back to the United States, they are labeled as "imports." Given these problematics, restricting imports from China via tariffs or other forms of trade protectionism will mean that US consumers will have to spend more for purely "Made in America" goods. Thus, to protect the significant savings American consumers derive from lower-priced Chinese imports, it is often argued that both levels of US government (federal and state) can help mitigate some of the adverse impact of cheap imports on the US labor market by strengthening protections for workers – as noted, something they have not done well. This way, workers made redundant by imports could improve their skills and reenter the labor market, and millions of consumers could continue to benefit from low-priced imports from China and other emerging economies. Finally, tens of millions of American workers are employed in industries and businesses that export a wide range of manufactured goods and services around the world, including China. Indeed, Beijing often reiterates that General Motors (GM) has sold more vehicles in China than in the United States each year from 2010 to 2016. In 2016, GM's sold 3.9 million vehicles in China, compared to 3.0 million in the United States.[22] In addition, growing numbers of American businesses and service providers are inextricably tied to global supply chains – without which they would lose their competitive edge. Clearly, global trade is hardly a zero-sum game. Yet because the benefits of economic globalization, especially unfettered trade, tend to be diffuse, and its costs usually concentrate and fall disproportionately on particular groups, sectors, and communities, the negatively impacted constituencies have strong incentives to mobilize against free trade and deepening global integration. Indeed, those adversely affected by the changes emanating from globalization tend to oppose it vociferously. Not surprisingly, free trade, open markets, and globalization writ large are increasingly hard sells politically in representative democracies.

US–CHINA ECONOMIC GLOBALIZATION "WARS"

The large US trade deficit with China, with its negative impact on American jobs and the nation's overall economic well-being, has long been a contentious issue and remains a sore spot with politicians (both Republicans and Democrats) and the public, who blame it on China's deliberate unfair trade practices and promise to hold Beijing accountable. During the 2016 Presidential election, the Republican candidate Donald Trump announced his intention to impose a 45 percent tariff on imports from China, which he blames for "robbing Americans of billions of dollars of capital and millions of jobs," while his Democratic counterpart Hillary Clinton pledged to hold Beijing responsible for giving its exports an unfair competitive advantage in the global markets. At its core, the criticism against China is that it engages in unfair "mercantilist" trade through its currency policies. That is, China's unprecedented export growth is to a large extent facilitated by Beijing's policy of preventing the appreciation of the RMB – which in turn keeps the prices of Chinese exports low. Such deliberate "currency manipulation" distorts trade and in the process transfers jobs and wealth away from the United States.

Specifically, Beijing buys large volumes of foreign currency and then lowers the price of the RMB vis-à-vis the foreign currency in order to make Chinese exports cheaper in the United States and other global markets. Therefore, by keeping the value of its currency artificially low, including a highly selective adherence to WTO principles and its Protocol of Accession, Beijing makes its exports much cheaper and in the process undermines the competitiveness of American manufactured goods. Bergsten (2016), who now believes that China has not manipulated its currency for the past two years, notes that "China was the champion currency manipulator of all time from 2003 through 2014. During this 'decade of manipulation,' China bought more than $300 billion annually to resist upward movement of its currency by artificially keeping the exchange rate of the dollar strong and the renminbi's exchange rate weak. China's competitive position was thus strengthened by as much as 30 to 40 percent at the peak of the intervention. Currency manipulation explained most of China's large trade surpluses, which reached a staggering 10 percent of its entire GDP in 2007." Scott (2014, 1–2), who believes that China remains a currency manipulator, echoes the widely held view, noting that "currency manipulation, by about 20 countries (mostly in Asia), is the most important cause of our trade deficit. These nations have been exploiting our markets and stealing US jobs for over a decade. Ending currency manipulation would reduce US trade deficits by between $200 billion and $500 billion per year within three years, creating between 2.3 million and 5.8 million U.S. jobs … China is by far the largest currency manipulator, and it has increased its holdings of foreign exchange reserves by at least $359 billion per year, on average, between 2006 and 2012." Some have even gone a step further to link China's underhanded policies to the skyrocketing US national debt. It is claimed that until 1989, the United States enjoyed the status of the net creditor to the world, but in the early 2000s, the United States became the world's biggest debtor. In the period December 2011 to December 2015, the foreign holdings of US Federal debt increased by $1.1 trillion to approximately $6.1 trillion – while the domestic total publicly held debt increased by about $3.5 trillion to $15.1 trillion. As of December 2015, the People's Republic of China is the single largest foreign holder of US federal debt, owning approximately $1.2 trillion, or 20.3 percent of all foreign investment in US privately held federal debt.[23]

Two caveats should be noted. First, there is no international (or national) agreement on what constitutes "currency manipulation." Not surprisingly, countries can (and do) readily accuse each other for engaging in currency manipulation. For example, Brazil, India, and other nations have criticized the US Federal Reserve's post-crisis monetary policies for "deliberately" weakening the US dollar to boost imports. And, second, a key role of central banks is to conduct domestic monetary policy, including adjusting the value of the national currency by expanding or contracting the money supply. In fact, every central bank has legal and monopoly power to create money and fix one nominal price (the exchange rate) and a nominal interest rate to achieve stated policy objectives such as price stability or full employment. Like many other central banks that fix a nominal exchange rate, the US Federal Reserve targets the federal-funds rate, while China's Central Bank (Peoples Bank of China or PBC) has the authority to fix the RMB-US dollar rate. Indeed, the PBC fixes the exchange value of the RMB within a narrow band of 2 percent, within which it allows market forces to operate. Given such wide powers, the actions of central banks can (and often do) generate controversy and policy disagreement.

Yet, does this means that China engages in currency manipulation – or more specifically, deliberately manipulates the RMB in order to keep it consistently undervalued in order to make its export "cheaper" in relation to exports of other countries, in particular, its largest market – the United States? At the outset, it should be noted that China's currency has gone through different policy regimes: it has been pegged to the US dollar and allowed to float – albeit not entirely freely. For example, from 1994 to 2005, the yuan was fixed at around 8.28 to one US dollar. This artificially depressed rate made Chinese exports cheaper than US goods, including American exports to China. Not surprisingly, American manufacturers with the backing of lawmakers in Congress argued that the artificially low yuan placed American companies at a huge competitive disadvantage *inter alia*, contributing to the bankruptcy of US companies and the loss of tens of thousands of American jobs.[24] The contention was that the yuan was so undervalued (by some accounts by as much as 40 percent) that it amounted to an unfair trade subsidy. This unfair advantage permits a flood of cheap Chinese-made goods into the United States but makes American products expensive in China.[25] Thus, some claim that if the yuan were traded at its true market value, the bilateral imbalance would be substantially reduced, if not altogether eliminated. This is because China's exports to the United States would become more expensive in dollars and would therefore decrease, while China's imports from the US would become less expensive in yuan and therefore increase. To make matters worse, China's unwillingness to allow the yuan to appreciate, in turn made other Asian Pacific Rim countries reluctant to allow their currencies to appreciate because of their fear of losing further export sales to China.[26] As the US trade deficit with China soared to record levels in first-quarter 2005, the Bush administration came under intense pressure to take unilateral action to address the problems associated with the artificial undervaluation of the yuan. US Treasury Secretary John Snow called for an immediate Chinese exchange rate adjustment, but many other lawmakers called for punitive tariffs on cheaply priced Chinese imports unless China revalued its currency.

In May 2005, the US Senate by a margin of 67 to 33 voted to consider a proposal to impose a 27.5 percent tariff on all imports from China unless Beijing stopped inflating its currency. In May 2005, the US decided to reimpose quotas on seven categories of clothing imports from China, limiting their growth to no more than 7.5 percent over a 12-month period. On 23 June 2005, the Bush administration, which until then had insisted that diplomacy was working in getting China to allow the yuan's value to be set by currency markets rather than controlled by the government, finally warned China that it could be cited as a "currency manipulator" and face economic sanctions unless it switched to a flexible exchange system. Labeling China's currency policies "highly distortionary," the Bush administration warned that it was going to closely monitor China's progress towards adopting a flexible exchange system.

It seems that the pressure worked. On July 21, 2005, Beijing made its biggest monetary shift in more than a decade by revaluing the yuan and dropping the currency's peg to the US dollar, announcing that the yuan's exchange rate would become "adjustable, based on market supply and demand with reference to exchange rate movements of currencies in a basket" composed of the dollar, the yen, the euro, among few other key currencies.[27] This was an important, albeit modest shift. As noted, from 1994 to July 2005, the value of the yuan was pegged to the US dollar at a rate determined by the People's Bank of China. The yuan traded within the range of 8.27 to 8.28 to the dollar because the People's Bank maintained this peg by buying dollar-denominated assets in exchange for the yuan in order to reduce excess demand for the yuan. As a result, the exchange rate between the yuan and the dollar remained largely the same – despite changing market conditions. When Beijing abandoned the peg by moving to a system that now linked the yuan to a basket of currencies, it effectively raised the yuan's value by 2.1 percent.[28] This meant that prior to the revaluation, US$1 bought 8.28 yuan, and following revaluation US$1 would buy roughly 8.11 yuan. Beijing made it clear that it had set tight parameters on how much the yuan could rise. Clearly, the aim was to make sure that the yuan did not float by a big margin, but appreciated[29] by

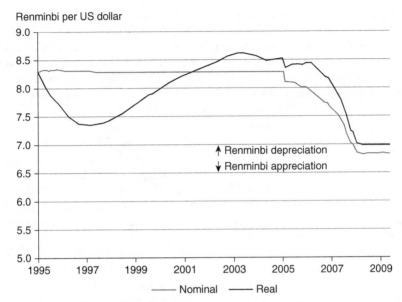

Renminbi per US dollar

FIGURE 2.9 Renminbi-dollar exchange rate.
Source: Humpage and Herrell 2009.[31]

a modest 2 percent by moving within a tight range of +/– 0.3 percent against a group of foreign currencies that represent China's top trading partners.[30] Thus, unlike a true floating exchange rate, the yuan was allowed to fluctuate by only 0.3 percent on a daily basis against the basket. However, this modest and gradual appreciation (called "managed float") allowed China to continue to accumulate foreign reserves – implying that if the yuan was allowed to free float, it would appreciate much more rapidly. The fact is that during July 2005 to May 2008, the yuan appreciated by 14.4 percent in terms of the US dollar – but much less in real effective terms (since most other major currencies appreciated against the dollar), despite China's large and growing trade surpluses.

In adopting more market-based system under which the value of the yuan was allowed to fluctuate relative to a basket of currencies, and by allowing the RMB to modestly appreciate from 2005 to 2008, China managed to placate the critics.[32] However, facing intense pressure during the subprime-induced global financial crisis, Beijing was forced to resume its earlier practice of pegging the renminbi to a nearly fixed rate to revive its faltering export-dependent economy. Since the PBC tightly controls the renminbi movements through its interventions in the market, Beijing kept its currency pegged at nearly 6.83 per dollar from mid-2008 through July 2010 to help its companies compete amid weak global demand.[33] To the critics, this was just the latest of Beijing's underhanded acts. By deliberating keeping the yuan undervalued,

Beijing gains unfair advantages for its exports, while a free-floating yuan would erode China's advantage and much of the global imbalance in world trade.

Predictably, Beijing's decision only galvanized the critics and triggered a torrent of sharp condemnations. In March 2010, some 130 members of the House of Representatives (both Democrats and Republicans) sent a strongly worded letter to Treasury Secretary Timothy Geithner, demanding that he take immediate action by declaring China a "currency manipulator" and imposing tariffs and other punitive measures to force Beijing to stop manipulating the value of its currency to gain an unfair trade advantage. A number of influential lawmakers, including senators Charles Schumer (Democrat) and Charles Grassley (the top Republican on the Senate Finance Committee), even proposed legislation to effectively threaten China with trade sanctions for deliberately undermining global trade through its undervalued currency – claiming that a yuan undervalued by some 40 percent gave Chinese exporters an unfair price advantage.[34]

Beijing's response was equally swift and uncharacteristically terse – adding fuel to an already explosive subject. Commerce Minister Chen Deming accused the United States of politicizing and exaggerating the issues and, in a blistering public statement, made clear that China would not take kindly to such actions, stating that "If [the Treasury Department's] reply is accompanied by trade sanctions and trade measures, we will not ignore it." Chen warned that "If some congressmen insist on labeling China as a currency manipulator and slap punitive tariffs on Chinese products, then the [Chinese] government will find it impossible not to react ... If the United States uses the exchange rate to start a new trade war, China will be hurt. But the American people and US companies will be hurt even more." Chen also indignantly dismissed US criticisms, reiterating Premier Wen Jiabao's earlier statement denying that the yuan was undervalued or that China's exchange-rate policies were behind American deficits and the trade imbalance. Rather, Chen blamed restrictive US export policies, especially on high-tech dual-use goods such as supercomputers and satellites, for the US trade deficit problem.[35] In similar vein, Vice Premier Wang Qishan has repeatedly stated that the United States trade deficit reflects a low US savings rate and profligate spending – a problem that even a moderate rise in the yuan's exchange rate will not resolve. He urged the Obama administration to "take all necessary measures to stabilize its economy and financial markets to ensure the security of China's assets and investments in the US." Most notably, Wang publicly lectured Geithner and other senior US officials to take "credible steps" to protect the value of the dollar and said that "high attention should be given to fiscal deficits."[36]

On April 3, 2010, the Obama administration announced that it would delay publication of the semiannual exchange rate report to Congress (due on April 15), containing the international economic and exchange rate policies of America's major trading partners. The report was eagerly awaited because it would officially state the Obama administration's position on

China's exchange rate policy, and in particular, whether Treasury Secretary Geithner would declare China a "currency manipulator." Instead, striking a measured tone, Geithner tactfully noted that "China's inflexible exchange rate has made it difficult for other emerging market economies to let their currencies appreciate. A move by China to a more market-oriented exchange rate will make an essential contribution to global rebalancing." Geithner noted that "the best avenue for advancing US interests at this time" is via discussions in multilateral and bilateral forums, including that of the G-20 finance ministers and central bank governors in late April, the semiannual Strategic and Economic Dialogue between the United States and China in May, and during the meeting of G-20 leaders and finance ministers in June.[37] To further assuage Beijing, on April 7, Geithner made an impromptu 75-minute stopover at the VIP terminal of Beijing airport (on his trip to India) to meet with Vice Premier Wang Qishan (China's leading finance official) to "exchange views on US–China economic relations and the global economy."[38]

No doubt, the Treasury's conciliatory message was intended to de-escalate tensions that had been brewing for months between Beijing and Washington. In fact, the war of words began during Geithner's confirmation hearing (in January 2009) for Treasury Secretary when he bluntly stated that both he and "President Obama – backed by the conclusions of a broad range of economists – believe that China is manipulating its currency."[39] Geithner's tough rhetoric brought nods of approval from the members of the Senate Finance Committee – many of who have long rallied against Beijing's alleged malpractice and were now hoping for a firm stance against China from the new Obama administration. However, to the markets, Geithner's accusatory tone signaled a potential confrontation between the world's largest and second-largest economies. The already jittery markets responded almost immediately as investors became concerned that China might scale-back its purchase of US debt if the new administration pushed Beijing to further revalue its currency: the dollar promptly fell, the price of gold jumped by $40, and the price of Treasury debt was driven further down.[40] Although Geithner tried to gloss over his remarks by stating that what he actually meant was for China to adopt "market exchange rates," it only brought a short respite to this sensitive subject.

On May 24, 2010, during the start of the second round of the "US–China Strategic and Economic Dialogue," Beijing once again repeated its commitment to reforming its currency regime – but based on "independent decision-making" and at its own pace. Not surprisingly, on June 10, 2010, during a heated Senate Finance panel hearing on US–China trade relations, both Democratic and Republican lawmakers heaped criticism on Geithner and the Obama administration for their lack of progress in dealing with Beijing's mercantilist economic and currency policies. Senator Schumer angrily noted that "billions and billions of dollars, millions and millions of jobs flow to China simply because their currency is manipulated." He warned that Congress is now working on legislation that would impose tough trade sanctions on China. Schumer noted: "China's mercantilist policies continue to undermine the health of US industries, so this is fair warning ... despite the administration asking us not to do it, we are going to move forward with our bipartisan legislation ... I am confident that this bill will pass the Senate with overwhelming support. The issue here is not US protectionism but China's flouting of the rules of free trade."[41]

Seemingly in response, on June 19, 2010 (a week before the Group of 20 summit), China's central bank released a statement signaling the possible end to the yuan's 23-month-old dollar peg (which was ended in July 2010).[42] Beijing made clear that domestic economic conditions were behind the shift by stating that "the recovery and upturn of the Chinese economy has become more solid with the enhanced economic stability ... It is desirable to proceed further with reform of the renminbi exchange-rate regime and increase the renminbi exchange-rate flexibility."[43] However, the statement remained vague with regard to when the central bank would implement the change. Beijing ruled out a one-time revaluation by noting that there is no basis for "large-scale appreciation." Beijing's move helped deflect criticism from the Obama administration and other G-20 nations at the June 26–27 G-20 meeting in Toronto. While Geithner called the move an "important step," he also added that "the test will be how far and how fast they let the currency appreciate."[44] However, Senator Schumer cynically noted that "this vague and limited statement of intentions is China's typical response to pressure ... Until there is more specific information about how quickly it will let its currency appreciate and by how much, we can have no good feeling that the Chinese will start playing by the rules."[45] Schumer warned that "we hope the Chinese will get more specific in the next few days. If not, then for the sake of American jobs and wealth, which are hurt every day by China's practices, we will have no choice but to move forward with our legislation."[46]

China's growing foreign exchange reserve does suggest that the PBC has been engaged in a large-scale and one-way intervention in the foreign exchange market by selling the yuan and buying dollars and that the RMB has been undervalued to the dollar (by how much is debatable) compared to where it would be if it were left purely to market forces. Nevertheless, it is not always clear whether the movements in the RMB's nominal exchange rate affects long-term trade flows and employment creation in the United States, and it is true that currency movements can be the result of several factors. On the one hand, it can be argued that the PBC actively prevented the value of the RMB from rising during the years 2005–2014 via "sterilization" measures – and in the process accumulated a massive $4 trillion in reserves by early 2014. On the other hand, it is reasonable to say that as China's exports expanded and it amassed huge trade surpluses relative to the US, its holdings of US dollars also skyrocketed, making it exceedingly difficult for the PBC to maintain the peg to the dollar and forcing the authorities to allow the RMB to appreciate relative to the dollar – at least until 2014. As the trade-weighted dollar exchange rate appreciated more than 20 percent against virtually all currencies from the second quarter of 2014 to the first quarter of 2016 because of robust growth in the US economy, the unwinding of monetary easing by the Federal Reserve, and similar actions in the Eurozone and Japan, the currencies of the US major trading partners declined on their own due to market forces.[47] Since mid-2014, China's foreign currency reserves have been falling, in keeping with the PBC's efforts to strengthen the exchange rate – in part because of Beijing's concern that a declining currency could result in capital flight from the country. Hence, because Beijing has been more frequently selling rather than buying dollars, manipulation has been less of the problem since 2014 (Bergsten 2016).

In fact, on August 11, 2015, the PBC announced a surprise devaluation, depreciating the RMB 3 percent against the US dollar overnight. Beijing's move was to make the official exchange rate more market oriented by basing its determination on market rates in step with its declared policy objective of full exchange rate flexibility. To this end, China's central bank announced new measures to improve the market orientation of its daily central parity rate of the RMB. Since the August 2015 announcement, the RMB has depreciated further and will most likely continue to face depreciation pressure against the dollar, especially if the Federal Reserve raises its rate and in the process strengthens the dollar relative to other currencies, including the RMB. More specifically, from July 2015 to December 2016, the RMB depreciated by 13.6 percent against the US dollar. While to some the RMB's depreciation against the dollar (as well as other major currencies) was evidence of problems in the Chinese economy – in particular, a slowdown of its export engine – to others the depreciation of RMB was yet another move by Beijing to boost economic growth at the expense of its trading partners. This argument has long being echoed by Donald Trump and some members of Congress. Indeed, in February 2016, the US Congress passed the "Trade Facilitation and Enforcement Act of 2015," issuing new and "enhanced" provisions for the Department of Treasury in their monitoring of foreign exchange rates – or more specifically, when to list a country as a currency manipulator.[48] The three new and enhanced provisions include (a) the size of the country's current trade surplus with the United States, (b) the size of the country's trade surplus with the rest of the world, and (c) the number of times the country has intervened in currency markets in recent months. If a country meets all three provisions and is labeled a currency manipulator, the Treasury Department is required to demand special talks with the country to guide them away from such practices – with penalties (such as imposition of tariffs) if the country fails to comply. In April 2017, the Treasury concluded that China met one of the criteria (a large trade surplus with the United States) and placed China under "monitoring list" – which is one step below being labeled a currency manipulator. The Treasury noted that it "will be scrutinizing China's trade and currency policies very closely" because China still "needs to demonstrate that its lack of intervention to resist appreciation over the last three years represents a durable policy shift by letting the RMB (yuan) rise with market forces once appreciation pressures resume."[49]

In July 2016, following the International Monetary Fund's assessment that the RMB was "broadly in line with fundamentals," the RMB was added to its basket of international reserve currencies known as special drawing rights (SDR). This has put the RMB (effective from October 2016) in distinguished company, as only four other currencies (the euro, the US dollar, Japanese yen, and the British pound) are included in the SDR basket. Even as this vividly underscores the deepening integration of the Chinese economy into the global financial system, it also highlights the challenges China faces – after all, the IMF's decision was based partly on Beijing's stated commitment to continue "market-oriented exchange rate reform" of the RMB. Yet, given President Trump's view that China continues to manipulate its currency, this issue is hardly settled.

THE DOLLAR AS RESERVE CURRENCY

Of course, the particular US concerns regarding currency manipulation, trade deficits, and the national debt should be seen in the larger context of the United States' share of the world economy (27.5 percent in 2010) and the world's seemingly insatiable appetite for dollar-denominated assets. After all, the US dollar is the world's reserve currency (the currency held by foreign central banks as protection against balance of payments crises). A large portion of international payments are made in dollars and a substantial portion of international trade (even trade not directly involving the United States) is denominated in US dollars. In addition, globally traded commodities (such as oil and food grains) are priced in dollars, thereby making it necessary for foreign banks to hold portfolios of dollar assets and liabilities. Overall, some two-thirds of the world's official foreign exchange reserves of 6.7 trillion dollars are held in dollars. This means that central banks around the world not only hold more US dollars and dollar securities than they do assets denominated in any other foreign currency, they also know that these dollar reserves are essential to stabilizing the value of their own national currencies. In other words, the US dollar is used and held by foreign central banks as the essential medium of exchange.

However, the US dollar's status as the world's reserve currency is a mixed blessing. Certainly, the dollar's status gives it what has been referred to as an "exorbitant privilege" – or the unique ability to borrow and trade in its own currency. In addition, it allows the United States to benefit from *seigniorage*, or reduced transaction costs, thereby giving American banks and businesses competitive advantages in international commerce, including foreign exchange risk and low interest rates, as countries using their currency can accumulate fiscal debts denominated in their currency at relatively low interest rates. As Kirshner (1995) has noted, foreign governments that hold large dollar reserves are "entrapped," as they depend on US prosperity for their own continued growth. Not surprisingly, the assumption that if the American economy went into a sharp downturn, foreign central banks would be reluctant to invest their national savings into the dollar has so far proven to be incorrect. Rather, the dollar has been repeatedly affirmed as the global reserve currency. The massive "flight to safety" by panicked investors following the collapse of Lehman Brothers into US Treasury instruments underscored that the US government is still the safest investment in the world, and that, for all its flaws, the US dollar and dollar-denominated assets are today akin to what gold was during the Bretton Woods era.

Nevertheless, as Druck, Magud, and Mariscal (2015) point out, the US dollar's status as the world's reserve currency can often be a "double-edged sword." Drawing on data for 1970 to 2014, the authors found that during periods of dollar appreciation (which tend to be about six to eight years in duration and usually occur when the US economy is growing), real GDP growth in emerging market economies (especially those that are net commodity exporters) slows down despite the fact that US growth is driving global demand. By contrast, during periods of a depreciating dollar (which tends to last for about nine years), emerging economies tend to perform much better. What explains this counterintuitive outcome? Druck and his coauthors note that as the dollar appreciates, dollar-denominated commodity prices tend to fall, and the weaker commodity prices results in falling incomes – which negatively impact domestic demand growth and ultimately a deceleration in real GDP growth. Thus, when the world's largest economy is growing and pulling in imports, some emerging economies also suffer from the unintended "collateral damage."

Moreover, the dollar's status as the reserve currency also means that financial shocks can be rapidly transmitted across borders. For example, during the 2007 global financial crisis, as American and other investors (both private and sovereign) seeking a safe-haven began to bring their dollars home (placing them in the safety of US government bonds), it helped lift the value of the dollar.[50] Yet for the rest of the world this meant a dollar crunch and an exacerbation of economic woes, especially in countries attempting to refinance debt, and those who experienced a roll-back of foreign investment and aid. In addition, because the massive accumulation of US dollar assets around the world saddled banks with significant funding requirements, the acute shortages of dollar liquidity (particularly in the weeks following Lehman's collapse), both within and outside the United States, created serious problems for financial institutions, as many could not access dollars when they needed them most.[51] This not only undermined the interbank money markets, but also resulted in a sharp rise in the cost of exchanging foreign currency for dollars in the FX swap markets. If not for the far-reaching policy measures adopted by central banks around the world, including international swap arrangements with the US Federal Reserve, they would not have been able to provide dollars to financial institutions in their respective jurisdictions. Regardless, the massive deleveraging also contributed to large and wild swings in the currencies of many emerging economies, including India (see Chapter 4).[52]

In addition, although the dollar's status allows the United States to finance its huge trade and fiscal deficits without transaction costs, it has also created "global imbalances" as emerging economies (most notably, China), in order to gain a trade advantage, have pegged their exchange rates to the dollar, often at undervalued levels – amassing vast amounts of foreign exchange reserves (much of which are denominated in dollars) in the process. Indeed, in a prescient speech in 2005, the then US Federal Reserve Governor Benjamin Bernanke (2005) warned that the mushrooming international imbalances in the trade of goods and assets was a potential source of vulnerability for the United States and the world economy. Bernanke blamed these imbalances directly to the "global savings glut" ostensibly accumulated by China and the developed East Asian and oil-exporting countries. He argued that the flow of these excess global savings into the United States was not only responsible for the persistently low long-term interest rates in the United States and other industrial economies, the low interest rates also created distortions in the US real estate sector. In addition, the massive capital inflows also pushed up the value of the dollar and helped create the very large US trade deficit – pushing the US current account deficit to more than 6 percent of GDP at its peak.[53] As these inflows were primarily invested by central banks in safe but lower-interest-earning US securities, they fed directly to new investment in interest-rate-sensitive areas like residential housing construction. To Bernanke, in the United States the key asset price effects of the global saving glut occurred in the market for both residential and commercial investment because low mortgage rates not only triggered record levels of home construction, but also a sharp rise in house prices. Thus, the global savings in the form of foreign exchange reserves became inexpensive capital once they were ploughed back into the United States, and directly contributed to the sub-prime housing mortgage crisis and ultimately the Great Recession.

Bernanke's claim that the rapid rise of US trade deficit and distortions in the US economy is not America's making, but Asia's – in particular, China's – is unduly one-sided. The more important question is: why did China and other emerging economies accumulate such large volumes of US dollars in the first place? Certainly, the dollar's reserve status is a key factor. Also, because there is no guarantee that the US Federal Reserve will serve as lender of last resort (a lesson that many countries have learned the hard way over the years),[54] they chose to build up enormous buffers of foreign currency, mainly dollar reserves in the form of US Treasury bonds – with China going a step further by also pegging its currency (albeit at a cheaper rate) to the dollar.[55] This requires the

United States to run a large trade deficit, as it has to continually extend the supply of dollars abroad – which can also lead to exchange-rate appreciation – thereby adding to the cost of exports. Not surprisingly, the US trade deficit had been growing rapidly since the early 1990s, reaching 6 percent of GDP at its peak on the eve of the global financial crisis in 2007. It is also not surprising that over the past two decades the United States has run massive current account deficits, while China, East Asia, and the oil-exporting countries have run up correspondingly large current account surpluses. It also explains why, despite the United States' massive debt burden (estimated at over $19 trillion, or 107 percent of the total US GDP in 2016), foreign governments continue to increase their holdings of US financial assets – which in mid-2016 totaled some $6.1 trillion, up from about $1 trillion in 2000. Owning roughly $1.2 trillion in US government securities, China is by far the largest holder of US debt.

In fact, China is now the world's leading creditor nation (replacing Japan in 2003), while the United States is the world's largest debtor.[56] What explains how and why the world's once most prosperous and still largest economy has become so structurally reliant on external financing – or more bluntly, what explains the United States' decline to debtor's status? In part, since the mid-1990s, the US Treasury has met its borrowing needs by purchasing debt from abroad. At the end of 1998, the foreign holdings of Treasury securities totaled about $1.2 trillion (or roughly 37 percent of all debt held by the public); in 2008, the dollar value of foreign-owned debt had jumped to just over to $2.9 trillion – or almost 50 percent of outstanding publicly held debt. The largest foreign holders of US debt are countries that run persistent trade surpluses with the United States. Until September 2008, Japan was the largest holder of Treasury debt, only to be replaced by the Chinese, whose holdings of Treasury debt have skyrocketed, making Beijing the largest foreign holder of US government debt. It is also, in effect, the US government's largest creditor. Indeed, Washington has become increasingly dependent on Beijing to raise money to cover its ever-growing list of expenditures.

To many American policymakers this is an ominous sign, because America's growing dependence and Beijing's growing financial leverage as a creditor grants it extraordinary influence over the US economy. If for economic or strategic reasons Beijing decided to move out of US government bonds, it would force other investors to do the same, and in the process drive up the cost of US borrowing and undermine Washington's ability to manage the nation's economy. Similarly, if China stopped buying – or, worse, began selling – US debt, it would sharply raise interest rates on a variety of loans in the US (Setser 2008a, 2008b; Burrows and Harris 2009). Despite Beijing's growing global economic clout, what is not always appreciated is that economic interdependence also generates countervailing forces that tend to push towards a more balanced equilibrium. For example, on one hand, China purchases US bonds (which are denominated in dollars) to make the dollar stronger against the yuan, as an artificially weak yuan helps to boost Chinese exports, in addition to making Chinese exports cheaper relative to US exports.[57] On the other hand, the growing Chinese investments in the United States have helped to bring down interest rates, besides assisting in the financing of the $1 trillion annual US deficit. Also, there is truth in the oft-repeated mantra that China needs the United States more than the United States needs China because when the debts become too massive, there are always more risks for the creditor. In other words, underscoring the old adage, "if you owe the bank a thousand dollars you worry, but if you owe the bank a million dollars, the bank worries," this means that China's growing financial clout is also profoundly limited by its major debtor – the United States. Beijing not only depends on a strong dollar to keep its export engines humming, it has also put itself in the unenviable position of having to literally defend the dollar's value.

In fact, reminiscent of Japan, which also had the bulk of its foreign assets denominated in US dollars rather than yen, and them saw the value of those assets drop when the US dollar depreciated sharply following the Plaza Accords in 1985, China today faces the same risks – and more. China is often referred to as an "immature creditor" because it does not lend in its own currency, but in the currency issued by the borrower (the loans China makes are denominated in US dollars). It is exposed to exchange rate risks as the value of the debt fluctuates with the dollar's rise and fall. Since an unprecedented 80 percent of China's reserves are estimated to be in dollars, even a modest depreciation of the dollar will translate into significant losses for Beijing. Martin Feldstein captures this irony lucidly when he says, "consider what a decline of the dollar relative to the yuan would mean for the Chinese. If the Chinese now hold $1 trillion in their official portfolios, a 10% rise in the yuan-dollar exchange rate would lower the yuan value of those holdings by 10%."[58] As a result, China has much incentive to defend the US dollar – and the fastest and easiest way to do this is to buy even more Treasury bonds. Indeed, McKinnon (2005) boldly predicted that Beijing will maintain its informal dollar peg and continue to accumulate dollar reserves as long as the dollar remains a useful monetary anchor – which he feels it will indefinitely.

This also means that the argument that Beijing can punish the United States by dumping its holdings of Treasury debt (the resulting market disruption would lead to higher US interest rates and a collapse of the dollar on foreign exchange markets) is not compelling. The Congressional Research Service has persuasively argued that such a sudden and highly disruptive strategy is not in the cards because it is unlikely to be effective.[59] This is because even the largest foreign holdings of US government debt are smaller than the daily volume of trade in Treasury securities. If the Chinese did employ such a strategy, the resulting decline in the value of US Treasury securities would generate substantial losses to all debt holders, including those attempting to use their debt holdings as leverage.

Similarly, Beijing's repeated call (if not subtle "threat") for the creation of a new international reserve currency, the use of IMF's SDR, and the establishment of the renminbi as an international alternative to the US dollar is not yet credible. Indeed, there is little danger that the dollar will be replaced as the world's dominant foreign exchange reserve anytime soon. For starters, before the yuan can be brought into competition with the dollar as a medium of international trade, it must first be made into a convertible currency whose value is determined by the market. Beijing simply cannot allow this, as it would not only mean loss of control by the party-state, it would also mean that China would have to lower or remove all manner of financial and trade barriers – which it is not prepared to do. Regarding SDRs, although a country can convert its reserves into SDRs, this does not mean that the SDRs can automatically function as an international currency. Specifically, until the private sector adopts SDRs, countries that adopt the SDRs will still need to acquire dollars or euros or some other national currency in order to spend their reserves. Suffice it to note, the private sector will only adopt the SDR if it provides tangible benefits – something it does not do at the moment. Despite the bold claims, Beijing realizes this, too. The reality is that even while the dollar's weakness undermines the value of China's existing reserves, Beijing really has no interest in exacerbating or precipitating a crisis by moving out of dollar assets. In other words, although there is nothing to prevent China from diversifying its reserves away from the dollar, such an action is not without risk. Given the fact that China now owns so many dollars, any massive sell-off will also push the dollar down, with huge losses in China's dollar-denominated assets. Yet, as Prasad (2014) warns, the dollar's role as a medium of exchange and unit of account are likely to erode over time because innovations in financial markets and technological advancements will make it easier to conduct cross-border financial transactions using other currencies, reducing dependence on the dollar. In fact, China has already signed bilateral agreements with several of its major trading partners to settle trade transactions in their own currencies.

3

Rising Prosperity and Widening Inequality in the People's Republic of China

From 1990 to 2010, the Asian region saw its average per capita GDP (in 2005 purchasing power parity (PPP) terms) increase from $1,633 to $5,133 and the proportion of people living on less than $1.25 a day fall from an estimated 54 percent to below 22 percent. Overall, by the end of 2010, some 715 million people had been lifted out of poverty (ADB 2012). Leading this charge has been the People's Republic of China (PRC). Home to some 1.3 billion people, China has been among the world's fastest growing economies over the past three decades, notching an unprecedented 10 percent annual growth rate. With its GDP doubling every seven to eight years, China became the world's largest economy on a PPP basis in 2014.[1] China's phenomenally high and sustained economic growth (in both absolute and per capita terms) has translated into significant increases in per capita GDP – which between 1990 and 2015 increased from under 5 percent of US per capita GDP to about 25 percent – substantially improving the incomes and purchasing power of the average Chinese citizen.[2] Table 3.1 shows China's rapid GDP per capita growth and Table 3.2 confirms that these sustained and high growth rates translated into a sharp reduction in poverty rates and significant improvements in living standards.

Indeed, the rate of poverty reduction and improvements in the average individual's standard of living in China has been simply unprecedented. This is largely because China's much higher growth in average income has translated into concomitant increases in average incomes and success in poverty reduction. For example, on the eve of the reforms in 1978 the incidence of poverty in the People's Republic was among the highest in the world. As an IMF study notes, in 1981 an estimated 84 percent of the Chinese population lived on less than $1.25 a day, but by 2008, China's poverty rate had declined to around 13 percent – far below the developing country average (Balakrishnan, Steinberg, and Syed 2013, 6). This means that across China there were over 500 million fewer people living in "extreme poverty" in 2008 than 20 years previously.[3] The experience of China (which has successfully reduced absolute

TABLE 3.1 *GDP per capita (in current $US)*

	2008	2009	2010	2011	2012	2016
China	3,414	3,749	4,448	5,442	6,188	8,123

Source: World Bank http://data.worldbank.org/indicator/NY.GDP.PCAP.CD

TABLE 3.2 *Number of people living on less than $1.25 per day (at 2005 PPP Prices)*

	Percentage of population		Number (millions)	
	1990	2008	1990	2008
China	60	13	683	173
Rest of Asia	58	31	427	287

Source: World Bank cited in Balakrishnan, Steinberg, and Syed (2013, 4)

poverty via its turbo-charged economic growth and resultant massive job creation) unequivocally confirms that the most powerful force for the reduction of poverty and improvements in living standards is robust and sustained economic growth.

Nevertheless, China's impressive achievements in economic growth, poverty reduction, and improvements in living standards mask an alarming trend: namely, that even as sustained increases in aggregate GDP growth have sharply reduced absolute poverty and brought greater affluence to all socioeconomic groups, economic inequalities – in particular, income and wealth inequality (or the unequal distribution of assets across households) – have not only been rising, it continues to worsen, underscoring the unmistakable trend that a disproportionate share of the national income is going to a relatively small percentage of the population (Chen and Ravallion 2010; Knight 2013; Li, Sato, and Sicular 2013; Ravallion 2013). This paradoxical trend, where countries are becoming less poor, but also more unequal, is particularly stark in China. Of course, this does not mean that the livelihoods of all socioeconomic groups have not improved, nor does the rise in inequality mean stagnation of incomes. To the contrary, over the past two decades real household incomes have averaged annual growth of 10 percent and more. Rather, what this means is that even as the purchasing power of most of the populace has increased, the major beneficiaries of growth have been the already well-off (especially those at the high-end of the income scale), especially the politically and economically well-connected as well as an array of parvenu businesspeople in the regions. These groups, by capturing a disproportionately large share of the overall income gains, have seen an astronomical growth of their income and wealth.

Naughton (2007, 218) has aptly noted that "in the course of two decades China has gone from being one of the most egalitarian societies about as equal as Japan, to being more unequal than the United States ... There may be no other case where a society's income distribution has deteriorated so much, so fast." The extensive national and micro-level data gathered by the "China Household Income Project" (CHIP, an international collaborative survey project started in the late 1980s to track changes in incomes, poverty levels, and inequality) and published in Li, Sato, and Sicular (2013) unambiguously confirm these troubling trends. The CHIP data show that during the period 2002 to 2007, sustained growth in per capita household income of the poorer deciles or the bottom 20 percent. More specifically, overall incomes increased by some 50 percent for the poorest decile and by 60 percent for the second-poorest decile. However, the incomes of richer deciles grew at an even faster rate. Specifically, the richest two deciles of the income distribution saw their incomes almost double. As a consequence, the income gap between the richest and poorest deciles widened from 19:1 to 25:1. Similarly, a recent IMF study (see Ding and He 2016), using as its main dataset the annual Urban Household Survey (UHS[4]), as well as drawing from the CHIP data to measure wealth inequality, provides a comprehensive analysis of the evolution of inequality in earnings, income, and consumption in urban China for the period 1986 to 2009. The authors find that economic inequality "has been increasing drastically in China ... For example, the variance of log household disposable income in China increased from 0.14 in 1986 to 0.43 in 2009, almost threefold over 24 years ... and that total consumption inequality is higher than disposable income inequality for most of the period" (Ding and He 2016, 5). These findings corroborate the data from a nationwide longitudinal survey carried out by China Family Panel Studies (CFPS) at the Institute of Social Science Survey at Peking University. Since 2010, the CFPS has been collecting data on household wealth in China. As a longitudinal nationwide survey, the CFPS not only captures a cross section of wealth holdings (the CFPS dataset contains comprehensive measurements of assets, including housing assets, financial assets (such as savings, stock, funds, bonds, financial derivatives, and other financial assets), agricultural machinery, business assets, detailed items of durable goods and liabilities from housing and other sources), but also enables researchers to better understand the patterns of wealth growth and wealth dynamics over time at the family level. Drawing on this rich dataset, Xie and Jin (2015) find that the share of wealth held by the top segment of the income distribution has been rising sharply. In 2012, the richest 1 percent owned more than one-third of the total national household wealth, while the poorest 25 percent owned less than 2 percent – with housing assets accounting for over 70 percent of household wealth. They estimate that the wealth Gini coefficient of China in 2013 stood at 0.73. Despite such hard evidence, it is reasonable to state that the level of income inequality in China is hugely understated. In other words, the level of inequality is much higher than official estimates show – the study of Xie and Jin is a case in point. Not only do official figures try to downplay the problem of growing inequality (until recently, the Chinese government simply refused to release official figures on inequality, given that the ground reality is so sharply at odds with party's socialist-egalitarian ideology), but more importantly, China's wealthy have every reason to hide or not disclose their wealth – in particular if it is "earned" through rent-seeking, kickbacks, and other illicit means. This unreported income makes estimating the extent of income and wealth levels in China difficult. The Asian Development Bank (ADB) has lucidly captured this trend by noting that the "rising inequality in developing Asia is closely associated with very rapid increases in the very top income groups . . . That is, the rich are getting richer much faster" (ADB 2012, 15).

Not surprisingly, the Gini coefficient (a common measure of income inequality based on per capita consumption expenditure) vividly highlights that China has experienced a much steeper rise in income inequality based on household income per capita.[5] Citing official estimates, Balakrishnan et al. (2013, 6) note that "China's Gini increased from 37 percent in the mid-1990s to 49 percent in 2008. It has since ticked down to 47.4 in 2012 but remains higher than that in the United States and close to levels in parts of Africa and Latin America." However, non-official sources indicate even higher levels of income and wealth inequality. For example, a survey conducted by China's Southwestern University of Finance and Economics concluded that the Gini had actually jumped to 0.61 by 2010. In regard to wealth inequality, Li and Wan (2015) note that with the protection of private property rights and the growth of private enterprise, including the privatization of public housing and the development of the real estate market, household income and wealth have increased substantially. Drawing on an extensive dataset composed of the 2002 China Household Income Project and the 2010 Chinese Family Panel Survey, they analyze the level of wealth and wealth inequality in China during 2002 and 2010. Their "analysis decomposes the evolution of wealth inequality during that period in terms of the structure and composition of wealth. The findings show that there was a large increase in the quantity of wealth and wealth inequality between 2002 and 2010. The level of wealth in 2010 was four times that of 2002, and housing assets were the greatest component of overall wealth in 2010. Wealth inequality also rose dramatically after 2002, with the Gini coefficient of the distribution of wealth increasing from 0.538 in 2002 to 0.739 in 2010" (Li and Wan 2015, 264). These discrepancies are mainly due to the fact that non-official surveys look at a wider range of income sources rather than just wages. Nevertheless, it is important to reiterate that inequality in China is not due to stagnant or declining incomes among poorer households, but is instead the result of substantial gains in income made by the top decile of income earners. As the Li, Sato, and Sicular's (2013) study points out, China's high and growing inequality has not meant a deterioration of living standards for poorer groups. To the contrary,

TABLE 3.3   *Income inequality in Asia (2000 to 2011)*

Country	Gini coefficient
China	0.474
Vietnam	0.376
India	0.368
Sri Lanka	0.403
Philippines	0.44
Bangladesh	0.31
Pakistan	0.327

Source: Zhou and Song (2016, 205)

TABLE 3.4   *Gini coefficient of income inequality for selected countries (1988 to 2007)*

Country	1988	2007	Change
China (World Bank)	0.30	0.43	0.13
China (CHIP Survey)	0.38	0.49	0.11
Brazil	0.61	0.56	−0.05
India	0.32	0.33	0.01
Indonesia	0.29	0.34	0.05
Russian Federation	0.24	0.43	0.19

Source: Zhou and Song (2016, 206)

during the years 2002 to 2007 (period of the available CHIP data), growth in the per capita household income of poorer deciles was quite significant – as noted, increasing by about 50 percent for the poorest decile and by nearly 60 percent for the second-poorest decile. Indeed, it is the sustained rise in the incomes of poorer households that contributed to the sharp reduction in poverty rates (Kanbur and Xiaobo 2005; Knight 2013).

INEQUALITY AMID HIGH GROWTH

A vast corpus of research has long claimed that economic growth and inequality follow an inverted-U pattern, with inequality rising sharply in the early stages of development but gradually declining as the economy matures and ultimately settles into some sort of virtuous equilibrium. Therefore it is not unusual for socioeconomic inequalities, in particular the income gap, to widen as countries embark on the road to modernity – meaning rapid industrialization and urbanization. For example, in the early

1950s Nobel laureate Arthur Lewis (1955; 1954) argued that the process of economic development is never uniform, but painstakingly uneven, with different sectors of the economy and some regions growing faster than others. Hence, rising inequality is endemic to the process of economic growth and development. Similarly, Simon Kuznets (1955) argued that although underdeveloped countries tend to have a relatively equal income distribution in their "initial" stage of development, it becomes more unequal once these economies begin to modernize. Hence, Kuznets would hardly be surprised by the fact that, as China makes the transition from a rigidly centrally planned economy to a market-based one, inequality would widen even with sustained growth in per capita incomes. However, Kuznets also claimed that inequality would eventually decline, once an economy matures. That is, inequality in income tends to decline once an economy attains a certain level of average income. Although the current patterns of income and wealth inequality in China (and India) seem consistent with Kuznets' hypothesis (at least as reflected in the increases in the Gini coefficient), it remains to be seen if such a growth-inequality trade-off exists and whether income inequalities will gradually flatten out as these economies mature.[6] The fact that over the past few years China's Gini coefficient has seen a marginal decline (reaching 0.463 in 2015) has led some to suggest that China has reached the "Kuznets turning point" where income inequality peaks and then starts to fall. However, it is too soon to reach this conclusion.

Lee, Syed, and Wang (2013) persuasively argue that the widening economic inequality in China is an inevitable by-product of the country's investment and export-led growth model. This model that China has assiduously followed for the last three and a half decades has to a large degree involved a trade-off between rapid economic growth and inequality. Specifically, China's growth model has generated ostensible wealth through investment-induced capacity growth, especially in the manufacturing sector. Although the resultant rapid capital accumulation in the manufacturing sector has kept the value-added per worker in the industrial sector high throughout much of the last three decades, a disproportionately large share of this value-added has gone to the corporate sector rather than to the workers – explaining the only modest increases in household income. This is because wages were "suppressed" by the continuous influx of younger workers into the labor market associated with China's favorable demographics, including the large-scale transit of migrant workers into the major urban centers where much of the country's industrial base is concentrated. However, an issue not mentioned in Lee, Syed, and Wang (2013), but which compounded this problem, has been China's inadequate labor protection for workers. Although Chinese trade unions provide workers (or the proletariat) the right to legally fight for their rights, in practice, trade unions are subordinate organizations to the Communist Party and the central government. As a result, workers represented by unions in public-sector enterprises and SOEs (state-owned enterprises) do not have an organization that can independently represent them – which explains the relative ease with which the authorities have restructured SOEs and why workers have experienced slow wage growth – thereby contributing to the widening of income inequality within China's cities.

However, Lee, Syed, and Wang (2013) cogently argue that an inevitable outcome of this "unbalanced growth strategy" is that it has generated income gaps based on *skills, sectors, and location*. With the introduction of market reforms (and the dismantling of the fixed-wage system that existed under central planning), wages became more reflective of workers' skills and educational levels (Deng and Li 2009; Knight 2013; Knight and Song 2003). Indeed, widening income gaps were inevitable under the growth model that placed a premium on skills and education – sharply pushing up the wages of a relatively small number of highly skilled workers and managers, but keeping the wages of the majority young and unskilled workers (including migrants from the countryside) low and stagnant. Also, larger corporations were able to pay their workers much higher wages due to their stronger competitiveness and gains from natural economies of scale, but also because they enjoyed cheaper access to financing under China's state-led banking system. Finally, and predictably, workers in the booming manufacturing sector received higher salaries than workers in the agricultural sector because of productivity differences. Of course, it should also be noted that China's difficulty in effectively moving beyond low-cost manufacturing into the more lucrative (and competitive) capital goods and high-tech sectors has served to limit the creation of better and higher-paying jobs and more opportunities for its labor force.

It is inevitable that a large continental-sized country like China will have sharp spatial variations in income levels. In terms of location, geography has favored the eastern region – or the coastal provinces. Specifically, the coastal provinces' proximity to global capital and markets, coupled with favorable government policy, led Beijing to establish special economic zones (SEZs) along the coast where tax-breaks, coupled with government subsidies and other incentives, attracted hordes of foreign business to set up shop, especially in low-wage assembly work. In the process, the coastal regions not only drew enormous benefits from the rapidly expanding export-driven trade and foreign direct investment, but also helped transform the region into a global industrial and manufacturing hub. As China's manufacturing and export-based heartland, the coastal regions provided unprecedented opportunities for nonagricultural employment and income. Not surprisingly, in less than a generation the income and wealth gap between China's eastern coast and the sprawling central and western provinces (which was already significant) widened even more sharply because of external trade and larger productive capital stocks. Although it is inevitable for continental-sized countries such as China (and India) to have large spatial or geographical differences in income and wealth levels, China's unbalanced growth model has served to accentuate regional imbalances with greater regional economic divergence and polarization rather than convergence (Song 2013). In fact, economic divergence, which tends to be more pronounced during the early stages of development but gradually to give way to convergence as competitive advantages become narrower, remains pervasive in the case of China.

Similarly, the gap between the average urban and rural income remains high, with the average urban disposable income more than three times the average rural total income. Households residing in the coastal urban centers, by virtue of "being at the source of wealth creation," receive higher wages and benefits, including better access to educational and medical facilities, including other social services, than those in the country's sprawling rural hinterlands, not just because they happen to be urban residents, but also because explicit public policies have contributed to rising disparities within geographical areas. Specifically, China's "Household and Residence Registration System" or *hukou* has exacerbated inequalities as it hinders the free movement of rural inhabitants, besides providing highly disproportionate benefits in matters regarding employment, residence, education, health care, and other social services to urban residents, with only a minimum of such benefits available to rural residents (Knight 2013). In placing these punitive constraints on geographic mobility, the *hukou* system denies rural migrants and their families not only the right to live in urban centers, but by extension the ability to secure better-paying jobs, educational opportunities for their children and social services, and ultimately socioeconomic mobility. Bureaucratic constraints on rural to urban migration have prevented market pull and push factors from mitigating the urban-rural income gap.

Seen against this backdrop, it is hardly surprising that China's rural–urban income gap is the largest in the world. Indeed, the Asian Development Bank's (ADB 2012b) claim that the face of poverty in China (and in many Asian countries) is mainly rural makes sense. The ADB report *Framework of Inclusive Growth Indicators 2012* (2012b) documents that the ratio of rural poverty to urban poverty has worsened in 18 of Asia's economies between 1990 and 2010, with the imbalance particularly stark in China – where the rural–urban income gap accounts for close to half of total inequality.

The report notes that since 1998 the rural–urban income gap in China has reached a ratio of over 3:1, symptomatic of the country's dual economic structure comprising an urban sector based on industries, manufacturing and services and a rural sector that remains far less productive. Similarly, according to the CHIP study (Li et al. 2013a; 2013b), per capita incomes for urban households were, on average, more than three times higher than those for rural households by 2002. The study finds that China's urban–rural income ratio (measured as the average income per capita of urban households divided by the average income per capita of rural households) has remained high for some two decades, and is worsening – its contribution to overall inequality increasing from 45 percent in 2002 and 51 percent in 2007 (also see Knight and

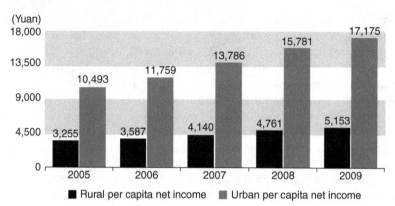

FIGURE 3.1 Widening urban-rural income gap.
Source: http://en.wikipedia.org/wiki/Income_inequality_in_China

Song 1999; Song 2013). In addition to the unbalanced growth model, the widening divergence is also due to a marked slowdown in growth in China's agricultural sector and dissipation of the "one-time" gains from efficiency-enhancing reforms such rural de-collectivization and the introduction of the incentive-based "household responsibility system" in the early reform era. Invariably, slower growth in the countryside has translated into slower growth in rural job creation and incomes, including the further widening of the rural–urban income gap (Yang 1999). However, as the CHIP study makes clear, the rural–urban income gap in China is not due just to stagnation in rural incomes, but is also the result of higher growth in urban incomes. Specifically, although during the period 2002 to 2007 rural incomes grew at an remarkable average annual rate of over 7 percent, urban incomes grew by a whopping 11 percent (in constant prices). As noted, this is partly because the rural–urban divide is embedded in China's urban–rural "Household Registration System."

Because China's economic growth is largely driven by an over-reliance on exports, excessive capital accumulation, sectoral imbalances with a large industrial and manufacturing sector and an underdeveloped service sector (at least when compared with countries of similar income levels), it has resulted in rapid growth in fixed-asset investment, with resultant structural imbalances such as the growth in total private and public debt which by the end of 2016 exceeded 250 percent of GDP – up from 150 percent prior to the onset of the 2008 global financial crisis. This partly explains why domestic consumption has failed to keep up with the pace of GDP growth. It also explains China's rather excessive reliance on the manufacturing sector for output growth at the expense of the services sector – which can generate new sources of employment. According to Guo and N'Diaye (2009), China's undervalued exchange rate explains the relatively low share of services related employment creation because Beijing believes that an exchange rate appreciation would undermine job creation in the manufacturing sector. Lee, Syed, and Wang (2013) note that as China's unbalanced growth model has become increasingly dependent on liquidity rather than productivity gains (especially in the post-global financial crisis period), it has further exacerbated economic inequalities. This is because "monetary policies that create excess liquidity beyond that warranted by cyclical considerations can have a differential impact on different sectors of the economy, benefiting those with access to credit and those holding assets whose price rises beyond fundamentals." Furthermore, excess liquidity has tended to generate greater profits for the corporate sector, with only temporary and limited spillover onto household incomes.

POLITICAL ECONOMY OF INEQUALITY

In his study, *Capitalism with Chinese Characteristics*, Yasheng Huang (2008) blames pervasive top-down political control and regimentation for distorting China's macroeconomic development, and in the process exacerbating economic inequalities. Huang divides China's economic reform trajectory into two distinct periods: the "entrepreneurial capitalism" in the 1980s and the "state-led capitalism" in the 1990s. In the first phase (in the early 1980s), the Communist Party led by Deng Xiaoping atrophied decades of Maoist central planning and enforced egalitarianism by introducing market reforms which enabled private-owned businesses to flourish. In turn, this unleashed decades of pent-up entrepreneurial activity and innovation. This shift to entrepreneurial capitalism spurred rapid economic growth and helped to dramatically improve incomes and living standards of millions of Chinese citizens, in particular the rural dwellers and the peasantry. However, the state took a regressive step in the 1990s, during and since the Jiang Zeming era. During this second phase, idiosyncratic statist policies, by deliberately favoring large urban-based SOEs including their foreign and domestic subsidiaries at the expense of the smaller (and more nimble) rural private and collective enterprises, served to stifle individual initiative and undermine private enterprise. In addition, the changes in the control and ownership rights of state-owned assets enabled the Communist Party cadres and their benefactors, the so-called "princelings" (the sons and daughters of influential party officials), including well-connected government officials, bureaucrats and parvenu business and entrepreneurial interests, to illicitly capture much of the state-owned assets, such as the lucrative real estate and industrial and manufacturing units. Huang persuasively illustrates that the policies introduced during the second phase disproportionately benefited the party and business elites, including sections of middle-class urban residents.

On the other hand, workers made redundant from SOE layoffs under labor market and related structural reforms, including increased competition from the swelling ranks of migrant rural labor, experienced job losses and downward pressure on wages.[7] Overall, the majority urban and rural poor were adversely impacted – they not only experienced declines in their incomes, but also the gradual dismantling of the socialist era "iron rice bowl" (under which rural communes and SOEs guaranteed employment, housing, education, health care and social services), which translated into a lowering of living standards, including erosion of the previous gains made in education, health care, and social services. Cumulatively, greater statist control and regulation, besides exacerbating inequalities (especially the rural-urban divide), also created further opportunities for rent-seeking, cronyism, and corruption.

In a similar vein, Minxin Pei's (2016) original recent study, *China's Crony Capitalism: The Dynamics of Regime Decay*, blames "incomplete" political and economic reforms since the post-Tiananmen era – namely, the decentralization of "the control of public property without clarifying its ownership," for the problems of "an incipient kleptocracy, characterized by endemic corruption, soaring income inequality, and growing social tensions." Drawing on an extensive array of evidence, Pei argues that "beginning in the 1990s, changes in the control and ownership rights of state-owned assets allowed well-connected party and government officials and businessmen (including criminal gangs) to amass huge fortunes through the systematic looting of state-owned property, in particular land, natural resources, and assets in state-run enterprises" at the expense of the majority shareholders or the "people." This was because the decentralization of the rights of control over state property took place without clear rules and laws regarding the rights of ownership. Predictably, this enabled the powerful and well-connected with "maximum advantage to extract wealth from society." With "crony capitalism" deeply entrenched through both rent-seeking and targeted repression, the party-state and the array of obsequious vested interests or cronies it serves and benefits have no incentives to reform the existing arrangements. For example, they have every incentive to keep SOEs in operation (although the majority remain highly inefficient and loss-making) via generous government grants and subsidies, including protection from competition via selective use of industrial and trade policy. Also, given the complex and opaque structure of the SOEs, not to mention the perplexing shareholding structure between state and non-state companies, the system also supports (and has created) an array of vested interests of well-connected party insiders, made up ostensibly of the privileged, imperious and entitled princelings. The gains hardly go to the shareholders (the "masses"), but to SOEs managers and their political bosses who usually happen to be the princelings and the entrenched "hardliners" in the Communist Party hierarchy. As Pei bluntly notes, the pervasive "crony capitalism" the system has spawned has fostered "an illicit market for power inside the party-state, in which bribes and official appointments are surreptitiously but routinely traded. This system of crony capitalism has created a legacy of criminality and entrenched privilege that will make any movement toward democracy difficult and disorderly," including a more balanced and equitable distribution of economic growth.

Thus, Beijing's stifling of the private sector (which has been the engine powering economic growth and job creation) and its singular retreat from markets during the decade-long (2003 to 2013) administration of President Hu Jintao and Premier Wen Jiabao and movement toward greater reliance on state capitalism has only exacerbated income and wealth inequality, including corruption. For example, with active state support, the state-owned enterprises have become even more monopolistic and inefficient, squeezing both the domestic private and foreign companies. Indeed, continued lending by state banks to unprofitable SOEs has only added to the skyrocketing pile-up of non-performing loans (NPLs). Yet, because the SOEs are connected to the central and local governments and serve as reliable cash cows for China's ruling elite, and in particular the Politburo members (and their families, courtiers, and cronies), they continue to drain resources and stifle growth. Thus, as Huang and Pei show, Chinese authoritarian state capitalism has a dark side. The array of vested beneficiaries, including obsequious cronies, it has spawned not only face few constraints against self-aggrandizement and arbitrary intervention, they are also active in all manner of rent-seeking activities, including outright plunder, besides opposing and gutting reforms that are perceived as inimical to their interests.

As noted earlier, a unique feature of Chinese state capitalism is that the economy is simultaneously market based and decentralized, with key sectors controlled and regulated by the party-state. Knight (2016, 138) argues that although China's "political control is centralized and economic management is decentralized," the central authorities have responded to this "serious principal-agent problem, in which the agents are often better informed than the principal" (not to mention having agendas and interests that do not always correspond with that of the principal) with the creation of "a semi-marketized economy involving targeted state intervention." Moreover, this order is further undergirded by the "Cadre Management System" – a promotional system under the Chinese Communist Party (CCP) that not only institutionalizes both obligation and quiescence, but also characteristically rewards and punishes local officials for their "performance," usually on a quid pro quo basis. Conspicuous and tight political surveillance and control by the central government means that "local governments are in many respects agents of the central government" (Knight 2016, 139) because the career advancements of local bureaucrats and party cadres, as well as access to the party's extensive patronage networks (and largess), depends on how incessantly they extol the virtues of and disseminate and promote the party's and the central government's political and economic agendas: namely, supporting the central authorities' single-minded pursuit of economic development to further advance the epistemological foundations of a "harmonious socialist society." Nevertheless, the decentralization of economic management coupled with the reality that China lacks an effective rule of law and legal protections (making the network of personal relationships (or *guanxi*) with party and government officials critical) has further given local officialdom much discretionary leeway, allowing them to balance the sometimes-competing imperatives of Beijing with local exigency, including opportunities for rent-seeking, corruption, and self-aggrandizement. As the following sections illustrate, this incongruity has generated both intended and unintended outcomes: rapid economic growth, but also rising income and wealth inequality, including pervasive corruption.

The structure of central–local relations in China has served to promote both rapid economic growth and widening income and wealth inequality. In other words, fiscal decentralization has been a double-edged sword. Certainly, as Qian and Weingast (1997) argued years ago, economic decentralization by generating inter-jurisdictional competition has functioned as a disciplinary mechanism against imprudent intervention by subnational officials as well as provided incentives to local governments to pursue economic development. On the other hand, the differences in the initial level of physical and human development, natural endowments, and revenue base, the weakened market position of labor (due to weak worker protection laws and SOE restructuring and competition from migrant labor, which has compressed wages),[8] the self-serving imperatives of local officialdom and the "growth first and redistribution later" mindset have tended to distort development, waste valuable resources and exacerbate inequalities.[9] As Wu (2016, 5) notes, "local government officials compete with each other on economic performance, motivated by concerns over promotions and political pressures from higher levels of government. Pressures to outperform have led to unachievable goals and in some cases to overinvestment … when making the twelfth 'Five-Year Plan' (2011–2015), the Chinese central government targeted a 7 percent national GDP growth rate. However, all of the provinces set higher GDP growth rate targets, ranging from 8 percent to 13 percent. Those pressures appear to have resulted in inflated provincial statistics."

A number of reforms in the 1990s also had the unintended outcome of creating budget constraints for local governments. Prior to these reforms, taxation was largely the purview of local governments under the "fiscal contract responsibility system," which allowed local governments to keep the bulk of the collected revenues (about 80 percent) after making a fixed (and regressive) payment to the central government. However, the "tax-sharing reform" of 1994 removed local governments' control over the allocation of local tax revenues (with the bulk now going to the central government), and the "1994 Budget Law" made it illegal for local governments to incur budget deficits. In other words, China's fiscal system became highly centralized when it comes to revenue generation, but highly decentralized on the expenditure side. On one hand, this gives local governments much latitude and discretion with respect to the use of public expenditures, but on the other hand, local governments, particularly those in less prosperous and poorer provinces, are heavily depended on intergovernmental transfers from the central government to meet their expenditure needs. Indeed, the expenditure responsibilities of local governments, especially the need to provide some measure of social safety protection, have multiplied with the systematic hemorrhaging of the already-precarious "iron rice bowl" guarantee of the Maoist era. Specifically, the costs of the cradle-to-grave welfare support known as the "iron rice bowl," once shouldered by communes, collectives, and state-owned enterprises, have increasingly fallen on local governments, especially following the 1994 fiscal reforms, which sharply reduced the revenue allocated to local governments – who now receive, on average, about half of the fiscal revenue. Yet local governments, which remain responsible for more than 80 percent of expenditures, face hard budget constraints (given the 1994 Budget Law), and often prioritize economic development, including pet projects, at the expense of social welfare – further compounding the regional income and fiscal divide. In fact, Dollar (2007) presciently warned, given China's highly decentralized fiscal system where local governments depend mainly on locally generated tax revenue to fund basic social services including, education, and health care, and where the central government allocates or transfers inadequate resources to local governments, that widening regional and income inequality was inevitable.[10]

In addition, given the already-large variations in initial economic conditions, endowments, and revenue base among provinces, the diminishing role of the central government as an equalizing and redistributive agent and the absence of transparency and accountability (that is, the absence of electoral accountability, which makes local officialdom seemingly indifferent to the needs of local residents, especially the poorer households) give local authorities substantial discretion over the generation and use of revenues, including inter-governmental transfers. They can either choose to capture or divert revenues, prioritize economic "development" at the expense of more equitable redistribution, or simply decide not to allocate adequate resources for the provision of public goods, in particular, social-welfare related services. The case of China's massive social assistance/safety-net program, the *"Dibao"* (Minimum Livelihood Guarantee), is illustrative. Following its implementation in Shanghai in 1993, the *Dibao* was extended nationwide to all "urban areas" in 1999 and to the "rural areas" in 2007. Although the central and provincial governments make fiscal transfers to fund the *Dibao* (albeit, local governments with resources and the necessary fiscal capacity are required to commit a budget), local governments at the municipal level are responsible for both the administration and the implementation of the program, including conducting the needed means-test to identity the recipients who are "low-wage families" – or whose income falls below the local *Dibao* line. In other words, their income is insufficient to sustain their basic livelihood. Despite the significant expansion in coverage of the number of beneficiaries (making the *Dibao* the world's largest safety-net program),[11] the program nevertheless suffers from the usual logistical problems associated with poor and haphazard targeting of recipients, including the exclusion of rural migrants living in urban areas who do not hold urban household registration (and are thus ineligible for the urban *Dibao*), and the fact that the actual assistance packet (albeit, it tops up a recipient's income to a basic level below the minimum wage) tends to be rather low relative to average consumption costs (Gao 2017; Golan, Sicular, and Umapathi 2015). More fundamentally, given that implementation is decentralized, it gives local authorities tremendous discretion not only regarding who meets the eligibility criteria to receive the transfer payments, but also to whom and how to allocate the funds, including diverting the funds away from their intended use.

Moreover, as the state can sell land-use rights to business and commercial developers, many party insiders have been able to rapidly accumulate wealth through land/property transactions. Indeed, the use of revenues generated from land sales highlights the complex ground reality. In 1989, with the end of state ownership of land, local governments came to enjoy what Tian, Sheng, and Zhao (2015, 88) have referred to as the "exclusive power . . . in the chain of land collection, conversion, and land supply. With such monopoly power, local governments can easily convert rural land into urban land and sell it [that is, user rights] for their own purposes. Meanwhile, local governments can retain most of the land revenues rather than transferring them to the central government." Not surprisingly, local governments have a strong incentive to expropriate, if not outright confiscate, and convert land for sale. Indeed, they routinely have, through deceit and intrigue, but more often through the use of strong-arm tactics, forced rural residents to forfeit their rights, if not outright evicted them. In fact, land sale has become a convenient way for local governments to generate revenue – which grew "from RMB 542 billion in 2004 to RMB 3.21 trillion in 2012" (Tian, Sheng, and Zhao 2015, 89).

Yet, being de facto agents of the central government was never supposed to be an equal relationship. Hence, collaboration has never been a fixed practice, but one that adapted to Beijing's shifting priorities. As agents of the central government, local officials can hardly ignore Beijing's seemingly never-ending exhortations, fiats, and directives. Therefore, even as they deftly acquiesce to the center's perennial and seemingly unequivocal demand to meet development targets (usually measured by industrial output, infrastructural expansion and volume of domestic and foreign investment) in order to secure Beijing's imprimatur and favor (which translates into promotions and other perks), their relative autonomy from official scrutiny and punishment also allows them to routinely invest their energies in what they consider best to advance their own careers – in addition to lining their pockets and those of their courtiers and patronage networks. After all, it is common knowledge that officials who prove fastidious and resourceful in securing funds and have a good track record in generating economic development (broadly defined) tend to move up the bureaucratic and administrative ranks more quickly and effortlessly. In such a permissive environment, the central authorities' repeated exhortations (the need to balance growth with equitable distribution and create a more harmonious society via the provision of public goods) often fall on deaf ears among the opportunistic and unenthusiastic local agents – who only grudgingly follow Beijing's demands for greater social and economic equity. Fewsmith and Gao (2014, 178) succinctly note that "instead of improving the quality of governance at the local level, the decentralized fiscal system has created a strong motivation for local governments to maximize their revenues. Case studies show that local governments respond to the central government's demand for service-oriented construction in name only." Thus, the Chinese fiscal system has served to unintentionally increase regional and income inequality. Differentiating between what he calls "revenue and spending decentralizations," Song's (2013, 294) econometric analysis "shows that the increase in revenue share of local governments from mid-1980s to 1994 indeed increased regional inequality, while the revenue re-centralization in 1994 only had a modest effect on reducing regional inequality."

Exacerbating this, China's tax structure also contributes to the widening income and wealth gap. As Lam and Wingender (2015, 4) note, "the redistributive effect of taxes and transfers is relatively limited in China." What explains this? First, before the 1994 fiscal and tax reforms, the central government negotiated with local governments in regard to the percentage of locally collected taxes to be paid into the central coffers. The 1994 reforms substantially extended Beijing's control over the economy under a "tax-sharing system" that increased the central government's share of the tax revenue. This, in effect, helped to double the central government's revenues, but sharply reduced those of local governments. Because China's taxation system is highly centralized, local governments have no autonomy to set tax rates to increase taxation. Predictably, over time, this imbalance in the center-local fiscal and tax regime has worsened, with the central government having greater fiscal power and the local governments becoming more dependent on central government for transfer payments, or finding alternative sources of revenue – as noted earlier.

To local governments, squaring the mismatch between their revenues and expenditures has meant getting around prohibitions on borrowing – forcing many to find off-budget revenue sources to finance their budgets, including using land as collateral (which poses a major debt risk for local governments) and reliance on land sales (which partly explains the increasing volatility of China's property market) and borrowing via "local government financing vehicles" (LGFVs) – which has become more widespread as revenues from land sales are leveling off, given that land is a fixed and limited resource. As a result, local governments (with the tacit approval of central authorities) created LGFVs (also sometimes called "local government financing platforms" or LGFPs) as well as UDICs (urban development and investment companies) to serve as their principal financing agents, to facilitate borrowing as well as tap the stimulus largesse (during 2009 to 2010, China undertook a massive fiscal stimulus program totaling 4 trillion yuan) by issuing bonds.[12] By the end of 2010, over 6,500 LGFVs had been set up (IMF 2013). Indeed, Zhang and

Barnett (2014, 6) note that "many local government financing vehicles (LGFVs) were established as intermediaries to channel funding from the financial market, mostly banks." Because local governments are responsible for implementing the infrastructure investments funded by the stimulus, they enjoyed a free rein when it came to borrowing – and they borrowed heavily via the LGFVs. As their responsibilities, not to mention the outsized ambitions of local authorities, have far outstripped their revenues, local governments have accumulated massive debts. At the heart of the problem is that the LGFVs have built up huge mismatches between their short-term borrowing and the long-term investments they have financed (and are financing). Investments in infrastructure and real estate may not generate sufficient cash flow to service the debts. This is because the majority of the LGFVs are depended on land sales and high property prices to meet their obligations. Also, the significant misallocation of resources at the local level due to politically motivated lending in wasteful "white-elephant" ventures, including "missing funds" through graft, corruption and malfeasance, has only exacerbated the debt problem. In short, most local governments lack a sufficient cash flow to service their debt and related obligations – forcing them into the arms of "shadow banks" to meet their funding needs and to service their debts. Inevitably, this has meant that funds available for social and economic welfare spending have substantially declined. Indeed, today many local governments faced with declining revenues (as land sales shrink) and debt levels increase are forced to further cut back on basic human development and social welfare spending.

China's fiscal policies – in particular, income redistribution through taxation and transfers – have had limited impact in responding to the widening income and wealth inequality. As Zhuang and Shi (2016, 5) note, "the pre-tax and pre-transfer income inequality is not very different from the post-tax and post-transfer inequality in China while the latter is one-third lower in high-income countries. The limited role of redistribution through fiscal measures in reducing income inequality in China is consistent with the fact that the country's total personal income tax revenue currently amounts to less than 1.5 percent of GDP, compared with high-income countries' ratio of 10 percent on average." In addition, China's heavy reliance on indirect or transaction-based taxes such as the value-added tax (VAT) on goods and some services and on property taxes has also served to worsen inequality. Overall, indirect taxes accounted for just over 73 percent of China's tax revenues (net of tax rebate) in 2012. In contrast, direct taxes, including personal and corporate income tax, contributed about 25 percent of the total tax revenue – with corporate and individual or personal income taxes accounting for 19.5 percent and 5.8 percent, respectively.[13] China's heavy reliance on indirect taxes makes its taxation system highly regressive, as these taxes are levied on consumption rather than income (personal income tax has a greater positive impact on equalizing income distribution), thereby imposing a higher tax burden on low-income and poor households because they spend a larger percentage of their income on meeting their daily consumption needs. Moreover, the fact that "income" is taxed under different rate schedules has meant that "capital income" (which includes dividends, interest, and royalties) is subject to lower taxes on average than is wage income. This enables individuals and households with higher incomes (and who tend to have more diverse asset portfolios) to take advantage of the lower tax brackets. Of course, such options are not available to average wage earners, who end up paying a disproportionately larger percentage of their incomes in taxes. Not surprisingly, Wang and Piesse (2010), drawing on three comparable national representative household surveys for 1988, 1995, and 2002, confirm the regressive nature of China's tax system. Specifically, they show that a regressive taxation system and skewed allocation of subsidies have contributed to the urban–rural income gap and exacerbated inequality. They note "that the relatively poorer rural population has a net tax liability, whereas those in the richer urban areas receive net subsidies. This pattern is common in China, although the extent of the bias varies. This skewed system of tax and welfare payments is a major cause of the persisting urban-rural income gap and contributes to the overall income inequality in China" (Wang and Piesse 2010, 36).

Prasad (2014) notes that China's financial system remains heavily bank-dominated, with the central government directly controlling most of the banking system. Domestic credit allocation is controlled largely by state-owned banks and disproportionately directed towards state-owned enterprises. Because the government controls almost all banks and financial institutions, it can (and does) set interest rates independently of market factors. And, because Chinese households (which tend to save a high proportion of their incomes, given the weak welfare system) have few alternatives to bank deposits, they deposit their money in the banks. Such "financial repression" has enabled the government to cap their citizens' savings at about a zero real rate of return. According to Lardy (2008; 2012), the imperative of maintaining an undervalued exchange rate to facilitate export growth, domestic banks' solvency and profitability, and the availability of cheap credit for SOEs and local governments has led Beijing to engage in "financial repression," reflected in the maintenance of very low or even negative real return on household deposits. Lardy measures this by examining the differential between the nominal interest rate households receive on their net savings deposits and the rate of consumer price inflation. He argues that a decline in the real return on savings deposits can be viewed as an implicit tax imposed on households. According to Lardy, between the years 2002 and 2008, the implicit tax imposed on households was around 4 percent of GDP, while during the same period banks and the corporate sector benefited from the low-interest-rate environment at estimated rates of 1 percent and 0.9 percent of GDP, respectively. Lardy argues that by setting the benchmark nominal interest rates on bank deposits and loans at artificially low rates (in large measure designed to shield the margins of the banking sector and to make it easier for banks to roll over their debt and to enable them to lend to the SOEs and local governments), the People's Bank of China (PBC) indirectly forces bank depositors to subsidize the banking sector and the government – in what amounts to a significant redistribution of income away from households to the government's preferred sectors of the economy.[14] To Lardy, this confiscation of household income is a major reason for the weak consumption demand in China, including a more efficient allocation of capital.

GLOBALIZATION'S JANUS FACE

China is the veritable poster child for globalization. Its continental size, large and diverse markets, rich resource base, and human capital have given the People's Republic a huge comparative advantage. To its credit, China's ability to expeditiously utilize these endowments and opportunities to navigate its way to prosperity in an increasingly enmeshed, integrated, and interconnected world accounts for much of its economic renaissance. Indeed, in 1978, when China's new paramount leader Deng Xiaoping announced his ambitious "open-door policy," the opening of China to the global economy, he could not have imagined that in 2014 China (whose share of world exports was close to zero in 1978) would become the world's largest exporter and second-largest importer of goods – or, to put it bluntly, would become the world's leading trading nation.

China's integration into the world economy was accelerated considerably, not only by its accession to the World Trade Organization (WTO) in 2001 as tariff reductions and trade facilitations greatly improved the market access of Chinese exports, but also because China's opening to the world coincided with the unprecedented opportunities offered by the revolution in information and knowledge-intensive technologies and the resultant sharp drop in communication and transportation costs. In a relatively short period, China has fundamentally transformed both the nature and patterns of global trade. If on one hand, China's imports of commodities, inputs, and final finished products directly raise partner countries' export receipts, then on the other, its large and diverse exports also negatively impact its competitors' net exports. Indeed, as China's economy has expanded and become more deeply integrated in the global economy, spillovers from China have intensified. According to recent IMF (2016, 59) estimates, "a 1 percentage point slowdown in Chinese growth translates into a 0.15–0.30 percentage point decline in growth for other Asian countries in the short term ... Financial spillovers from China to regional markets are on the rise, in particular in equity and foreign exchange markets, and are stronger for those economies with greater trade linkages with China. They are likely to rise further with rapidly growing financial linkages with

China, including through the ongoing internationalization of the renminbi and China's gradual capital account liberalization."

Similarly, the creation and proliferation of the ubiquitous multi-layered integrated "global value chains" or GVCs (under which a country imports "foreign content" consisting of raw materials and intermediate goods in order to add greater value to domestically produced goods for export, rather than for domestic consumption) has revolutionized the process of "vertical specialization," with several countries becoming part of an closely integrated import and export network system. China's export success lies in its ability to position itself as the "downstream" end of the value chain – that is, importing intermediate goods to assemble final products for export to the United States and Europe. Xing (2016, 192) notes that "GVCs are particular relevant to China's exports, as about half of its manufacturing exports are assembled with imported parts and components." Using panel data on bilateral processing exports covering more than 100 of China's trade partners, Xing (2016, 192) shows "that GVCs have been functioning as a vehicle for Chinese exports entering international markets, especially markets of high-income countries. By successfully plugging into GVCs, Chinese firms have been able to bundle their low-skilled labor services with globally recognized brands and advanced technologies of MNEs, and then sell them to consumers of international markets." As these linkages have deepened, countries' economic and business cycles have also become more correlated. Moreover, even countries that are not fully part of the value chains – especially the "least developing countries" – have benefitted from China's growing investment and commodity market linkages.

Although the boom in China trade has been the catalyst behind the dramatic growth in global trade and rising prosperity (albeit with gains varying at different stages in the supply chain), China has also failed to fully reap the rewards such intimate integration and dependence bring – in particular, improvements in human capital and the resultant creation of more skilled and higher-paying jobs. China's growing technological capacity and rising wages are rapidly shifting a growing list of activities to lower-cost producers, with negative implications for employment. Moreover, the imperatives of state capitalism, which has conspicuously protected SOEs from competition via trade barriers, discriminatory regulations, including tax breaks, access to cheap credit and preferential loans, have constrained China's ability to effectively transition from the so-called first-generation, low-cost manufacturing, with its concentration on textiles and consumer goods, into the more complex second-generation exports of capital goods and high-tech sectors. As Ghemawat and Hout (2016, 92) note, "Although China does lead the world in the export of smartphones and personal computers, it accounts for only 15 percent of these products' value at most. That's because Chinese companies typically just assemble and package semiconductors, software, cameras, and other advanced high-tech components fabricated abroad." Not surprisingly, Han, Liu, and Zhang's (2012) study of the impact of globalization on wage inequality in China from 1988 to 2008 shows that in the aftermath of two trade liberalization shocks (Deng Xiaoping's Southern Tour in 1992 and China's accession to the WTO in 2001), regions with greater exposure to globalization experienced larger changes in wage inequality than the less-exposed regions. Namely, their findings confirm that WTO accession "was significantly associated with rising wage inequality ... [and] that both trade liberalizations contributed to within-region inequality by raising the returns to education (the returns to high school after 1992 and the returns to college after 2001)" (Han, Liu, and Zhang's 2012, 288). Indeed, Scott (2014) argues that Chinese workers have gained relatively little from the huge trade surpluses, as wages have remained low and stagnant. Rather, the bulk of the profits has gone to Chinese and multinational companies, including well-connected government and party officials – further exacerbating income and wealth inequality.

These trends go against the long-accepted conventional wisdom going back to nineteenth-century economist David Ricardo's "theory of comparative advantage," which predicted that free-trade would benefit all parties and that the poorest workers should benefit most from trade expansion. No doubt, freer trade, and deepening global economic integration have resulted in significant gains for developing economies – with countries like China (and India) experiencing sharp increases in GDP per capita, improved living standards, and reductions in poverty levels – albeit workers in the manufacturing sector in the advanced economies have experienced prolonged period of job losses and stagnant wages (see Chapter 2). Nevertheless, the global financial crisis of 2007 to 2009 also painfully underscored that China and countries in the supply chain have an unhealthy dependence on their growth on the continued demand in the United States, Europe, and Japan. The sharp decline in global trade resulted in massive job losses and rising social tensions in China and elsewhere. In the post-crisis era, continued weak demand, but also a much stronger Chinese currency, has further depressed exports (Bems, Johnson, and Yi 2010; IMF 2016). Compounding this, the post-crisis slowdown of the Chinese economy has also sharply reduced demand for raw materials and commodities, negatively impacting the receipts of commodity exporters – in particular, agricultural products and raw materials used in industrial production.

Although the Chinese economic juggernaut has slowed because of the unstable and weak post-crisis economic environment, and as Beijing tries to rebalance the economy away from investment and towards consumption, it still remains a formidable export machine. The sharp rise in the growth and share of US Merchandise Trade with China and China's manufacturing exports (see Table 3.5 and Figure 3.2) has enabled Beijing to accumulate significant surpluses with its trading partners (both huge current account surpluses and foreign reserves), in particular, the United States – which has the largest merchandise trade deficit with China, totaling some $365.7 billion in 2015. Over the past decade, China has had the largest volume of foreign exchange

TABLE 3.5 *United States merchandise trade with China:*
1980 to 2016 (in billions of $US)

Year	US exports	US imports	US trade balance
1980	3.8	1.1	+2.7
1990	4.8	15.2	−10.4
2000	16.3	100.1	−83.8
2010	91.9	365.0	−273.0
2011	104.1	399.4	−295.3
2012	110.5	425.6	−315.1
2013	121.7	440.4	−318.7
2014	123.6	468.5	−344.9
2015	116.1	483.2	−367.2
2016	115.8	462.8	−347.0

Source: US International Trade Commission (USITC) Data Web

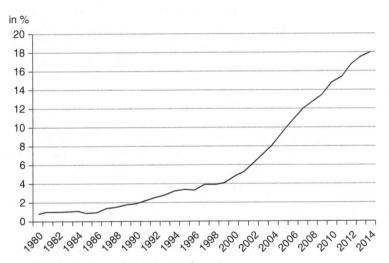

FIGURE 3.2 China's share of global manufacturing exports.
Source: World Trade Organization 2015.

reserves in the world – which increased from about $2 trillion in 2008 to around $3.2 trillion in July 2016. China is also the largest foreign holder of US Treasury securities, totaling an estimated $1.26 trillion in mid-2016.

Why has China, still a very poor country in terms of GDP per capita (China's GDP per capita ranks around 100th in the world) and relative scarcity of capital, become a global creditor and exporter of capital to the world's richest nation? More provocatively, why is China subsidizing the United States – the world's richest country? The problem, in part, is reflective of China's deeply rooted institutional and structural weaknesses. China's woefully underdeveloped capital markets, a weak banking sector, highly speculative stock markets, a rudimentary government bond market, poor resource allocation, and non-existent social security system prevent effective utilization and investment of the country's national savings. China must effectively address its many domestic economic problems, including restructuring banks' balance sheets, strengthening domestic capital markets, creating foreign-exchange hedging instruments, and improving corporate governance, among other things, to overcome the domestic constraints to investments. While these processes have begun in some sectors, it will take time. Beijing, it seems, is well aware that at present there are few viable alternatives to US dollar holdings. Yet they also know that China must fundamentally deepen its economic reforms and allow market forces to play the decisive role in resource allocation, including modernizing and opening the domestic financial markets to better mediate the nation's wealth (Wang 2007). In the meantime, Beijing must heed Deng Xiaoping's sage admonition and "bide its time" to facilitate its "peaceful rise.

As discussed in Chapter 2, to the United States, the origins and persistence of its massive trade deficit with China is due to Beijing's neo-mercantilist economic policies. The US contention regarding China's mercantile behavior is rather straightforward: Beijing engages in gratuitously unfair trade practices via inadequate adherence to WTO rules (if not engaging in outright protectionism), and most perniciously by deliberately manipulating its currency. Specifically, in maintaining an undervalued exchange rate, Beijing has been able to dramatically increase its export growth and pile up large current account surpluses – the latter by aggressively intervening in foreign exchange markets to keep its currency from appreciating. This in turn has resulted in a massive build-up of foreign exchange reserves. However, if Beijing allowed market forces to determine the value of its currency, its current account surpluses would be much lower and American trade balances would be much healthier.

Arguably, the aftermath of the global financial crisis of 2008 has forced Beijing to rethink its currency's close links to the US dollar. Although the exponential growth of China's massive foreign exchange reserves has been the result of trying to sustain a stable exchange rate between the yuan and the dollar – even in the face of strong economic pressures for appreciation (given China's strong productivity growth, it is natural for the yuan to appreciate), this linkage is becoming increasingly burdensome. To prevent appreciation and avoid loss of export competitiveness, the People's Bank has been forced to aggressively buy dollars and sell renminbi. However, this strategy has not been without pain. Besides making domestic macroeconomic management difficult (China's controls on private exchanges of renminbi for other currencies are not always effective), concentration on exchange-rate stabilization has meant that Beijing has largely ceded the ability to use monetary policy to target domestic objectives such as controlling inflation. Consequently, the swings in the US dollar has not only increased uncertainties associated with capital movement, weakening the dollar by driving up commodities prices in dollar terms exerts upon China the pressure of imported inflation. The sharp hike in food prices in China in recent years has already eroded the gains made in economic development, especially inequality and poverty reduction. Moreover, the subprime-induced general tightening of the global credit markets and the resultant "credit crunch" have reduced capital flows to China. Over the short term, this may not be a serious problem, as China has a fair amount of liquidity in the domestic economy. However, if the problem persists over time the credit crunch could have a negative impact. For example, an impact on the business sector's ability to raise funds from international sources can impede investment growth, as these businesses would have to rely more on costlier domestic sources of financing, including bank credit. This could in turn put further upward pressure on domestic interest rates.

Beijing is aware that it would be more prudent to adopt a more flexible exchange rate. After all, China's emphasis on exchange rate stability in the face of rising current account surpluses has not only generated intense protectionist pressures in the United States and elsewhere, it has also forced the central bank to accumulate massive foreign exchange reserves, with negative domestic consequences. Keeping the yuan from rising against the dollar not only means that China's central bank has to print more money to keep interest rates low; as noted, such a strategy can also exacerbate the problem of inflation if more money ends up chasing too few goods. It also means that China is exposed to large capital losses on its foreign reserve holdings (which, again as noted, are largely held in US dollars) as the renminbi appreciates. Moreover, an appreciation of the exchange rate would also boost domestic consumption – something China needs as it tries to wean the economy away from excessive reliance on investment. The adoption of a flexible exchange rate would give China greater leverage to limit deviations of inflation and growth from chosen targets by means of a monetary policy focused on domestic objectives. Of course, such a policy does not imply totally ignoring the exchange rate, as it may require the authorities to intervene in the exchange market to limit short-run currency fluctuations. Nor does it mean that a move towards a more flexible rate is an argument for capital account liberalization. Suffice it to note there are numerous cases of countries operating managed floats while maintaining capital controls. Rather, the adoption of a monetary policy aimed at domestic objectives would help China develop a more balanced and resilient financial system. Indeed, facing growing protectionist pressures from the United States and elsewhere, Chinese policy makers increasingly recognize the upside of reducing reliance on exports as a main growth engine by strengthening domestic demand.

As noted earlier, on November 11, 2008, Beijing approved a massive 4 trillion yuan ($586 billion) stimulus package over two years. Totaling some

TABLE 3.6 *China's stimulus package (total: RMB 4 trillion)*

Area	Amount
Infrastructure	*2.87*
General infrastructure	1.50
Reconstruction of Sichuan earthquake area	1.00
Rural area infrastructure	0.37
Technology and environment	*0.58*
Technology and structural adjustment	0.37
Energy savings and emission reductions	0.21
Social measures	*0.55*
Construction and renovation cheap houses	0.40
Social security and health	0.15

Source: National Development and Reform Commission (NDRC 2009). www.ndrc.gov.cn

14 percent of annual GDP, it is arguably the biggest peacetime stimulus ever. As Table 3.6 shows, the stimulus package targeted seven core spending areas. The general infrastructure category included construction and expansion projects of high-speed railways, new expressways and highways, airports, city subways, and nuclear power plants. Through targeted social spending, the authorities hoped to increase investment in the public health care system, education and subsidized housing, as well as to raise unemployment benefits and other welfare benefits in keeping with Beijing's policy to promote "harmonious growth."

Naughton (2009, 278) points out that "disbursement began almost immediately. The Chinese government and Communist Party sent an emergency directive to government departments at all levels, emphasizing the need to prop up domestic demand and start new construction projects. Literally within weeks, local governments throughout China were meeting to compile lists of shovel-ready projects that complied with central government directives. As a result, resources began flowing through the pipeline by the end of 2008, and expanded government investment began to have a discernible impact on the economy during the first quarter of 2009." However, in practice, not only were the bulk of the stimulus funds channeled through local governments, as Table 3.6 shows, the program privileged investment. As a disproportionate share of the stimulus funds were injected into state-owned firms and local infrastructure projects, the growth rate of fixed capital formation nearly doubled compared to the pre-crisis period (Wen and Wu 2014).

Given this, Beijing's expectation that the stimulus would dramatically boost domestic consumption and help rebalance an economy unduly skewed towards exports was unduly optimistic – as "social measures" represented a mere 5 percent of the package, not enough to stimulate domestic consumption.

In fact, the stimulus did the very opposite, as it subsidized exports and targeted infrastructure despite the fact that China already has overcapacity in industrial production and infrastructure (De Haan 2010; McKissack and Xu 2011). Moreover, the massive capital injection not only led to sharp increases in local government debt (which jumped from around 6 trillion RMB in 2008 to roughly 27 trillion RMB in 2016), it also crowded out private sector investment – in large part because private firms fund their investment from savings, while the more inefficient and less productive state-owned firms depend on cheap credit for their existence (Song, Storesletten, and Zilibotti 2011). Exacerbating this, the flow of easy credit also contributed to the rapid proliferation of shadow banking – or financial institutions that are not regulated as banks (Sharma 2014a). Not surprisingly, the multiplier effects of the stimulus have been much lower than expected. Indeed, as some had suggested, a more prudent way to stimulate domestic consumption would have been to send tax rebates directly to mid- and low-income families, as these rebates would produce faster and targeted results (because income is a key determinant of households' consumption and saving behavior). Equally perplexing, the stimulus package did little to improve the social safety net – which stands at less than 1 percent of GDP. Chinese citizens are prodigious savers because they are justly concerned about the prohibitively high medical, education, and housing costs and lack of social security and other safety nets when they retire (Ma and Yi 2011). This is particularly true for poorer households, who try their best to save because they fear the consequences of serious illness, unemployment, and old age in a country lacking effective government safety nets.[15]

In order to discourage precautionary savings and boost consumption, on January 21, 2009, Beijing announced additional spending of some RMB 850 billion over three years. This was designed to improve health care provision by initially covering some 200 million uninsured citizens, with the goal of achieving universal coverage by 2020, and improving access to primary health care in underserviced areas. Also, beginning in February 2009, a pension plan for rural workers was initiated and the level of pensions to the elderly poor modestly increased. To encourage spending by rural households, the authorities unveiled the "household appliances going to the countryside" (*jiadian xia xiang*) and "exchanging old for new" (*yi xiu huan xin*) programs. Under these initiatives, rural residents would receive subsidies and rebates on purchases of goods such as refrigerators, TVs, and washing machines for four years. Furthermore, to help the struggling property sector, minimum down payments were reduced from 30 to 40 percent of a home's value to 20 percent, and the transaction tax was waived for properties held for at least two years. The 12th Five Year Plan (2011 to 2016) further committed to construct 36 million low-income housing units by 2016. However, an IMF study (Ahuja et al. 2012, 12) notes that "there are few signs in the data that the initiatives to build out the social safety net and increase the provision of social housing have led precautionary savings to decline or have created sufficient momentum for household consumption to reverse the secular decline as a share of GDP that has been seen over the past several years."

Arguably, without effective privatization of state and collective-owned land and state assets, the stimulus efforts may be a one-time boost only. As noted, spending by Chinese households as a percentage of GDP remains significantly below private spending levels in other emerging economies. However, China's private consumption has failed to grow, not because Chinese consumers do not like to purchase goods and spend on vacations, but because most do not own property and collateral assets. Rather, most households are wage-earners who have not felt enough "wealth effect" to boost their consumption levels. Unless these concerns are effectively dealt with, consumers will not be spending their rainy day savings anytime soon. It also means that financial stimulus is one-time shot designed to alleviate immediate problems in the economy by giving it a boost. More sustained growth must come less from government-backed capital infusion and more from balanced growth, including productivity growth.

Since the political legitimacy of the Communist Party rests on continuing to deliver high economic growth and improve the lives of the people, Beijing's decision to put so much of the nation's hard-earned savings into low-yielding dollar-denominated bonds (despite the growing needs at home) has generated public anger. According to Martin Feldstein (2008), "the value of the dollar portfolio is equal to about $1,000 per person in China, about the level of the total per capita income in China at the official exchange rate." Arguably, popular resentment against the party elite, official corruption, and the growing economic inequalities partly explains why in recent years one of the best-selling books in the People's Republic is Song Hongbing's *Currency Wars* – an angry, half-baked account that blames financial crises on "conspiracies by the rich national elites and the Jews seeking world domination," and that "China should be prepared to fight 'bloodless wars' waged by evil forces like the U.S. Federal Reserve aimed at destroying China's economy." Even if Beijing dismisses the rantings of a crackpot, it realizes that the fruits of economic development need to be more widely shared – and the best way to do that is to foster domestic demand.

No doubt, Beijing is deeply concerned about the trajectory of the American economy. They have every reason to be worried. If the current trends continue, China's huge dollar-denominated foreign reserves could lose significant value in coming years. The literally unrestrained printing of money by the United States has the real potential for generating run-away inflation – which, in turn, can significantly erode the underlying value of China's hard-earned dollar holdings. Compounding this is the genuine fear of the United States imposing ever more onerous conditions on Beijing. Not surprisingly, these gnawing concerns have made Beijing increasingly irritated by the "self-serving" statements coming from Washington. This very much explains the growing assertiveness on the part of China, especially its willingness to roundly criticize US economic policies, especially, those pertaining to China. In a sense, the tables are now turned. For years, Washington has pushed China (and other emerging economies) to emulate US-style free-market capitalism. Among other things, this has meant that China should liberalize capital flows and let its currency appreciate in line with market forces. Not long ago, such American "advice" had sympathetic the ear of reformers in Beijing. As the so-called "Anglo-American model" of capitalism is increasingly out of favor, critics have become increasingly emboldened (Stiglitz 2008). China will not be alone in criticizing – sometimes sharply – its erstwhile debtor.

The acrimonious debate regarding China's trade and currency policies underscores the fact that economic interdependence and convergence does not necessarily mean the absence of conflict. After all, the gains of interdependence are not always aligned in a perfect equilibrium. As Sino-US economic relations have become disproportionately one-sided (at least in terms of trade and surplus), acrimony and discord have intensified. Apparently, anticipating a more adversarial or "hardball" US position, Beijing is clearly reassessing its economic relations with the United States with an eye on reducing its dependence. There are a number of possible scenarios. At the extreme, intense pressure by the United States could force a beleaguered Beijing to retaliate. For example, if China is declared a "currency manipulator" and faces punitive measures, that could push Beijing to liquidate some of its US Treasury bonds. Contrary to conventional belief, it would not be as difficult as one might think. After all, not only is China's foreign assets held as "official" foreign exchange reserves, the Chinese party-state, via its control of the banking sector, has a pervasive command over the economy. It can act quickly and decisively. Moreover, in contrast to Japan, China does not have to be deferential (or more aptly, *kowtow*) to the United States. Despite being a creditor, Japan, a member of the western alliance and beneficiary of the American security umbrella, was under American tutelage and "indebted" to its major debtor. However, China, a competitor to American power and influence, and whose relations with its major debtor can best be described as a "marriage of convenience" has a freer hand to utilize its economic leverage as a tool of foreign policy. No doubt, Beijing's actions would inflict just as much pain on investors in US Treasury debt (both foreign and domestic), as on China – a case of cutting off its nose to spite its face. However, investors would also lose faith in the ability of the US government to meet its obligations in the face of unsustainable, long-run structural deficits. Thus, to reiterate, since the lion's share of China's foreign exchange reserves is invested in US Treasury securities (and has helped keep down interest rates in the United States, despite chronic budget deficits and weak domestic savings), any significant changes in China's management of its foreign exchange could have a profoundly negative impact on US securities markets.

Of course, China could reduce its dependence in a more measured and gradual manner. Arguably, Beijing has been examining its options regarding the cost of maintaining the dollar-based system. It is rightfully concerned that the exploding US government deficits has the real potential to lead to inflation and sharply reduce the purchasing power of its dollar-denominated financial assets. As a hedge against this, Beijing has been contemplating and experimenting with a number of strategies, including short-term arrangements to diversify its investment portfolios away from US dollars. On this issue, China is hardly alone. Both Russia and India have also called for an end to the dollar's dominance in the international monetary system.[16] Like China, both have claimed that world currencies need to adjust to help unwind trade imbalances that have contributed to the global financial crisis.

However, unlike Russia and India, China is not waiting. In 2009, Beijing signed currency swap agreements totaling about 650 billion yuan (or about US$95 billion) with Hong Kong, Argentina, Indonesia, South Korea, Malaysia, and Belarus. This will now allow these countries to settle accounts with China using the yuan rather than the dollar. In July 2009, the People's Bank took another step towards internationalizing its currency and reducing reliance on the US dollar with the announcement of new rules to allow select companies to invoice and settle trade transactions in renminbi through financial institutions in Shanghai, Hong Kong, and Macao. This means that importers and exporters will now be able to place their orders with approved Chinese companies and settle payment in renminbi. In addition, Hong Kong banks will now be allowed to issue yuan-denominated bonds – a step towards building an offshore yuan market, while foreign banks will be allowed to buy or borrow yuan from mainland lenders to finance such trade. While the central bank has assured that this does not mean full convertibility of the renminbi but to provide stability for local exporters hit hard by the dollar's widely fluctuating value, it does underscore Beijing's growing concern about the future of the greenback and in line with its ambition to make the yuan an internationally traded currency. In the meantime, China continues to be a significant net buyer of US bonds, mainly treasuries.

Again, contrary to conventional wisdom, bitter historical legacies are not necessarily a barrier to deep economic cooperation. Despite their painful recent past, China, Japan, and South Korea (the region's three biggest economies) have formed an ambitious "united front" to counter the adverse effects of global financial turmoil. On December 13, 2008, the leaders of the three nations held their first-ever summit in Japan. The summit signaled an unprecedented phase of cooperation between the three nations – with Japan and China expanding credit lines for currency agreements with South Korea to strengthen the won. Again, on February 23, 2009, against the backdrop of the deepening financial crisis, the Finance Ministers from China, Japan, South Korea, and ten Southeast Asian nations agreed to create a US$120 billion pool of foreign exchange reserves to be used by countries to defend their currencies from speculative attacks. The agreement significantly broadens the earlier arrangement called the "Chiang Mai Initiative" (which only allows bilateral currency swaps),[17] by functioning as a de facto system of regional macroeconomic monitoring and cooperation.[18] In a joint statement, Chinese Premier Wen, Japanese Prime Minister Taro Aso, and South Korean President Lee Myung-Bak also vowed to boost regional trade and investment. Their communique reaffirmed the importance of close regional cooperation to counter the financial crisis. On March 24, 2010, Chiang Mai Initiative Multilateralization (CMIM) formally came into effect. The body's responsibility include monitoring the ASEAN+3 countries' (Association of Southeast Asian Nations, plus China, Japan, and South Korea) economic and financial status and providing guidelines regarding the use of the foreign currency reserve pool. In addition, the ASEAN+3 countries also agreed to create a regional credit guarantee and investment fund with an initial grant of $700 million to promote the issuance of bonds in domestic currencies within the region. Clearly, China is increasingly looking beyond the United States.

China has also been actively engaged in "strategic economic expansion" (Rui and Yip 2008). Specifically, Beijing has become an active participant in the international markets for mergers and acquisitions (M&A). Its gross foreign holdings acquired through M&As, "basically nonexistent 20 years ago, reached over $87 billion by the end of 2008 ... two main types of foreign direct investment are 'greenfield' in which a company builds a plant in a target country, and direct investment through mergers and acquisitions, in which a company purchases a large stake in an existing foreign firm" (Alon, Hale, and Santos 2010). More significantly, Beijing has been transferring part of the nation's wealth into "sovereign wealth funds." Since 2007 Beijing has allocated some $200 billion into a sovereign wealth fund under the management of the government-sponsored China Investment Corporation (CIC) to be used for investment abroad. It is the largest state-owned fund in the world. This financial power provides Beijing a unique opportunity to extend its reach globally by enhancing its ability to purchase or gain major ownership stakes in businesses, financial institutions, resources, and technology. One of the first announced investments of the CIC was a 10-percent stake in the US-based private equity firm, Blackstone Group. Although this raised concern on Wall Street at the prospect of "growing Chinese influence" on US corporate operations through the stock market, Washington could do little to stop it. As a large investor in US Treasuries, China claimed that it was simply trying to earn a higher return on its foreign investments by dividing its assets into stocks, bonds, and commodities such as oil and gold. This trend will continue. Chinese financial institutions have come under intense criticism at home for bad investments in the United States, including the $5.6 billion share in Morgan Stanley purchased by the China Investment Corporation and the large paper losses on the $3 billion the CIC invested in Blackstone Group in June 2007. As a result, Beijing's top priority is to broaden investments and reduce risk – which, at its heart, means a reduction in the purchase of US Treasuries. Not surprisingly, China, a large foreign investor in bonds from Fannie Mae and Freddie Mac, has been sharply reducing its holdings of that debt. After making direct net purchases of $46 billion in the first half of 2008, Beijing was a net seller of $26.1 billion in the second half of 2008. In fact, it was the weak demand from China and other foreign investors that led the US Federal Reserve to announce in November 2008 that it would buy up to $600 billion in debt from Fannie, Freddie, and other US government-related mortgage companies.

In 2013, China launched the Asian Infrastructure Investment Bank (AIIB) – a new multilateral development institution to finance infrastructure development. The US refused to join the AIIB (although many allies of the United States, including the UK, Canada, France, Germany, Australia, and others have joined), on the grounds that Beijing's real agenda was to construct a China-oriented body that served not only as an alternative to the IMF and the World Bank, but also went against established liberal norms by offering assistance to countries without imposing the requisite human rights, anticorruption, and environmental standards. Similarly, Washington views President Xi Jinping's ambitious "One Belt, One Road" initiative (announced in 2014) with suspicion. To the United States, the initiative, which has committed more than $1 trillion in development projects spanning some 85 countries, is hardly benign. Rather, it underscores China's determination to export its model of state-led development by establishing deep economic and diplomatic ties across Asia, Eurasia, Africa, and Europe. Whether the initiative will eventually shift the center of the global economy from the West and towards China and provide an alternative to the American-centered global economic order remains to be seen. Of course, it is difficult to know if Beijing's actions are part of its strategy to replace the current international economic order or to increase its influence within it. What is certain is that for the foreseeable future both China and the United States will have to cooperate constructively to resolve their bilateral and multilateral concerns.

TOWARDS MORE BALANCED GROWTH

It is now conventional wisdom that once a country crosses over into the ranks of the "upper-middle income" group ($7,000 to $17,000), its growth rates tends to decline by about 2 percentage points. In 2014, China made the transition from the "lower-middle income" country category to the upper-income one, with a per capita income of $7,593, or about $11,850 in PPP terms. As predicted, its growth rate has dropped from above 10 percent to about 7.5 percent since 2014. China now is at a crossroads, and the stakes cannot be higher. If China fails to make the transition to a "high-income country," it will mean that it has become caught in the "middle-income trap" with its per capita GDP hovering perennially around the middle-income range.[19] If this were to happen, China would not only have missed the opportunity to become relatively rich, but would also continue to suffer the indignities that plague many middle-income countries: protracted low growth, stagnant living standards, declining job opportunities, and political discontent. Hence, the key challenge facing China is whether it can move past the middle-income trap and become a high-income economy over the next few decades.

Clearly, a middle-income country's growth drivers have to change if it hopes to move to the high-income category. China enjoys certain advantages, but also faces formidable challenges. First, China's economy is blessed with foreign exchange reserves of over $3 trillion and is burdened with only modest budget deficits. Nevertheless, Malkin and Spiegel (2012) predict that an economic slowdown is inevitable as China becomes an established middle-income country. However, its vast geographical size and, in particular, the country's "uneven development" may help it escape the middle-income trap. Specifically, Malkin and Spiegel suggest that growth in China's more-developed provinces may slow to 5.5 percent by the end of this decade, but this decline will be compensated by a more robust 7.5 percent growth in the less-developed provinces. Nevertheless, they caution that China should not become complacent as the country's long-term growth projections show a downward trend.[20] Their analysis (Figure 3.3) highlights both the observed and forecast growth for the two types of regions ("advanced" and "emerging" provinces) since 1990. Clearly, in the developed provinces, the forecast slowdown is rapid.

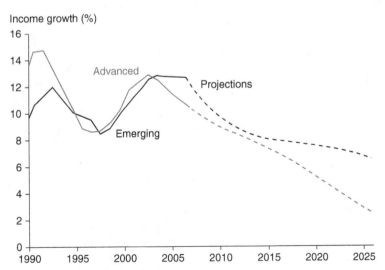

FIGURE 3.3 China's regional growth projections.
Source: Malkin and Spiegel (2012)

This means that in a few years, China's growth "will be concentrated primarily in the Chinese interior rather than in the more advanced areas near the coast" (Malkin and Spiegel 2012, 4).

Now the bad news: for starters, constrained external demand in the United States and other advanced economies has already (and will continue to) negatively impact China's exports. Also, China's massive investments in fixed assets are already producing diminishing returns – not only because of over-investment and massive misallocation of resources, but also because as the marginal productivity of capital declines, excessive reliance on factor accumulation only produces diminishing returns. China's state-owned enterprises, which dominate the industrial and manufacturing sector, are not only less profitable than many of the small private-sector companies, they are also inefficient, with a poor track record for innovation and profitability. Indeed, given the size of its economy, China has very few companies with international reputation. As a result, the bulk of China's high-tech exports are produced by foreign firms. To their credit, the Chinese leadership, in particular, Xi Jinping, the current General Secretary of the Chinese Communist Party, President of the People's Republic, and Chairman of the Central Military Commission, has repeatedly stated that reform of SOEs – plagued by poor performance, high-levels of debt and pervasive corruption – is an essential first step in reforming the Chinese economy. Yet, to date, the authorities have taken rather tentative and relatively "easy" measures such as regrouping SOEs by function to reduce redundancy and overcapacity, consolidating SOE assets (and debt), restructuring the management structure and promoting "mixed ownership" to improve profitability. However, as noted, Chinese state capitalism is driven as much by political imperatives as by rational market logic. With powerful, vested groups and an array of courtiers embedded within the party/state and outside in the private sector – with many who view these reforms as threatening to their interests – reforming the SOEs will not be easy.

Similarly, the blessings of "demographic dividend" bestowed on China and a number of East Asian economies are a one-time boost. Like Japan before it, for China the demographic window of opportunity is now fast closing (Bosworth 2012). Although it is not clear whether China has reached the "Lewis turning point" (that is, when rural-to-urban migration begins to tighten rural labor markets and reduce the rural-urban wage differential), what is clear is that the large pool of surplus rural labor that provided the engine of China's export-led boom is fast shrinking, and urban China growth in labor cost (as measured by real wage growth) has been consistently exceeding growth in labor productivity since 2008 (Cai 2012). With China's working-age population likely to peak in a few years (Zhuang 2012), and coupled with a rapidly aging population, labor costs will become even more expensive. Eichengreen et al. (2013) point out that economic slowdown is more likely for countries that maintain undervalued exchange rates (and China's currency manipulation and neo-mercantilist strategies have been the subject of much criticism) because they "provide[s] a disincentive to move up the technology ladder."

How can China avoid the middle-income trap? In its ambitious 12th Five-Year Plan (2011 to 2015) and the 13th Five-Year Plan (2016 to 2020), Beijing has targeted seven strategic sectors as investment priorities. These are green energy and environmental protection, next-generation information technology, biotechnology, advanced equipment manufacturing, new energy, new materials, and new-energy vehicles. If these targets are to be realized, there is broad consensus that China must simultaneously invest in human capital to upgrade worker skills to enhance productivity and innovation and reform the institutional order to allow for greater individual creativity and experimentation. Although China has a good track record when it comes to overall student enrollment and in recent years has increased financing for education, these have not effectively translated into improved educational outcomes. Like Malaysia and Thailand, China's educational system is not producing the number of skilled workers needed for knowledge- and technology-intensive sectors. To mitigate, Beijing will have to invest massively in its educational system at all levels to dramatically improve not only the quantity, but, more importantly, quality, which is so essential to successful competition in a high-tech and knowledge-based economy. Eichengreen et al. (2013) note that growth "slowdowns are less likely in countries where the population has a relatively high level of secondary and tertiary education and where high-technology products account for a relatively large share of exports." The implications are clear: growth in China, and in particular its move from a low-cost to a high-value economy, cannot be achieved by simply adding more capital and labor. Rather, growth will increasingly be driven by productivity improvement through innovation and skills upgrading. For this to occur, investment will need to flow into sectors with the highest returns on capital. Of course, this also means that the financial sector must improve credit allocation and ensure that productive firms have access to essential financing.

Beijing will also have to limit government intervention in the economy, especially the state's pervasive control over the financial sector, and provide real incentives for private enterprise. Moreover, the authorities will have to directly confront the pervasive problem of corruption and establish a well-regulated and transparent institutional legal and administrative system, which is essential for private enterprise to thrive. In 2012, when Xi Jinping assumed the office as President of the People's Republic and General Secretary of the Central Committee of the Communist Party of China, he embarked on a wide-ranging anti-corruption campaign – arguably motivated by his concern that corruption and its resultant ills were undermining and distorting China's economic growth. Xi and his inner circle are well aware that since the legitimacy of the party depends much on economic performance, removing obstacles to growth and building the necessary institutions to support a modern and increasingly globalized Chinese economy are essential. On the other hand, Xi has also reversed much of the political and economic liberalization of the past several decades. Whether China's Leninist political order will be able to move the economy up the technological ladder to the coveted high-income status remains to be seen.

In addition, China will have to "rebalance its economy" by reducing its current investment and export-led growth model to one that is based on domestic consumption. Indeed, Chinese policy makers acknowledge that economic growth, which over the past three decades has been driven by high levels of investment in export-oriented industries and infrastructure, needs to shift to a "consumption-driven growth model." Of course, a successful shift to domestic demand will first require a more equitable income distribution. As noted, China's Gini coefficient is amongst the highest in the world. Such a high level of inequality severely limits household consumption, and coupled with the absence of a social safety net, especially in health care and education, forces households to engage in discretionary savings. Finally, as Acemoglu and Robinson (2012) argue, China's extractive political and economic institutions are not compatible with equity, innovation and, ultimately, sustained high growth rates over the long run. That is, China's "extractive state" will have to become more "inclusive." Put more bluntly, China must democratize in order to make its political and economic institutions more inclusive. As Acemoglu and Robinson (2012) note, democracies provide the foundations for inclusive economic and political institutions.

4

Democracy, Prosperity, and Inequality in India

In 2015, India was the world's second most populous nation with an estimated 1.27 billion inhabitants. In 2016, the Indian economy was estimated to be the seventh largest in the world by nominal GDP and the third largest in purchasing power parity (PPP) terms (Table 4.1).[1] As Table 4.2 shows, the high and sustained growth rates over the past two decades coincided with the introduction of market reforms (or "economic liberalization," in the Indian lexicon) beginning in 1991 – when faced with an acute fiscal crisis, the authorities enacted dramatic structural and trade reforms at the urging of the International Monetary Fund. Since then, India's growth rate has averaged around 7 percent during 1993/1994–2009/2010, around 6.5 percent during 1993/1994–2003/2004, and 8.5 percent during 2004/2005–2009/2010, before accelerating to an impressive average annual GDP growth rate of 10.2 percent during 2002–2007, a rate that was higher than that of the People's Republic of China. Despite a sharp decline in economic growth in fiscal year 2008–2009 because of the global financial crisis,[2] growth gradually resumed to 7.6 percent in 2015 – making India the fastest growing large economy in the world.[3]

On balance, robust and sustained economic growth has been broad-based across India. In fact, under both the Eleventh (2007–2012) and Twelfth (2012–2017) Five-Year Plans, several of the country's poorest or "low-income states" grew at a record clip – with Bihar (one of the poorest states) outperforming even the most prosperous or "advanced" states. Similarly, the GDP of Madhya Pradesh and Rajasthan (both low-income states) have grown faster than India's overall GDP. Although the fruits of this economic growth have been broadly shared, they has also been disproportionally distributed. Although the India–wide Gini coefficient (a measure of income inequality) masks substantial variations in income inequality levels across the 29 states, what is unambiguous is not only that faster-growing states have seen larger increases in wealth inequality, there have been sharp differences in the growth rates of wealth holdings in the middle- and upper-income states and the poorer states (Jayadev, Motiram, and Vakulabharanam 2007). Clearly, rapid

TABLE 4.1 *GDP in purchasing power parity (PPP) of top five countries (US$ trillion) in 2015*

China	19.52
United States	17.95
India	7.98
Japan	4.74
Germany	3.85

Source: World Bank, *World Development Indicators* database, July 1, 2016, http://databank.worldbank.org/data/download/GDP_PPP.pdf.

TABLE 4.2 *GDP growth rates and per-capita GDP in India*

Period	GDP (%)	Per-capita GDP (%)
1951–1981	3.6	1.4
1981–1988	4.6	2.4
1988–2003	5.9	3.8
2003–2013	7.9	6.4

Source: Panagariya (2013, 7).

economic growth has generated higher levels of inequality – and as if to underscore Kuznets – with income and wealth inequality rising more sharply in the richer states.

With rapid growth serving to further exacerbate income and wealth inequality throughout the country (Motiram and Naraparaju 2015), the gap between the top, middle, and bottom income quintiles has sharply increased with the India-wide Gini coefficient between early 1990s and late 2000s, increasing from 30.8 to 33.9. Basole's (2014) detailed analysis of wage and asset data for India using the World Top Incomes Database finds that although average incomes have grown significantly since the mid-1980s, most of the gains have gone to those at the very top of the income scale – noting that "the 1990s saw an increasing divergence between the rich (top 1%) and the rest of the country."[4] Similarly, studies by Credit Suisse (2015a; 2015b) reveal that the richest 1 percent of Indians owned about 53 percent of the country's wealth and the richest 5 percent owned 68.6 percent. Altogether, the top 10 percent owned 76.3 percent of the country's wealth. At the other end of the scale, some 90 percent of Indians owned less than a quarter of the country's wealth. Finally, Jayadev, Motiram, and Vakulabharanam (2007) provide important insights on the patterns of wealth disparity in India using the all-India debt and investment surveys (for 1991 and 2002). In particular, they examine the differences in wealth holdings by state and income as well as disparities based on specific socioeconomic categories. The authors "find that there have been increases in wealth levels in the country across virtually all groupings, accompanied by a small but perceptible rise in the level of interpersonal wealth inequality, whether examined by summary measures such as the Gini coefficient or by centile shares of wealth." Specifically, the top 10 percent of households possess just over half of the total wealth (whether measured in terms of assets[5] or net worth,[6] with the top 10 percent owning 51.94 percent of the wealth in 2002 compared to 50.79 percent in 1991), while the bottom 10 percent possess only 0.2 percent of the total wealth. Overall, the bottom 50 percent of the population own less than 10 percent of the total wealth.

Nevertheless, sustained per capita income growth (Table 4.3) – from a per-capita income of around $375 per year in 1991 to $1,700 in 2016 (or $6,261 on PPP basis), has moved India from the World Bank's designation of "low-income country" to a "middle-income country" – albeit, India lags far behind China, whose per-capita GDP in 2015 was $8,154 in nominal terms and $13,801 in purchasing power parity terms (IMF 2015). Yet, the substantial rise in incomes in India has contributed to improvements in overall living standards, including a sharp reduction in the country historically pervasively stubborn poverty levels.

According to the Government of India's Planning Commission, in 1981 an estimated 60 percent of India's population lived on less than $1.25 a day. By 2008, this poverty rate had dropped to about 33 percent (Table 4.4). The proportion of Indians living in "extreme poverty" (on $1 a day or less) has fallen from 40 percent in 1990 to about 25 percent in 2007, although the

TABLE 4.3 *GDP per capita (in current US$)*

Country	2008	2009	2010	2011	2012	2016
India	1,042	1,147	1,419	1,534	1,489	1,709

Source: World Bank http://data.worldbank.org/indicator/NY.GDP.PCAP.CD.

TABLE 4.4 *Number of people living on less than $1.25 per day (at 2005 PPP prices)*

	Percentage of population		Number (millions)	
	1990	2008	1990	2008
India	47	33	433	395
Rest of Asia	58	31	427	287

Source: World Bank, cited in Balakrishnan, Steinberg, and Syed (2013, 4).

country's overall population has increased. Similarly, research by the IMF (Anand, Tulin, and Kumar 2014, 4) notes that the "the poverty headcount rate, measured using the national poverty line, declined by 1.5 percentage points per year in 2004/05–2009/10, double the rate of the preceding decade. More recent data suggests that between 2004/05–2011/12, poverty declined by 2.2 percentage points per year which is about three times the pace of the poverty reduction of the preceding decade."

However, the methodology and measurements used to assess India's poverty rate are not without controversy, and there has been a long and heated debate on what constitutes an appropriate "poverty line." India's Planning Commission traditionally estimated "poverty levels" on the basis of consumer expenditure surveys conducted by the National Sample Survey Office (NSSO). For example, in the mid-1990s, India's official poverty estimates were made on the basis of the methodology developed by the 1993 Lakdawala Committee, which based the "poverty line" on per-capita consumption of "caloric intake" of 2,400 calories per day for rural areas and 2,100 calories per day for urban areas. However, the Tendulkar Committee appointed by the Planning Commission in 2005 revised the Lakdawala "poverty line." Namely, the Tendulkar Committee made adjustments for the difference in prices due to inflation – both spatially (across regions) and temporally (across time). By estimating poverty levels on the basis of expenditures in rupees required to purchase a bundle of goods for basic sustenance, the Tendulkar Committee's revised estimates put the national "poverty headcount ratio" for "rural areas" to 42 percent (up from 28 percent) – or an increase of 105 million people in absolute terms (Table 4.5).

Yet, another official panel chaired by the former Reserve Bank of India governor C. Rangarajan tasked to revisit the findings of the Tendulkar committee following a massive public protest over the "abnormally low poverty rate" predictably revised the "total number of poor" to 363 million people, or 29.6 percent of the population against 269.8 million people, or 21.9 percent, set by the Tendulkar committee – sharply underscoring Nobel laureate Angus Deaton's (2013) pithy observation that "poverty measurement is ultimately a question of democratic consensus, not scientific calibration – a continuing exercise based on what is acceptable to policy makers and the public, including the poor themselves."

TABLE 4.5 *India's poverty rates (percent)*

	Lakdawala Committee			Tendulkar Committee		
	Rural	Urban	Combined	Rural	Urban	Combined
1993–1994	37.3	32.4	36	50.1	31.8	45.3
2004–2005	28.3	25.7	27.5	41.8	25.7	37.2

Source: Government of India (2011; 2013)

TABLE 4.6 *All-India poverty estimates: percentage below poverty line*

Year	Rural	Urban	Total
1993–1994	50.1	31.8	45.3
2004–2005	41.8	25.7	37.2
2009–2010	33.8	20.9	29.8
2011–2012	25.7	13.7	21.9

Source: Press Note on Poverty Estimates, 2011–12, Planning Commission; Report of the Expert Group to Review the Methodology for Estimation of Poverty.

In the end, this debate underscores that the question is not whether India's poverty levels have declined, but by how much. Arguably, the Planning Commission's figures for 2011–2012 are the most comprehensive. They estimate that those spending less than Rs. 27 (US$0.43) in the rural areas and Rs. 32 (US$0.53) in the urban areas were considered to be "poor." Specifically, 21.9 percent of the population (or 269 million people) were "poor" in 2011–2012 – a decline from 45.3 percent of the population (or 403 million people) in 1993–1994. These figures confirm that over 130 million Indians have been lifted out of poverty since 2004 (Table 4.6) – marking for the first time a meaningful decline in the absolute numbers of the poor.

Nevertheless, despite these impressive improvements, India still continues to have a large number of people (anywhere between 250 to 300 million) who live below the variously defined poverty lines. More specifically, even as India's overall poverty levels have declined, the absolute numbers of people still living in poverty is still unacceptably high. Not only do significant numbers of Indians continue live in abject poverty, an equally large number are negatively affected because of either the inadequacy or absence of essential public goods and services such as access to education, health care, housing, clean drinking water, and employment opportunities. In fact, various indicators of "broad deprivation" such as literacy, coverage of immunization, child mortality and access to clean water have not improved much and is no better than the average for low-income countries such as Bangladesh and Nepal.

Equally troubling, India has also witnessed a sharp rise in inequality (though much less pronounced than in China), with its Gini ticking up from 33 percent in 1993 to 37 percent in 2010. However, given India's rigid and entrenched system of socioeconomic stratification based on caste and gender, Balakrishnan and co-authors (2013, 6) appropriately caution that "other important dimensions of inequality in India that are not evident in conventional inequality indices based on consumption or income. These are inequalities associated with 'identity,' such as gender or caste, and inequalities in access to education and health." Also, as Bardhan (2009a) points out, "there are reasons to believe that the NSS data under-represent the rich, and in any case while for other developing countries the Gini coefficient often refers to income distribution, India's refers to distribution of consumption expenditure (as NSS does not collect income data), which is usually less than that of income (partly because the rich tend to save more than the poor)." However, income data occasionally collected by independent organizations show that in "a 2004–5 household survey, the Gini coefficient of income inequality comes to 0.535. Contrast this with the corresponding figure for China, 0.387 .... " Similarly, Kaushik Basu (2008, 36), a former senior adviser to the Indian government, warned that "the bulk of India's aggregate growth is occurring through a disproportionate rise in the incomes at the upper end of the income ladder." This observation is further underscored by Nobel laureate Amartya Sen (2011, 7), who has noted that "[India's] growth record is very impressive ... but there has also been a failure to ensure that rapid growth translates into better living conditions for the Indian people."

WHY RISING INEQUALITY?

What explains post-1991 India's simultaneous acceleration in economic growth (and rising prosperity) and rapidly widening income and wealth inequality, and why has a mature democratic polity ostensibly committed to promoting human development and socioeconomic justice failed to do a better job at reconciling economic growth with more equitable distribution of the fruits of that growth? The following sections unpacks this puzzle by juxtaposing two interrelated questions. First, it shows that the interactions between the forces of economic globalization and national politics (and the resultant policies) have created conditions conducive for sustained economic growth and rising prosperity, but also widening inequality. And, second, the failure to reconcile economic growth with distribution – or more specifically, growth with a more equitable distribution of income and wealth – has to do with both the peculiarities of India's fiscal federalism and the pathologies inherent in the actual practice of democracy in a deeply divided society. In particular, given the absence of political parties that structurally represent the poor (albeit, there is no shortage of popular movements claiming to represent the downtrodden), the deepening of democracy has only served to exacerbate the multiplicity of social cleavages, making collective action difficult. Indeed, the growing prevalence of increasingly uncompromising "identity politics" means that India's voters (the vast majority who are poor and who regularly vote) in the world's largest democracy often fail to get elected officials to serve the common good. Moreover, the exigencies of electoral politics in such a highly polarized setting has spawned a proliferation of "second-best" populist and palliative redistributive measures designed more to get incumbents reelected rather than to authoritatively address the problem of rising socioeconomic inequality and still-widespread poverty.

INCOMPLETE GLOBAL INTEGRATION

At the outset it is important to note that a distinguishing feature of the Indian economy is the country's agricultural sector – which makes up less than 15 percent of GDP, yet employs more than one-half of the total workforce. In 2011–2012, about 59 percent of male workers and 75 percent of female workers were dependent on agriculture (Government of India 2014, 14). Based on overall GDP, this means that the relative income per person engaged in agriculture is just about one-sixth of those engaged in non-agricultural activities. In addition to the unpredictability due to the vagaries of nature, India's agricultural sector has been beset with problems due to rising input costs and falling output prices, market instability (in particular, volatility in global demand for agricultural commodities), distortionary government policies (in particular, the excessive buffer stock build-up and the lack of a proactive stock liquidation policy), infrastructure bottlenecks, unviable size of landholdings and falling productivity (because of the continuous fragmentation of land holdings due to inheritance practices, the average farm size in India is small – with over two-thirds of farmers operating on a less than one hectare of land) making productivity gains difficult. As Table 4.7 shows, the relatively small and declining contribution of the agricultural sector in overall GDP is due to the fact that agricultural output has not only failed to keep up with overall growth in GDP, the growth rate of agriculture has continued to decline since 1999. This has contributed to reduced farm incomes, with adverse impacts on the small and marginal farmers – in particular, landless agricultural workers who make up the majority of the rural population.

The stagnation in the primary agricultural sector has had an adverse impact on rural employment and incomes, besides widening the gulf between the rural and urban areas. As Basole (2017, 40) notes, "there is an ongoing severe crisis of

TABLE 4.7 *Growth rate of GDP of agricultural sector 1981–1982 to 2013–2014*

Years	Growth Rate of Agriculture	GDP Growth
1981–1982 to 1989–1990	2.9	4.7
1990–1991 to 1999–2000	2.8	5.3
2000–2001 to 2009–2010	2.4	6.8
2010–2011 to 2013–2014	2.1	3.7

Source: (De Roy 2017, 68)

quality of livelihoods in the rural sector to the extent that 70% of agricultural households cannot meet their (low) consumption needs ...." Yet, paradoxically, available data from the "National Sample Survey on Consumption Expenditure" shows that inequality has not risen in the "rural areas," but has in the "urban areas." The Gini coefficient in rural areas was 0.28 in 1973–1974 and 0.29 in 2009–2010, while in the urban areas the Gini coefficient increased from 0.30 in 1973–1974 to 0.38 in 2009–2010. As will be discussed later, this underscores that although growth has been very much concentrated in India's urban areas, stagnant incomes and inequalities in the rural areas have been mitigated by both the national and state governments' various rural development and antipoverty programs. Specifically, government transfer initiatives to agriculture, including the "Minimum Support Prices" for agricultural commodities, subsidies for power and agricultural inputs, greater availability of institutional credit and antipoverty programs such as the Mahatma Gandhi National Rural Employment Guarantee Act (MGNREGA – a national government employment guarantee program), the Swarna Jayanti Shahari Rozgar Yojana, the National Rural Livelihood Mission, and the National Food Security Act (NFSA) of 2013 have helped to keep poverty and inequality in check – albeit, the government support and subsidies (the subsidies alone are estimated to consume anywhere between 2.7 to 3.0 percent of the country's gross domestic product) have come at a huge fiscal and economic cost, with only a modest impact on employment generation and poverty reduction.[7]

Second, the conventional view that economic globalization has been both a blessing and a curse for India is misleading. To the contrary, India is the poster-child of globalization. Since India opened its economy and began to gradually integrate into the global economic order in 1991, the Indian economy has expanded at an average annual rate of around 6.4 percent – a far cry from the anemic and near-stagnant 3.5 percent "Hindu rate of growth" during the "inward-looking" statist period from 1950 to 1980. As noted earlier, during 2002–2011, India's growth rate averaged 7.7 percent, and during 2005–2008, the average growth rate was an impressive 9.5 percent. Put bluntly, the post-1991 decision to open up and integrate into the global economy has been the catalyst behind India's economic renaissance – the engine behind its phenomenal GDP growth and emergence as an important global player.

Yet, counterintuitively, it is also India's rather unorthodox integration into the global economy – which, despite all the frenzy of reformist policy announcements and rhetoric of change, has meant that the Indian economy still remains relatively closed. This, in turn, has prevented the country from fully reaping the benefits of economic globalization. Thus, the problem is not too much globalization (as many critics allege), but rather too little of the right type of global economic integration. The legacy of the autarkic, inward-oriented policies of the pre-reform or "pre-liberalization" era, the half-hearted dismantling of statist and protectionist policies, and failure to deepen global economic integration by implementing "second-generation reforms" have prevented India from fully benefiting from globalization. Specifically, the following sections of this chapter will show that domestic policy choices, in serving to greatly limit, if not prevent, an overwhelmingly poor and underdeveloped agrarian-based economy's deepening and modernization of its essential manufacturing and industrial base have limited the economy from fully reaping the benefits of globalization. This is not to suggest that a nation's developmental fate is irrevocably linked to linear growth stages. However, it is worth noting that no country has become prosperous by skipping the critical manufacturing phase of development.[8] India, which currently enjoys a huge comparative advantage in young, low-skilled labor, has failed to fully exploit labor-intensive manufacturing that can provide jobs to its vast and growing labor pool. In fact, rising inequality and the modest reduction in poverty are due to India's singular failure to fully take advantage of the opportunities offered by economic globalization – namely, to create a wide range of basic and intermediate manufacturing jobs, which historically have served as a ladder out of low-income status.[9]

Certainly, India's and China's continental size, huge markets, rich resource base, and human capital give both a significant comparative advantage in this age of globalization. If China has benefitted from globalization because it serves as the "world's factory" and provides the world the requisite "hardware," then India has benefitted as a provider of "software" and related services such as business outsourcing. By riding the revolution in information-technology (IT), India has been able to fortuitously overcome the once-insurmountable constraints of geography and time. The global expansion of high-speed internet and related telecommunications networks have seemingly rendered "geography irrelevant" by creating linkages between nations, economies, and businesses that simply did not exist before. This has enabled India's entrepreneurs, including an array of parvenu business people, and the country's large pool of highly skilled and relatively inexpensive English-speaking "techies" to cash in on the IT revolution. In a relatively short period of time, India has become the location of choice for all sorts of IT-related activities best symbolized in "Electronics City" – Bangalore's main "tech-hub," where everything from advanced software production and programming, data processing, network management and systems integration, multimedia, business outsourcing, and call-center processing are performed.

Yet India's over-concentration due to its singular comparative advantage in the knowledge-intensive services sector has come with a cost. Unlike China's large and diverse labor-intensive manufacturing sector, which has created jobs for hundreds of millions of workers (especially unskilled labor from the countryside), India's excessive dependence on services and knowledge-intensive sectors such as banking, real estate, finance, and the information technology sector (computer programming, software development and production, communication networks, call centers, and outsourcing services) relies on a relatively small number of well-educated and skilled workers.[10] That is, unlike China's broad-based and deep integration in the global economy, India's comparative advantage in skill-intensive services and the technology sector rewards the "skill premium" – or individuals with advanced technical, managerial, and communication skills. This explains the widening earning differentials among individuals and households and the rapidly widening income inequality in India. Jaumotte, Lall, and Papageorgiou's (2013, 302) observation that "Both financial globalization and technological progress tend to increase the relative demand for skills and education. While incomes have increased across all segments of the population in virtually all countries in the sample, incomes of those who already have higher levels of education and skills have risen disproportionately more" is an apt description of India's experience.

It is important to also emphasize that the labor-intensive service sectors such as tourism, hospitality, and the retail trade can only create a certain number of jobs, and unlike labor-intensive manufacturing these sectors can only absorb relatively small numbers of low-skilled labor moving out of the countryside. Unlike China's large and diverse labor-intensive manufacturing sector, which has absorbed millions of workers, India's narrow dependence on highly specialized and cloistered service sectors like information technology and business outsourcing rely on a relatively small number of highly educated and skilled workers, thereby excluding the vast majority of the estimated 10 to 12 million young people who enter the labor market each year. As noted, the low levels of agricultural growth and resultant stagnant income growth in the countryside coupled with the absence of a dynamic industrial and manufacturing sector has meant that the scope for mobility for low-skilled labor out of the agricultural sector has been limited. Not surprisingly, according to the most recent available official data on labor force (the 68th round of the National Sample Survey on Employment and Unemployment in India), India's total workforce numbered 473 million in 2012. A whopping 70 percent were classified as "rural" – with 49 percent of this workforce employed directly in the "primary sector" (read "agriculture") and the rest in rural activities such as construction or casual labor. Table 4.8 shows the relatively small share of the manufacturing sector in gross GDP when compared to other key players. Compounding these problems, India's poor infrastructure, notorious for its delays and bottlenecks, coupled with the equally pernicious bureaucratic and regulatory red-tape, including restrictive labor laws and a less-than-welcoming environment for foreign investment, have served to limit the expansion of labor-intensive manufacturing. Predictably, this has resulted in India's experiencing prolonged "jobless growth."

POLITICAL ECONOMY OF INDIA'S MANUFACTURING SECTOR

Agriculture, manufacturing, and services make up the core sectors of the economy. Historically, labor has moved out of agriculture into manufacturing

TABLE 4.8 *Percent share of manufacturing value added in GDP 2000 and 2005*

	GDP Share (2000)	GDP Share (2005)
India	14.3	14.1
China	32.1	34.1
Malaysia	32.6	32.2
Thailand	33.6	36.1
Vietnam	18.6	22.5
Industrialized Economies	17.6	16.8
Developing Economies	20.5	21.7

Source: Zagha (2013, 139)

and then into services. For the advanced economies, this has meant moving out of agriculture and labor-intensive, low-skilled manufacturing into services. Japan, South Korea, and China's economic transformation took place because these countries were able to effectively leverage their comparative advantage in abundant low-wage labor to establish large-scale and competitive manufacturing industries specializing in exports. However, in the case of India, both labor and production have been gradually moving away from the agricultural sector, but not into manufacturing, but mostly into services. The Indian economy's truncated structural transformation, where it has seemingly skipped the second stage, means that it has a relatively small and uncompetitive manufacturing sector with a pronounced inability to generate mass employment. Goel and Restrepo-Echavarria (2015, 1) note that under "India's atypical structural transformation," the overall GDP shares of three sectors vary sharply: "the services share has increased dramatically and currently stands at 53 percent. In comparison, the manufacturing share has remained stagnant, growing only from 19 percent in 1970 to 23 percent in 2012" (Figures 4.1, 4.2, 4.3 and 4.4).

Not surprisingly, as Joumard, Sila, and Morgavi (2015, 6) note, "Productivity of the manufacturing sector is low ... the productivity of India's manufacturing sector is lower than in other emerging economies, and also lower than in the service sector. Measured in value added (in PPP) per hour worked, productivity of manufacturing in China and Brazil is 1.6 and 2.9 times higher, respectively, than in India." This is fundamentally because the dominant characteristic of India's manufacturing sector is the extraordinarily small scale of operations, as over 85 percent of manufacturing employment is in micro-enterprises of fewer than ten employees. Zagha (2013, 144) lucidly captures the reality by noting that "one of the distinctive features of India's manufacturing is its 'missing middle.' That is, the size distribution of firms is U-shaped rather

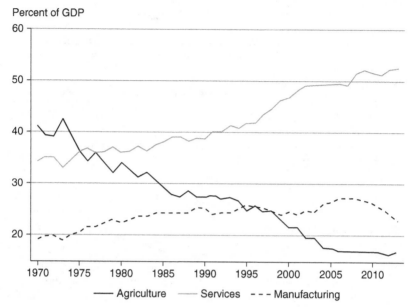

FIGURE 4.1 GDP shares in India.
Source: World Bank World Development Indicators. (Original)
Source: Goel and Restrepo-Echavarria (2015, 2).

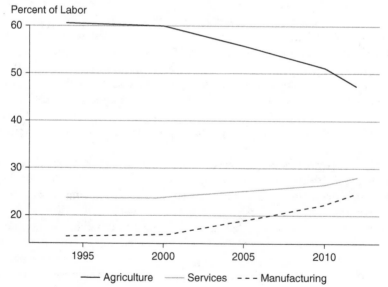

FIGURE 4.2 Labor shares in India.
Source: World Bank World Development Indicators. (Original)
Goel and Restrepo-Echavarria (2015, 2).

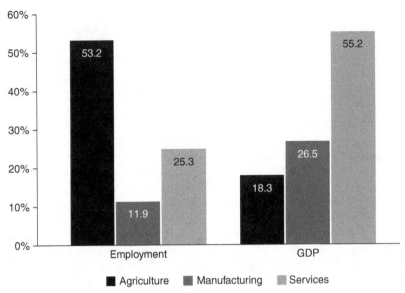

FIGURE 4.3 Sectoral contribution to the economy in 2010.
Source: Green and McAuley (2014, 2).

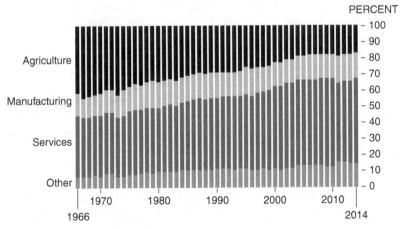

FIGURE 4.4 India's evolving economy.
Source: World Bank, Our World in Data 2015.

than the inverted U observed in most countries. The implication is that India has large numbers of small firms, mostly in the informal sector, and large firms. But medium-scale businesses, which in other developing nations account for the bulk of employment, are missing ... The relative dearth of mid-sized businesses has much to do with India's failure to develop an export-oriented low-skill-intensive manufacturing sector able to provide more employment and pull the economy ahead."

Dabla-Norris and Kochhar (2015, 160–161) note "the extraordinarily small scale of establishments in India relative to any major emerging market when measured in terms of employment and output. Almost 90 percent of manufacturing employment is in enterprises with fewer than 10 workers, and 60 percent of manufacturing occurs in establishments with fewer than five workers ... the disproportionately small size of industrial firms in India is a serious drag on manufacturing productivity, and growth." Similarly, Joumard et al. (2015, 7) note that "the productivity problem in manufacturing partly stems from the preponderance of small firms with low productivity, which cannot exploit economies of scale ... Employment in manufacturing firms with less than 10 employees – the so-called unorganised sector ... accounted for about 65% of employment in the sector in 2011–12, compared to 14% on average in the OECD and 9% in Brazil ..." Moreover, "the share of manufactured goods in total merchandise exports fell from 77% in 2003 to 65% in 2013 ... India's share in world manufacturing export stood at 1.7% in 2010 compared to 14% for China ... The latest competitive industrial performance index ranks India 43rd out of 133 countries, far behind China, but also behind Thailand, Brazil and Indonesia"(Joumard et al. 2015, 9).

The dismal state of Indian manufacturing is the direct result of the central and state governments' policy distortions that have placed numerous restrictions on private enterprise through licensing laws, directed credit, preferences for small-scale industry, anti-monopoly regulations, small-scale industry reservations policy, and stringent if not punitive labor laws – which make it very costly to reduce the number of workers in enterprises of more than 100 workers. According to McKinsey Global Institute report (2014, 15), "At least 43 national laws – and many more state laws – create rigid operating conditions and discourage growth in labour-intensive industries."[11] The result of this policy is that formal-sector firms (those that are registered and that pay their taxes) loathe taking on new employment. Subramanian (2013) notes that "India's panoply of regulations, including inflexible labor laws, discourages companies from expanding. As they grow, large Indian businesses prefer to substitute machines for unskilled labor." This explains why India's manufacturing sector is capital and skill-intensive – and not labor-intensive as expected from a labor-abundant economy. Hasan, Kapoor, Mehta, and Sundaram (2017, 85) note that "India's labor regulations have contributed to keeping apparel firms relatively small and in the informal sector."

During China's three-decade boom (1978–2010), manufacturing accounted for about 34 percent of China's economy. In India, this number peaked at 17 percent in 1995 and is now around 14 percent. For example, India's textile industry dominated by many small producers that are not only excessively regulated, the average firm in both the formal and informal sectors is also constrained from fully exploiting scale economies and new technologies. As a result, little foreign capital has flowed into these sectors, and because Indian firms are less well integrated into global production networks than are Chinese firms, they have benefited little from technology transfer. Similarly, the production of goods such as garments, toys, shoes, leather, and related textile products continue to be reserved for the small-scale producers, although large firms have a potential comparative advantage, given their greater ability to exploit the optimal scale of production. This has placed domestic producers at a disadvantage when competing against foreign producers who have no scale restrictions. Nothing underscores this problem better than India's famous textile industry. In 1950, India was the world's leading exporter of cotton textiles. However, currently India's textile industry trails far behind that of China. Even in 2005, India's exports of textiles and garments amounted to $9.5 billion and $7.5 billion, respectively, versus China's respective $77 billion and $40 billion (Winters and Yusuf 2007, 51).

Bhagwati and Panagariya (2014) succinctly argue that the fundamental reason why Indian manufacturing has failed to expand or "scale-up," why the vast majority of manufacturing firms start small and continue to remain small, and why Indian industry has failed to generate high-quality jobs is because the plethora of the country's restrictive and punitive labor laws (which are among the strictest in the world) have systematically hollowed-out the industrial and manufacturing base of the country, beginning with the Industrial Disputes Act of 1947, which required "large-scale enterprises" to obtain prior and compulsory state government approval before firing or laying-off workers ("large-scale" used to refer to firms with over 300 employees), and an amendment to the Act in 1976 which made it compulsory for firms with 300 or more workers to seek permission from the government before dismissing workers – even in the case of needed layoffs and retrenchment during economic downturns. A further amendment in 1982 reduced the ceiling for seeking prior government permission to 100 workers. An additional four dozen central laws and hundreds of state laws governing labor have all served to scuttle manufacturing growth (there are currently 44 labor-related statutes enacted by the central government and another 100 by the state governments).

The inconsistent and contradictory central and state labor laws not only make compliance and inspection exceedingly difficult (resulting in the running joke "that you cannot implement India's labor laws 100 percent without violating 20 percent of them"), they also discourage businesses from taking on or creating new employment. Predictably, only a small percentage of the labor force is employed in the formal private sector. Thomas (2013, 674) notes that "In the mid-2000s, the manufacturing sector provided employment to 56 million, or 12.2% of India's total workforce. Of the total manufacturing workforce, an overwhelming proportion worked in the informal or the unregistered sector. Only the remaining workers – 8.5 million in 2004–2005 – were engaged in the factory sector, which broadly represents organized manufacturing sector ... In India, registered factories comprise all factories that employ more than 10 workers and operate with the aid of electric power as well as factories that employ more than 20 workers without the aid of electric power." In effect, the relatively privileged and closed formal sector has had the unintended effect of pushing many workers into the informal sector, which provides limited or no job security and no benefits – and which, according to the International Labor Organization (2012), is the world's largest.[12] India's unorganized informal sector, made up of numerous tax-evading, small, and inefficient enterprises, employs the bulk of India's off-farm labor force – keeping millions outside the reach of labor laws ostensibly designed to protect them, including the social welfare schemes that could help offset their wages, and thereby, help increase income and reduce wealth inequality.

Moreover, the highly punitive labor laws also explain why Indian firms prefer industries that are automated. Although Joumard et al. (2015, 11) note that labor costs in India have "remained relatively low ... in 2009 were about 25% lower than in China. Nevertheless, Indian manufacturing is surprisingly capital intensive compared to China and Indonesia ... In 11 out of 14 manufacturing sub-sectors, India has the highest capital-labour ratio. India has also specialised in more skill-intensive production compared to its peers ... India's organised manufacturing has higher capital-intensities than countries at the same level of development and with similar factor endowments." Cumulatively, these restrictions have severely restricted export competitiveness, and also job creation, by forcing businesses to create more capital-intensive manufacturing jobs rather than what India needs – more labor-intensive manufacturing jobs that would raise wages and living standards for the vast majority of India's low-skilled workers. But, as Joumard et al. (2015, 9) note, "total employment outside of agriculture rose by about 51 million between 2004–05 and 2011–12, but only 6 million jobs were created in the manufacturing sector. Moreover, most of them were informal labour (i.e. not covered by social security arrangements)." The absence of a robust manufacturing sector has meant that "half of the 48 million non-agricultural jobs added from 2004 to 2012 have been dead-end construction jobs in rural areas" (Green and McAuley 2014, 2). Clearly, the Indian services-sector by itself will not be able to generate enough employment to meet the needs of a growing and expectant population. The stark reality is that India cannot grow into a major economy on services alone. Since the industrial revolution, no country has become a major economy without first becoming an industrial power. India will have to significantly expand and improve the competitiveness of its manufacturing base. Indeed, the most critical challenge facing India in the next few years is how to further develop manufacturing in order to create jobs for the more than 100 million people set to join the labor force in the next decade.

Unlike China, which has invested a significant volume of resources in building a world-class infrastructure (partly to assist manufacturing growth), India's infrastructure is decrepit, inefficient, and literally overwhelmed.

Inadequate and inchoate road and rail networks, crippling electric-power deficits, and overcrowded ports and airports where erratic service and long delays are a norm are a drag on economic growth – in particular, manufacturing growth. Because inefficient and weak infrastructural systems increase costs, manufacturing industries will continue to be uncompetitive even if labor laws are reformed unless the country's infrastructural networks improves. In fact, infrastructural bottlenecks have gravely hampered industrial expansion. For example, the pervasive delays in ports and roads relative to India's competitors have forced industries to shift operations to other countries. The World Bank (2013) estimates that it takes about 17 days to export from India, compared to 5 days from Singapore and other Southeast Asian countries. Specifically, the cost of a container shipped from India was $945, compared with $456 from Singapore. Exacerbating this is the lack of a reliable electricity supply. Persistent power shortages have translated into costly disruptions to production, and although key stakeholders agree that chronic electricity shortages constitute the country's greatest infrastructure deficit, little has to be done to alleviate this problem. Overall, burdened with chronically poor infrastructure, excessive regulations, and red-tape (which add to the production and transportation costs), the manufacturing sector remains uncompetitive and inefficient, and not commensurate with India's overall economic weight.

The May 2014 parliamentary election of a business-friendly government under Narendra Modi and his Bharatiya Janata Party (BJP) raised hopes that the new administration would finally implement the languishing economic reforms and roll back the Indian state's pervasive involvement in the economy – something the "can-do" pro-business Modi had aggressively carried out during his 15 years as Chief Minister of Gujarat state. Indeed, the replacement of the influential (if not, imperious) Planning Commission in January 2015 with NITI Aayog (National Institution for Transforming India), tasked to function as a think-tank to inform policy makers about "national development priorities," and Prime Minister Modi's aggressive attempt to woo foreign investment with his "Make in India," "Make for India," "Startup India," "Skill India," and "Digital India" campaigns further confirmed the view that market principles would play a greater role in the economy. The passage of 3 years since Modi's election have made clear that the Prime Minister's ambitious "Make in India" and related slogans have had the singular aim to transform India into a leading "global manufacturing hub." However, Modi's ambitions are hardly new, as previous administrations unveiled similarly bold initiatives – the most recent and equally lofty, the 2011 National Manufacturing Policy (NMP), with the stated goal to increase the share of India's manufacturing to 25 percent of GDP and to create an additional 100 million jobs by 2022.

Not to be outdone, the Modi administration has also committed itself to increasing the manufacturing sector's share of India's gross domestic product to

25 percent by 2022 and to add 100 million more manufacturing jobs, and, in April 2015, the Modi's government announced its aim to increase India's share of global trade from 2.1 percent to 3.5 percent and double exports to US$900 billion by 2020. In order to cut and streamline bureaucratic red-tape and to facilitate better coordination between New Delhi and the 29 state governments, the Department of Industrial Policy and Promotion has been empowered to coordinate across ministries and between the central and state governments to implement the program. However, translating the "Make in India" slogan into substantive outcomes will require India to deepen its integration into the global economy with the aim to generate sustained export growth. The first phase has been off to a good start. By relaxing Foreign Direct Investment (FDI) caps – with 100 percent now allowed in many sectors and with lower caps for defense, insurance, and multi-brand retail, coupled with Modi's numerous foreign trips ostensibly aimed at making India the world's favored destination for FDI, his government has been able to secure agreements for greater trade and investment collaboration with India's major trading partners, including leading foreign companies.[13] Yet expanding manufacturing and boosting exports will require more than FDI and pithy slogans. More specifically, it also requires an efficient infrastructure (it is estimated that upgrading India's basic infrastructure such as roads, airports, and rail networks will cost over $450 billion), and although FDI reached $78.5 billion in net inflows between 2014 and 2015 and $95.2 billion by September 2016, the post-crisis slowdown in global trade and the rise of protectionism around the world pose major challenges for global trade expansion.[14, 15]

Compounding these challenges are India's powerful lobbies and vested constituencies who favor protectionism over deepening global economic integration, which also pose a major obstacle to expanding manufacturing growth. Not surprisingly, the Modi administration's modest plan to merge 44 labor laws into four in order to "simplify" rules for hiring and firing workers triggered an immediate backlash from the opposition parties, labor unions, and various civil society groups. In fact, India's largest labor union (which also happens to be affiliated with Modi's Bharatiya Janata Party) made common cause with unions affiliated to the main opposition Congress party and the various leftist groups, calling for a nationwide strike on September 2, 2015 to protest the government's plans.[16] Indeed, the BJP and Indian National Congress-affiliated labor unions, representing an estimated 150 million workers, launched a nationwide strike to express their displeasure at the government's plan. In the end the government backed down – saving face by establishing a national panel to review national labor policy – and opting for "competitive federalism" by encouraging the legislatures of BJP-controlled state governments like Rajasthan and Madhya Pradesh to reform the labor laws in hopes that success in these states would encourage other states to do the same. In fact, the Modi administration has made a point to encourage India's 29 state governments to implement reforms via competitive federalism, hoping that "healthy competition" among the state governments as they vie for resources from the center, including investments from outside, would boost economic growth. Similarly, the Modi administration's proposed amendments to the "land acquisition bill," to ease the onerous rules to acquire land needed to modernize the country's crumbling infrastructure and create "industrial corridors," faces protracted uncertainty and gridlock in Parliament, with the Congress-led opposition denouncing the bill as "anti-farmer."[17] The Goods and Services Tax (GST) bill faced similar political gridlock (albeit, it was eventually passed in August 2016 and was scheduled to be implemented by April 2017), despite broad policy consensus that the GST, by replacing myriad local levies and the cumbersome indirect taxes (currently collected on goods and services by the state and federal government) with single tax on value added, would significantly reduce tax cascading, create a common and more integrated national market, encourage voluntary tax compliance, reduce tax collection costs, help the central government improve its fiscal situation, and provide a much-needed boost to economic activity by streamlining commercial activities.[18]

INDIA AND GLOBAL TRADE

The weak export competitiveness of India's manufacturing industries explains New Delhi's disproportionate reliance on protectionist measures to shield its "infant industries" (many of which are some 70 years old) from open global competition. Indeed, complementing some of these earlier measures, more recent measures such as those announced in November 2011 (as part of the National Manufacturing Policy) have called for more local content requirements (or "localization") in government procurement in the various manufacturing sectors, including electronics, energy, information, and communication technology. In fact, India's Preferential Market Access mandate (which is part of the National Manufacturing Policy) also requires local content requirements for government procurement related to electronic products. Cumulatively, India's localization policies, which are with some justification seen as a form of non-tariff trade barrier, have tended to further distort cross-border trade by restricting access to India's markets. Not surprisingly, India (according to the World Bank) in 2013 was ranked 134th out of 189 countries for the "ease of doing" cross-border business, and in 2017 ranked 130 out of 190 countries.[19] This is the lowest ranking for any G-20 country. According to the WTO World Tariff Profiles report, in 2016 India imposed a 48.5 percent simple average final bound tariff rate and a 13.4 percent simple average applied tariff rate – with particularly high tariffs on imports of agricultural products. India is also the world's leader when it comes to using "anti-dumping" measures (with 740 cases during 1995–2014, as compared to China's 218) against foreign competition – not to mention that New Delhi continues to impose high tariffs (when compared with other countries), and its foreign investment regime remains highly restrictive (Figure 4.5).

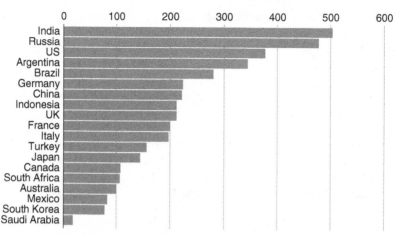

FIGURE 4.5 India, Russia, and the US the worst offenders.
Source: Financial Times.

India's protectionist trade policies and failure to deepen its integration into the global economy – especially with its major trading partner, the United States – has negatively impacted India–US economic relations. This is because the US market is largely open to India's exports, as India is a major beneficiary of the US Generalized System of Preferences (GSP) program, which allows most Indian goods to enter the United States duty free.[20] On the other hand, US exports to India lack "reciprocal access" via high tariff and non-tariff barriers such as foreign ownership restrictions and, as noted earlier, what Subramanian (2013) has aptly termed "protectionism through localization." Therefore, even as trade and financial linkages between the two countries have steadily grown over the past three decades (with the two-way trade totaling roughly $62.9 billion in 2012 and US foreign direct investment increasing from a meager $200 million in early 2000 to over $24 billion in 2013), it is far less than it should be between the world's largest and third-largest economies (see Table 4.9). Indeed, bilateral trade and investment between the two giants is shockingly tiny, with India accounting for less than 2 percent of total US exports of goods and services and less than 1 percent of the stock of US overseas investment in 2017. Comparatively speaking, India is the United States' thirteenth largest trading partner, but India–US trade is just one-eighth of China–US trade. Even Taiwan and South Korea trade more with the United States than does India.[21] The relatively miniscule size of India–US trade is not only due to India's sluggish manufacturing and narrow export base, but also because New Delhi has hampered the deepening of economic ties by creating roadblocks with complex, contradictory, and discriminatory regulations and rules that businesses and investors find infuriating and costly (both in time and energy) to navigate.

TABLE 4.9 *United States–India trade*

US Goods and Services Trade with India (in billions of dollars)

	1995	2000	2006	2012	2013	2014	2015	2016
Total	11.2	19.1	45.1	93.7	97.3	104.4	109.0	NA
Exports	4.6	6.5	16.2	34.4	35.1	36.7	39.6	NA
Imports	6.6	12.6	28.9	59.3	62.2	67.7	69.5	NA
Balance	-2.0	-6.1	-12.7	-24.9	-27.1	-31.0	-29.9	NA

US Goods Trade with India (in billions of dollars)

	1995	2000	2006	2012	2013	2014	2015	2016
Total	9.0	14.4	31.5	62.6	63.6	66.9	66.2	67.7
Exports	3.3	3.7	9.7	22.1	21.8	21.5	21.5	21.7
Imports	5.7	10.7	21.8	40.5	41.8	45.4	44.8	46.0
Balance	-2.4	-7.0	-12.2	-18.4	-20.0	-23.9	-23.3	-24.3

US Agricultural Trade with India (in billions of dollars)

	2006	2012	2013	2014	2015	2016
Total	1.4	6.2	4.4	4.2	3.9	3.4
Exports	0.4	0.9	0.9	1.1	1.2	1.3
Imports	1.0	5.4	3.5	3.2	2.7	2.1
Balance	-0.7	-4.5	-2.6	-2.1	-1.5	-0.8

US Manufacturing Trade with India (in billions of dollars)

	2006	2012	2013	2014	2015	2016
Total	29.1	57.3	58.8	61.4	60.5	61.9
Exports	8.5	19.0	19.5	18.9	18.5	18.8
Imports	20.6	38.4	39.4	42.5	41.9	43.0
Balance	-12.1	-19.4	-19.9	-23.6	-23.4	-24.2

US Services Trade with India (in billions of dollars)

	1995	2000	2006	2012	2013	2014	2015	2016
Total	2.2	4.7	13.6	31.1	33.7	37.5	42.8	NA
Exports	1.3	2.8	6.5	12.3	13.3	15.2	18.1	NA
Imports	0.9	1.9	7.1	18.8	20.4	22.4	24.7	NA

Source: "US–India Bilateral Trade and Investment," Office of the United States Trade Representative, 2016. https://ustr.gov/countries-regions/south-central-asia/india.

Even the landmark Indo–US civil nuclear agreement signed in 2008, which was supposed to generate billions of dollars in business for both US and Indian companies and their domestic suppliers, has to date failed to yield anything tangible except protracted disagreements over which partner would be liable in the event of a nuclear accident. Specifically, US firms are leery about entering the Indian market, given India's "strict" liability laws.[22] Similarly, disappointment with the long-awaited decision to open India's estimated $500 billion retail market to foreign companies such as Wal-Mart and IKEA has served to further limit New Delhi's ability to attract much-needed foreign direct investment, not to mention denying consumers the benefits from these deep-discount stores in the form of wider selection and cheaper prices.[23] The relative ease with which the populist Aam Aadmi Party (AAP, or the "common man's party"), which won an unprecedented election victory in Delhi in November 2013 and punitively reversed the decision of the previous government to disallow Wal-Mart and other global retail chains from opening stores in India's capital city, underscores the challenge India faces in attracting the FDI needed to modernize its infrastructure and industries, especially the lagging manufacturing sector.[24]

Not surprisingly, the US House Ways and Means Trade Subcommittee Chair, Devin Nunes (on March 13, 2013), concerned about India's growing protectionist measures, including creeping trade and investment barriers against US businesses, warned, "I am concerned that India has launched a series of alarming policies that harm US job creators and are counterproductive." He further said, "I intend to push India to remove barriers that prevent US companies, farmers, ranchers, and workers from competing on a level playing field and selling their world-class products and services to India's 1.2 billion consumers."[25] Similarly, the Indian government's "compulsory licensing" rules regarding foreign firms' intellectual property rights – specifically, pharmaceutical patents – have forced American industry associations to form a new organization: the Alliance for Fair Trade with India (AFTI).[26] Led by the US Chamber of Commerce, the National Association of Manufacturers, and several other industry groups, the AFTI directly appealed to President Obama and the Congress to take immediate and "purposeful" action against New Delhi's inhospitable, "mercantilist behavior." Incensed by what it sees as New Delhi's cavalier disregard for international rules and gross violation of the pharmaceutical industry's patent rights (namely, the February 2013 decision by India's Patent Office to revoke Pfizer's patent for the cancer drug Sutent by granting a domestic manufacturer, Cipla, the right to produce a low-cost generic; the March 2012 action by the Indian government to grant a "compulsory license" to a local company to manufacture a generic version of Bayer's Nexavar, a cancer drug, on the grounds that Nexavar was too expensive for Indian patients; and including the Indian Supreme Court's decision to deny a patent to Novartis for the drug Glivec to treat leukemia, despite the fact that its patent is recognized in more than 40 countries) led the AFTI to send an open letter on June 6, 2013 to the President and Congress. The AFTI charged that India has "systematically discriminated against a wide range of US innovative products," "has repeatedly ignored internationally recognized rights – imposing arbitrary marketing restrictions on medical devices and denying, breaking, or revoking patents for nearly a dozen lifesaving medications," and that India's decision to "undermine internationally recognized intellectual property standards is ... designed to benefit India's business and industrial community at the expense of American jobs."[27]

Similarly, as noted earlier, India's intrusive local content requirements, which mandate that foreign companies buy local content, led Washington (in February 2013) to approach the WTO for dispute consultations concerning the "domestic content" requirement of India's solar program. The US claimed that by requiring all companies producing solar-energy-related products to use locally manufactured solar cells (with New Delhi offering special subsidies) was in violation of WTO rules, which require members to treat both foreign and domestic producers and goods on an equal footing.[28] Moreover, erecting barriers to local market access via high tariffs and inconsistent tax requirements, including limits on foreign direct investment via foreign equity caps, restrictions on investment in banking, financial services, retail, and telecommunications, have served to hamper the expansion of trade and investment in India.[29] Clearly, New Delhi's actions have not gone unnoticed. In June 2013, more than 170 members of Congress wrote to President Obama to express their concern regarding "India's failure to protect intellectual property adequately and its attempts to implement local content requirements in technology purchases,"[30] and in August 2013, the Senate Committee on Finance and the House Committee on Ways and Means requested the US International Trade Commission (USITC) to launch an investigation into how Indian policies discriminate against US trade and investment.[31] Signaling that Washington's patience is running out, on February 10, 2014, US Trade Representative Michael Froman announced that the Obama Administration planned to take New Delhi to the WTO regarding India's "discriminatory" domestic content requirements on solar energy products. This marked the second time in less than a year when Washington had taken New Delhi to the WTO – the latest step potentially setting the stage for possible US sanctions if disputes were not resolved by the WTO.[32]

Although the official justification behind the use of protectionist measures such as anti-dumping is to prevent large foreign business interests from unfairly distorting domestic markets by cutting prices (often below cost) to capture market share and, in the process, driving out local producers, in practice the measures are often used to shelter politically well-connected, inefficient domestic businesses from foreign competition. Indeed, Rao (2015) has noted that bureaucratic and administrative capture, where "virtually every regulatory system has been captured by retired bureaucrats," has enabled vested interests to use an array of regulations to stifle reforms in the manufacturing sector. More broadly, Kohli (2012) has argued that the "state-business alliance," which dominates Indian policymaking, has privileged an economic strategy that is "pro-business" rather than "pro-market" because it promotes the interests of large firms such as those owned by the influential Tata, Birla, and Ambani houses. Their sprawling business empires have benefitted from policies that have liberalized the financial sector, as well as protectionist measures that have excluded foreign investors and smaller domestic firms. To Kohli's thinking, big business has gained a disproportionate influence in elite policy-making circles because of its active lobbying, because India's campaign finance system requires big donors, and because of the narrowing of elite policy-making that privileges technocrats over voters.

INDIA'S VULNERABILITY TO FINANCIAL GLOBALIZATION

In response to the global financial crisis of 2007–2009, the governments in several advanced economies – in particular, the United States, Great Britain, the Eurozone, and Japan – have employed both conventional and unconventional monetary policies, including injecting liquidity into the financial markets, undertaking large-scale asset purchases or "quantitative easing," and cutting short-term interest rates to near zero to influence market expectations and jumpstart economic growth. In the United States, since November 2008, the Federal Open Market Committee (FOMC) has regularly used bond purchases to reduce long-term interest rates to promote economic activity in support of domestic employment growth and to revive America's stagnant housing markets. The FOMC has varied these very large-scale asset purchases. referred to as "quantitative easing" (QE), based on its assessment of the United States' overall economic performance. In QE3 (announced first in September 13 and again on December 12, 2012), the Federal Reserve committed itself to monthly purchases of $85 billion in bonds.[33] However, in May 2013, when Federal Reserve Chair Ben Bernanke, during his testimony to Congress, raised the possibility of "tapering" or unwinding securities purchases from its current $85 billion a month, it had an immediate negative impact on several emerging country bond and currency markets, besides abruptly reversing credit flows to emerging economies with troubling debt loads – most notably, India.

This event underscores that the global financial environment is increasingly driven by monetary policy in systematically advanced economies like the United States, and emerging economies like India whose financial system have become more deeply interconnected with global financial markets are now vulnerable to cross-border spillovers and contagion (Sharma 2014a). The Fed, by printing trillions of dollars, had kept US interest rates near zero, besides boosting asset prices around the world (especially in emerging markets like India), forcing investors to turn to emerging markets for higher yields.[34] In turn, emerging market economies such as India (and also Brazil, Indonesia, and Turkey) welcomed the new inflow of liquidity, not only for investment, but also to finance an excess of consumption. In the case of India, this trend is reflected in the total government expenditures – which increased by an average of 15 percent each year between 2009 and 2013. Burdened with large current-account deficits and debt, economies such as India lay exposed and vulnerable, especially if foreign investors perceived any signs of weakness (real or imagined) such as slowdowns in economic growth or risks of currency depreciation or default. Given that the US dollar plays such an important role in the global economy, even modest changes in US monetary policy can have (sometimes significant) impact on global capital inflows and outflows.[35] In turn, the resulting exchange rate movements against the dollar can have very large and rapid effects on the level of inflation and exports, especially in emerging economies. Indeed, the reverberations stemming from the Fed's policy intention were felt far and wide, especially in emerging market economies' currency markets, as investors sold or "unloaded" emerging market bonds and currencies. The rupee (unlike the Indonesian rupiah or the Brazilian real) experienced a significant correction – or, more appropriately, a meltdown.

Predictably, the Fed's action led to howls of indignation from emerging markets. As Rodrik and Subramanian (2014) aptly note, "From Istanbul to Brasilia to Mumbai comes a crescendo of complaints about dollar imperialism. Heads of state and central bank governors allege that the policies of central banks in industrial countries, especially the US Federal Reserve, pursued in self-interest, are wreaking havoc in emerging-market economies. This allegation is mostly unfair. Emerging markets aren't hapless and undeserved victims; for the most part they are simply reaping what they sowed."[36] It is important to keep in mind that a large body of research confirms that the key determinants of capital flows to emerging economies are real growth-rate differentials and interest-rate differentials, including investor sentiments. Countries with high growth rates and those offering high interest rates (as least, relative to those in advanced economies) tend to encourage capital flows, especially portfolio flows seeking both higher and quick returns.

As India's growth rate faltered and then began a steady dip, foreign investors began to pay greater attention to the so-called "fundamentals" of the Indian economy. Clearly worried about New Delhi's perennially stalled economic reforms and unsustainable fiscal and current-account deficits, the footloose investors began to pull out their funds from India's equity, bond, and currency markets. It was this investor wariness about the Indian economy – in particular, concerns about the economy's structural flaws and the growing debt load – that explains the large and rapid capital outflows. Specifically, in March 2013, India's external debt stood at US$390 billion, an increase of US$44.6 billion or 12.9 percent over the level at the end of March 2012. More troubling for investors, the increase in the overall debt was primarily due to a rise in short-term trade credit – with the ratio of short-term debt to foreign exchange reserves rising to 33.1 percent by March 2013 from 26.6 percent from March 2012, and the debt denominated in US dollars jumping to

57.2 percent of the total external debt.[37] India's excessive dependence on short-term portfolio capital (which is intrinsically more volatile than FDI), the absence of a vibrant and competitive export sector (in particular, the failure of the manufacturing sector to earn sufficient foreign exchange to service its obligations), and a growing dependence on imported energy stood as big red flags. With India's imports increasing, and in order to make up for the shortfall (or trade deficit), New Delhi both borrowed excessively and encouraged short-term portfolio investments – ostensibly to shore up its own foreign currency reserves. However, the Fed's announcement and the potentially tighter credit in the US and other advanced economies triggered a sudden outflow of liquidity. Chastened footloose investors asked, among other things, how is New Delhi going to finance its imports and deficits? Their concerns only sped their exit from the Indian market. India's currency and capital accounts were adversely affected by the large outflow of portfolio investment (estimated at $15 billion during June-August 2013), vividly reflected in the plummeting rupee.

Like Brazil and Indonesia, both of which raised interest rates to prop up their currencies, India's central bank, the Reserve Bank of India (RBI), also increased the bank rate (i.e., the interest rate at which it lends money to other banks) to 10.25 percent, placed a cap on amount that banks could borrow or lend under its daily liquidity window, announced the sale of government securities through an open market operation, and imposed a 10 percent duty on gold imports.[38] However, these actions failed to bring much respite. To the contrary, put in an unenviable position, the RBI's policy decisions became contradictory, if not harmful. For example, the RBI's decision to reduce the amount of money Indian businesses and residents could send abroad had the unintended outcome of further spooking foreign investors, who became concerned that similar restrictions would be imposed on them. This served to trigger a further sell-off in the Indian financial markets. As capital outflows continued unabated, the depreciation of the rupee increased inflationary pressure, eventually forcing the RBI to raise interest rates. India's experience vividly highlights that, in this era of globalization, countries with large current-account deficits (such as India) are particularly vulnerable to shifts in investor sentiment.[39] In this case, an announcement by the US Federal Reserve that it planned to "taper" its loose monetary policy had far-reaching consequences, as capital flew out from emerging markets on expectations of greater stability and returns in advanced economies.

In a rapidly globalizing world, cross-border economic and financial shocks and spillovers are a fact of life. The Indian case also underscores that in such a fast-evolving global economy, emerging economies, especially those with glaring structural problems like India, will continue to have diminishing options unless they implement the necessary reforms. For example, the RBI correctly reasoned that if it allowed the rupee to weaken, it would not only push up the cost of imports, but also further widen the current account deficit and exacerbate the already-high consumer price inflation. Although a cheaper currency could help boost exports and help narrow the current-account deficit, unfortunately India, with its weak exports, could hardly take advantage of this opportunity. Still, further tightening of liquidity carried its own risks by undermining India's already-weak and sagging growth, besides worsening the financial conditions for corporations and banks by exacerbating their debt woes. Since growing numbers of private businesses in India have large outstanding foreign debts, their ability to service their debt was made the more difficult by the depreciated rupee exchange rate.

Indeed, the rupee's fast depreciation had an immediate negative impact. The rapid erosion in purchasing power meant that everything that India imported (which is a lot) suddenly became a lot more expensive. If India's estimated 300–350 million strong middle class – who have increasingly acquired a taste for a western consumer lifestyle, including annual vacations – saw their purchasing ability shrink, the vast majority of the populace would find it exceedingly difficult to afford basic necessities. However, as noted, the import that took a big chunk of change was the escalating cost of energy. India's heavy dependence on imported fuel (which can only be purchased in dollar-denominated prices) took a big toll. As the rupee plunged in value against the dollar, the fuel import bill surged. What was the government to do? It could either raise the price of fuel or subsidize the cost to consumers. The first option was seen as potentially politically risky (especially close to national elections), as raising fuel prices negatively impacts everyone – although it disproportionately impacts the poor, who, in India, go to the polls and vote. The second option for expansion of subsidies meant a further widening of the already-high fiscal deficit. With the national election campaign already in full swing, legislators predictably opted for greater subsidies and other populist measures, which are – to say the least – politically expedient but fiscally irresponsible. India (and other emerging economies) must have heaved a big sigh of relief when, in September 2013, the Federal Reserve announced its decision not to reduce its monetary stimulus after all. However, on December 18, the Federal Reserve announced that it would "scale-down" its bond-purchase program from January 2014, when it would buy $75 billion worth of bonds each month (down from $85 billion a month). The Fed's decision brought some respite to India and other emerging economies. Nevertheless, the damage caused by the Federal Reserve's earlier decision is a reminder of the risks of economic globalization and the importance of putting in place measures to make the economy more resilient to domestic and external shocks.

DEMOCRATIC POLITICS AND LIMITS TO EQUITY AND REDISTRIBUTION

As India is a federal union administratively divided into 29 states and 7 union territories, the central government and its constituent units (the state governments) have constitutionally delineated powers, obligations, and duties. For example, India's system of "fiscal federalism" is highly centralized, with the central government enjoying most of the revenue raising powers – albeit the state governments have specific jurisdiction to collect taxes. Yet the state governments are constitutionally obligated to shoulder much of the fiscal burden for financing a wide array of public services. Although the central government transfers resources to the states through a complex grants-in-aid mechanism (with priority given to the less-well-off states), this disproportionate fiscal asymmetry has placed tremendous pressure on the budgets of state governments – indeed, on all the various subnational units. Unable to meet their expenditures because of rising costs and government profligacy, including engaging in soft-budget constraints to remain in power, subnational governments have financed their fiscal deficits by borrowing from the central government (which has to be repaid from the state governments' own fiscal resources), and in recent years, through borrowing in the open market. In fact, since 2007, borrowing by state governments has seen a sharp rise. Between 2015 and 2017, 18 of India's state governments and territories exceeded the permitted gross fiscal deficit, which is limited by a 2003 national law to 3 percent of gross state domestic product. This cycle of constant borrowing has served to sharply increase the debt burdens of subnational units, with the resultant increase in interest payments for debt servicing – which already consume about one-third of the central government's tax revenue.[40] Predictably, the growing subnational expenditures on interest payments have translated into reduced state-level social welfare spending, including public service expenditures – further exacerbating the problem of rising inequality and poverty, and in particular, spatial and regional disparities.

Exacerbating this is the actual everyday practice of politics in India. As noted earlier, even the secure parliamentary majority that the Modi government enjoys, and an enfeebled and divided parliamentary opposition to boot, does not mean that pushing needed economic reforms will be easy in India's fractious polity – with multiple veto and decision making "centers." Rather, in this highly contentious, unpredictable, and unpropitious political environment, policy-making usually remains mired in gridlock, and implementing "agreed-to" decisions exceedingly difficult. It is commonplace for political parties to cynically and irresponsibly oppose the sitting government's policies, which they either championed or supported when in power.[41] Indeed, such political obstructionism and demagoguery are symptomatic of the larger malaise that afflicts India's body politic. More specifically, in practice, the gulf has widened between the procedural and deliberative aspects of democracy. On one hand, the democratic procedures and rules such as regular, open and competitive elections, the existence of political parties representing competing interests and viewpoints, broad electoral participation, and the rights to the freedom of speech, assembly, and association, among others, are deeply ingrained and taken for granted. On the other, the deliberative process, which requires commitment to political compromise and consensus-building, respect for the rules and procedures of representative institutions, and respect for the rule of law and individual rights and freedoms, is at best, perfunctorily followed. In fact, the substantive everyday practice of politics in India is hardly a deliberative one, but one that is boisterous, strident, and uncompromising and whose lifeblood is popular mobilization. It is a democracy of agitated and intransigent leaders (and political entrepreneurs) and followers – with all sides claiming to represent "the will of the people" – which usually means that their particular demands and wishes are just and legitimate – regardless of any other consideration. If in a "liberal democracy," the will of the majority is tempered with the protection of minority rights via constitutional, judicial, and other legal constraints, in India's increasingly "majoritarian democracy," the majority (often defined and mobilized along caste, regional, or religious lines) considers itself entitled to rights and privileges above all others – even if it means subverting or breaking "unjust laws."

As Vivek Sharma (2015) notes, this is in part because "neither the Indian state nor its society is liberal, although it is indeed democratic ... Indian society is profoundly *aliberal* in the sense that a variety of group identities, above all kinship but also caste, region, language and religion, are profoundly important to how society organizes itself and how it interacts with the state. Indeed, both the Constitution of India and its corpus of law, legislation and judicial precedent are permeated by aliberal notions of group and communal rights of varying sorts, including those that relate to religion." Hence, Fareed Zakaria's (2003, 3) earlier warning that "while democracy is flourishing; liberty is not" is apt. Zakaria notes that although the idea of democracy (in the sense of devolution of power to the masses) has spread rapidly, it is less clear the extent to which democratic consolidation or the institutionalization and routinization of democratic norms and values within the political system are taking place. In India (and elsewhere) the trend has been towards "illiberal democracy" – a form of governance that deliberately combines the rhetoric of liberal democracy with illiberal rule. That is, although regular and competitive multiparty elections are held, qualifying the country as an "electoral democracy," the everyday practices of the state are marked by arbitrariness and abuses. Similarly, political freedoms and civil rights may be formally recognized, but hardly observed in practice. The judiciary may be officially deemed independent, but it is easily compromised and the free press is harassed in numerous ways, making them compliant. Although democracy in India has meant "opening up its politics to a much broader group of people who were previously marginalized," and the creation of new political parties has enabled greater representation and made India "more democratic," it has also made it "less liberal" (quotes are from Zakaria 2003).

This evolution, which has gradually unfolded over the course of some seven decades, has helped democracy to acquire a mass appeal. Today, Indians from all walks of life have come to appreciate the power and utility of democracy. The universal right to vote instituted in 1951 had one very powerful effect: it empowered India's teeming masses by making their numbers count. The "deepening of democracy" reflected in the spread of democratic ideas, competitive politics, and universal suffrage has helped spur unprecedented political activism among formerly passive groups and has served as an effective vehicle for the political empowerment of the country's previously excluded and subordinate groups. A broad alliance of the lower castes and classes, collectively referred to as the "Other Backward Castes" or OBCs (estimated to be about 40 to 45 percent of the population),[42] the "Scheduled Castes" or Dalits (20 to 25 percent of the population),[43] Muslims (12 to 15 percent), and other groups and communities that had endured generations of neglect and oppression, have gate-crashed their way into the political arena, translating their numerical preponderance into political power. Today their representatives occupy influential positions, including some of the highest offices in the land such as the national cabinet, state legislative assemblies, and chief ministerial positions. Indeed, current Prime Minister Modi comes from a backward caste and the ruling BJP party now has more backward and scheduled caste members of Parliament than upper caste members. Furthermore, backward and scheduled caste political organizations and parties such as the Bahujan Samaj Party, the Samajwadi Party, the Rashtriya Janata Dal in the northern "Hindi belt," and the DMK (Dravida Munnetra Kazagham) and the AIADMK (All-India Anna DMK) in the southern state of Tamil Nadu are formidable political machines, forming governments or determining the nature and fate of governments. As the old certitudes of the Hindu order – in which the lower-caste "inferiors" were expected to show ritualized deference to their propertied, upper-caste and -class "superiors" – have crumbled, so have the days of de facto control of passive lower-caste voters by the upper castes and classes. This sharp erosion of upper-caste/upper-class political dominance is nothing short of a quiet revolution.

Yet, why has the extension of popular sovereignty and empowerment of the masses not translated into a more effective transformation to the structural foundations of socioeconomic and political domination in India? Part of the problem, according to some theorists, stems from the fact that Indian society – what Mohandas Gandhi once called that layer upon layer of inbuilt resentment, inequality, and oppression – is sorely lacking in "social capital."[44] In other words, although India is blessed with a robust civil society and a rich and vigorous associational life, the associations usually reflect narrow caste, ethnic, regional, and religious-communal loyalties (including patriarchy, class domination, and other parochial ties) that are deeply embedded in civil society. As a result, particularism and localism and other potentially divisive tendencies often define India's associational life.[45] These cleavages have prevented the development of ancillary networks of civic reciprocity and engagement, or what Putnam (1993) has termed "civic community" or "civicness," necessary for the articulation and aggregation of interests and collaboration. Not surprisingly, despite India's resilient democratic institutions and relatively long experience with constitutionalism, political participation (especially voting) still continues to be a largely collective behavior rather than the exercise of individual choice envisioned by liberal theory. Unlike in most western democracies, where political parties have clearly defined party ideologies and relatively stable constituencies, party identification is generally weak in India (among politicians and voters alike) and tends to be clientelistic with a fluid social base. Rather, the large groups of floating voters are up for grabs and major swings and upsets are common – such as the 12 percent nationwide swing in favor of the BJP in 2014, or the 25 percent swing for the BJP in the March 2017 assembly elections in Uttar Pradesh. Predictably, parties have strong incentives to aggregate votes through formation of strategic (if not opportunistic) alliances based on the sharing of the total number of contested votes in order not to split the votes. More often than not, ideological and programmatic compatibility take a back seat to the imperatives of electoral victory. Cumulatively, all these have constrained the representatives of the state and civil society from creating forums through which they could identify and agree on common goals.

Thus, contrary to the oft-repeated claims of India's "chattering classes" (the English-speaking elites), India has never been the paragon of genteel secularism and cosmopolitanism. Rather, its religiosity, social cleavages, and sectarian feuds based on faith, caste, and locality have always been real, volatile, and often non-negotiable. But, as Benedict Anderson (1983) has noted, all states create founding myths and traditions that become part of their collective memories. The Indian nationalists – in particular, Gandhi and Nehru – developed a distinctive narrative of India's past that privileged commemorative histories of religious tolerance, socio-cultural accommodation and assimilation, and pluralistic syncretism of faith and belief, while devaluing the more authentic and intimate folk traditions based on the vicissitudes of kith, creed, and caste. The "little traditions" spoke of recurrent partitions and pathological conflicts between Hindus and Muslims, high castes and low castes, and the uneasy coexistence between the mélange of peoples and communities that made the subcontinent their home. In India, where civic-based participation remains poorly developed (what Chhibber (1999) has described as "democracy without associations"), the democratic revolution by empowering the unlettered masses has, like never before, brought to the surface the seemingly latent hostilities and tensions between religions, castes, and regions.

Moreover, as Huntington (1968) recognized long ago, societies with highly active and mobilized publics and low levels of political institutionalization often degenerate into instability, disorder, and violence. In India, the high levels of political mobilization in the absence of a strong and responsive state and political parties have served to fragment rather than unite society. Instead of responding to the demands of an increasingly mobilized population, the country's weak and overburdened political institutions have reinforced, if not exacerbated, socioeconomic and political cleavages. Thus, even as the new political awakening has provided unprecedented opportunities to a diverse society once tightly regulated and governed by westernized political elites and by the strict rules and taboos of Brahminic Hinduism to explore its multifaceted and checkered histories, the problem is that the members of society seem to have become prisoners of their own discursive frameworks and narrative accounts. The nostalgia for the "politics of identity" has spawned controversial and acerbic "inventions of traditions" and of "imagined communities" that have reawakened and incited parochial emotions and pitched "communities" and "religions" against each other. Mirroring this jaundiced social reality, party competition has become even more based along caste, religious-communal, and ethno-regional lines – with such loyalties the most significant determinant of electoral outcomes. Not surprisingly, political parties of all stripes today place partisan interests above the public good, often pathetically outbidding each other (through promises of costly state entitlements and other guarantees) to consolidate their bases and garner support.

The trend is unambiguous. Members of the upper castes (20 to 25 percent of the population) have been gravitating towards the once-obscure Hindu-nationalist Bharatiya Janata Party, whose commitment to good governance, "traditional values," and the transformation of India into a disciplined Hindu nation-state has struck a particular chord, especially among the propertied classes in the Hindi-speaking heartland.[46] The Samajwadi Party, confined mainly to Uttar Pradesh, claims to be the party of the state's backward castes, and the Bahujan Samaj Party represents the interests of the Dalits (former "untouchables"). Meanwhile, the secular, or "modernist" Indians, who fear the BJP's parochial Hindu nationalism, continue to cling to the incorrigibly "top-down" Congress Party. The heterogeneous, vertically segmented low castes and classes, unified largely in their desire to settle scores with their former upper-caste "masters," suffer from many internal contradictions of particularism and localism that have made common cause extraordinarily difficult.[47] Backward caste and Dalit politics exhibit what the Rudolphs (1987) have termed as "involuted pluralism" – that is, deeply fragmented and factionalized from within, it faces serious collective-action problems. Indeed, in their strident campaigns against the *manuvadis* or upper-caste pieties and exploitation, the low-caste political nomenklatura rarely invoke universal principles of rights and justice. Instead of demanding that the state accord universal rights, protections, and provisions to all its citizens, especially the "weaker sections," they often insist that their particular communities and groups are most deserving of state entitlements, be they "caste reservations" or other special benefits. As a result, the various constituents of the erstwhile lower-castes in any given time are engaged in making a multiplicity of claims and in the perverse game of pursuing and jealously guarding their own prerogatives and narrow sectarian and clientelist interests.

Not surprisingly, such an unpropitious environment has produced a motley array of self-serving regional chieftains, political fixers (including criminal gangs, the so-called *goondas* and *dacoits*), local power brokers, and political freelancers. These typically pose as the saviors of their communities, promising to sweep away the debris of the past and usher in a new order. Yet, often unchecked by institutional constraints, they enjoy broad discretionary powers. Thus, they are often all too ready to circumvent institutional and legal procedures and, if need be, maliciously engage in political demagoguery to inflame their communities. Although it is important to repeat that social pluralism is not necessarily antithetical to the formation of an inclusive political community, weak political institutions and chauvinistic politics in contemporary India have engendered societal fragmentation and alienation rather than integration.

Ironically, from the start, the Indian state became an unwitting accomplice in creating and reinforcing religious and caste-based identities at the expense of common or national citizenship. Burdened by the trauma of partition and to appease the most fanatical elements in the Muslim community, the government failed to establish a uniform civil code for Muslims, and in its effort to correct the systematic injustices and deprivations suffered by the lower castes and other underprivileged communities, the constitution abolished "untouchability" and outlawed discrimination on the basis of caste and religion. The first amendment to the constitution (which became law in 1951) also introduced a wide array of "positive" or "compensatory discrimination" programs (India's version of affirmative action) by reserving 22.5 percent of all central government jobs for individuals belonging to Scheduled Castes and Tribes.[48] Soon after, similar reservations were made for admission to educational institutions. However, since the Indian constitution left open Article 15, which notes that the "socially and educationally backward classes" might also be considered and become eligible for reservations, a myriad of caste groups who deem themselves to suffer similar disadvantages have demanded similar "positive discrimination" in their favor. Over time (and given their numerical preponderance), these reservations were quickly granted to the "Other Backward Castes." In 1980, the report of the Backward Classes Commission (or the Mandal Commission), chaired by B. P. Mandal (a former chief minister of Bihar, and himself a member of a backward caste), proposed an even wider-ranging "compensatory discrimination" program for the 52 percent of the population, including Muslims, classified as "backward." The report recommended that 27 percent of all central and state government jobs and 27 percent of all spaces in government universities and affiliated colleges should be reserved for members of the 3,743 castes and sub-castes identified as "backward." For more than a decade, this report was shelved. Then, in 1990, the new OBC-dominated Janata Dal coalition government under Prime Minister V. P. Singh announced its plan to implement the commission's recommendations.[49] This decision aroused strong passions, convulsed Indian society (with some high-caste students immolating themselves in protest), fueled caste wars, and was instrumental in causing the government's downfall. Although implementation was stayed by the Supreme Court pending a ruling on the constitutionality of the measure, no political party has publicly opposed "reservations," since none wants to alienate itself from the large backward-caste "vote bank."

In 1991, the newly elected Congress Party government under Prime Minister P. V. Narasimha Rao sought to mollify opposition to the reservations issue by adding a 10 percent reservation for the poor of the higher castes. In November 1992, the Supreme Court upheld the reservation for OBCs, with the vague provision that it be "need-based," but struck down the additional 10 percent as constitutionally impermissible. Such public policies and decisions have only served to sharpen caste enmities – a classic case of how noble intentions can turn sour. Since the late 1980s, India has experienced renewed religious and communal discord, as the forward, or elite, classes and castes, the scheduled castes, the various backward castes and classes, and competing religious and regionally focused groups have fiercely contested and sometimes violently fought over every scrap of the state's largesse. Ironically, in order to gain from the lucrative "reservations" and related spoils, even the relatively privileged castes such as the Patels in Gujarat, Jats in Haryana, and the Marathas (in Maharashtra) among India's 3,000-plus castes have resorted to all manner of public protest to win inclusion in the official "Other Backward Classes" category (Deshpande and Ramachandran 2017). In August 2015, Patidars, a prosperous caste in Gujarat, staged a violent protest in Ahmedabad, the state's capital city, which left several people dead. In February 2016, the Indian capital, New Delhi and the surrounding state of Haryana were placed under siege after rioters representing the Jats (an influential and powerful community in North India) blocked roads and railways in and out of Delhi, including the canal that supplies much of the water supply to the capital. After some three dozen were killed in violent clashes with the police and with the city's water supply running dry, the authorities acceded (in fact, capitulated) to the Jats' demand by granting them the "reservations" they desired. Indian society, it seems, had been irreversibly realigned in ways so as to strengthen caste, communal, religious, ethnic, and regional identities.

SECOND-BEST SOLUTIONS TO INEQUALITY AND POVERTY

Even as India's national Parliament and some two dozen state assemblies have become more pluralistic and representative of the country's society, they have failed to effectively address the problem of widening income and wealth inequalities. To see it the other way, although the majority poor and subordinate groups actively participate in the country's political life (in particular, they vote in large numbers), they have failed to hold political parties and leaders accountable for their failure to deliver on their promises to improve the voters' material lives. In large measure this is because long-term investments to improve human and economic development have been preempted by what Bardhan (2009b, 349) has succinctly described as "competitive populism – short-term pandering and handouts to win elections." Indeed, crucial decisions regarding the allocation of resources are heavily influenced by political considerations, rather than by sound technical and economic criteria. The imperative of short-term political calculations (to get elected in the next electoral cycle) means politicians of all hues try to out-bid one another in their pandering to "vote banks" by promising costly, quick-fix populist solutions to complex problems.[50] In what is an all-too-common occurrence, politicians, with considerable fanfare, make regular visits to their constituencies to inaugurate projects and to receive petitions for new ones. Ruling parties routinely distribute government resources and perks to reward supporters and to create new bases of support, while withholding resources from opposition supporters and perceived "hostile" communities. Such a system has accentuated deep-seated communal and caste allegiances and antagonisms, besides spawning widespread graft and corruption. Moreover, competitive populism negatively impacts economic development by scuttling needed structural reforms, besides having a deleterious impact on social welfare and redistributive policies.

In such an environment, the government's social-welfare programs tend to be more leaky than usual. The 2011 World Bank report, *Social Protection for a Changing India*, notes that India devotes over 2 percent of GDP towards "anti-poverty and social protection programs" such as the Public Distribution System (PDS), the Mahatma Gandhi National Rural Employment Guarantee Scheme (MGNREGA), the Indira Awaas Yojana (IAY), and the Indira Gandhi National Old Age Pension Scheme (IGNOAPS), among others. However, the significant public investment devoted to these programs is not commensurate with their outcomes. As the World Bank report notes, although the PDS absorbs substantial public resources (almost 1 percent of GDP), its benefits have been limited, as the leakage and diversion of food grains from the PDS are high – with only 41 percent reaching needy households.[51] Similarly, and as noted earlier, the MGNREG scheme, despite its broad coverage, suffers from poor implementation, gravely diminishing the program's potential for poverty reduction and socioeconomic mobility. Indeed, two of India's leading economists, Bhagwati and Panagariya (2014), dismiss the US$6 billion a year MGNREGA program as an expensive palliative and symbol of government waste and incompetence – given strong evidence of the outright siphoning of the goods via layers of corruption and poor delivery and implementation. Their careful calculation shows that MGNREGA (after factoring-in corruption and waste) spends about Rs. 248 in order to deliver a net Rs. 50 per person per day. In other words, the entire scheme is highly inefficient and costly, as it takes about Rs. 5 to deliver Rs. 1 worth of benefits. According to the authors, the poor would have benefited far more from "direct cash transfers" because cash transfers have two distinct advantages over "in-kind transfers." First, they empower the recipient rather than placing them at the mercy of an array of middlemen, as is the case under in-kind transfers, and second, they are more efficient as they cut corruption and leaks in the long distribution chains typical under in-kind transfers. Bhagwati and Panagariya note that because direct electronic transfers of payments to beneficiaries through the Unique Identification Authority of India's (UIDAI) Aadhaar card-enabled bank or post office accounts will reduce bureaucratic red tape, corruption, government expenditures, and improve overall societal outcomes, it is now prudent to transit out of all in-kind government transfer programs, including health and education services, under a "conditional" cash transfer or voucher system.

Even Prime Minister Modi, a long-time critic of subsidies and government hand-outs, including those ostensibly aimed at "helping the poor," has not only quietly made a volte-face by supporting the previous Congress-led United Progressive Alliance (UPA) government-era social welfare programs, his administration, arguably to buttress Modi's pro-poor credentials, has introduced its own series of costly programs. For example, a long-time and vehement critic of MGNREGA, Modi was fond of ridiculing the program as a living example of the Congress' failure to improve livelihoods, often repeating "Let the people know that even after 60 years of Independence, they have to dig holes. This is what the Congress has achieved." But as prime minister, Modi has described MGNREGA in glowing terms as a "national pride" – with his administration even increasing the program's outlay, given its "essential" role in rural development. Similarly, the expensive, duplicative, and unduly bureaucratic National Food Security Act (estimated to cost the government approximately Rs. 1.3 lakh crore, or US$22 billion every year) was proposed by the previous UPA government[52] – despite the fact that a number of state governments already provide such food subsidies to the poor and despite strong evidence that hunger and malnutrition in contemporary India have more to do with households lacking enough income to afford sufficient food (rather than from a lack of food supply), in large part because of the inflationary pressure caused by the excessive food buffer-stock build-up due to distortionary government policies. All of this has not stopped the Modi administration, critical of policy distortions and populist dole-outs, from repackaging and expanding the Food Security Act – rather than creating productive employment opportunities for the poor. Again, Bhagwati and Panagariya (2014) note that the cost of the program will not only add to the country's already high and increasingly unsustainable fiscal deficit; like other well-intentioned entitlement programs, it will not produce the desired welfare outcomes. They point out that India can hardly afford another massive entitlement program. The sad tragedy is that the food and related goods will hardly reach the intended beneficiaries, given that it is to be distributed through India's notoriously corrupt and inefficient government-run nationwide network of over 500,000 "fair price shops."[53] It is widely known that anywhere between a third to one-half of subsidized rice and wheat are illegally diverted from the fair price shops and sold illegally in the open market. Bhagwati and Panagariya

(2014) aptly caution that huge and costly public programs like MGNREGA and Food Security, once established, are extremely hard to dismantle and replace with more efficient programs because of the rent-seeking opportunities they provide to a wide network of vested interests – including influential politicians. Sarcastically noting that good intentions do not always translate into good outcomes, they argue that the escalating costs of these programs mean there are fewer available resources for the government to invest in health care, education, sanitation, or in the country's decrepit infrastructure. Over time, such "well-intentioned" programs are self-defeating, as they contribute to declining economic growth and stagnation.

Why has India, despite having such an expansive safety net and social protection programs, failed to reduce the income and wealth gap? Why have these programs not proven to be effective in reducing dependence by enabling recipients to eventually graduate out of the programs? The conventional view attributes this ineffectiveness, if not failure, to the government's inability to judiciously implement and monitor the various welfare-enhancing programs, with some suggesting that greater decentralization and devolution of responsibility over anti-poverty programs to local governments and leaders will result in better targeting and delivery to needy constituents. This, however, misses the larger role of political calculations and expediency under competitive populism. As Kapur and Nangia (2015) note: "Of the two principal components of social welfare policy – basic public goods (especially public services) and social protection – India has focused disproportionately on the latter in the last two decades, expanding existing social protection programs and creating new ones. By contrast, the country's basic public services, such as primary education, public health, and water and sanitation, have languished. What explains this uneven focus?" (Kapur and Nangia 2015, 73). The authors succinctly note that the transformation in Indian polity, namely, the "stronger electoral competition in recent years has made political leaders favor highly visible social protection programs. In comparison, improving public services is a long, arduous, and less glamorous task that might go unnoticed by the electorate" (Kapur and Nangia 2015, 85). In other words, the increasingly zero-sum nature of political competition forces politicians to make short-term calculations. In such an unpropitious environment, "populist quick-fix policies rather than sustainable improvements in structural conditions become the order of the day" (Bardhan 2009b, 352). Thus, the second-best social protection measures are preferred because they are politically convenient. Yet the 2014 national elections do suggest a silver lining, as the verdict was widely seen as Indian voters finally rewarding incumbents who can deliver better economic outcomes. However, it is premature to conclude whether the positive association between economic growth and the electoral outcomes will hold.

5

Prosperity with Equality: Future Directions

A vast corpus of scholarship has long claimed that economic growth and inequality follow an inverted U-pattern – with inequality rising sharply in the early stages of development, but steadily declining as the economy matures and ultimately settles into some sort of virtuous equilibrium. Thus, it is not unusual for socioeconomic inequalities – in particular, the income and wealth-gap – to widen as countries embark on the road to economic development. In the early 1950s, Nobel laureate Arthur Lewis argued that the process of economic development is never uniform, but painstakingly uneven with different sectors of the economy and regions growing faster than others – making rising inequality inherent to economic development. Similarly, Simon Kuznets (1955) proposed an inverted U-shaped relationship in describing the connection between a country's average level of income and level of income inequality. Kuznets argued that although countries generally tend to have a relatively equal income distribution in their "initial" stages of development, it becomes more unequal once the economies begin to modernize and mature. However, as countries continue their growth and development trajectory, the growing wealth would enable them to provide resources for social protection and greater income distribution – with inequality following the shape of an inverted U curve. Thus, what soon became the celebrated "Kuznets hypothesis" claimed that (a) widening inequality was an inevitable by-product of economic growth and (b) that inequality would steadily decline once the economy matured. That is, income inequality tends to decline once the economy attains a certain level of average income. Arguably, Kuznets would hardly be surprised by the fact that when countries like India and China have made the transition from a rigidly centrally planned economy to an open and competitive market-based one, inequality has widened even with sustained growth in per-capita incomes. Although the current patterns of income and wealth inequality in China and India seem consistent with Kuznets' hypothesis (at least as reflected in the increases in the Gini coefficient), it remains to be seen if such a growth-inequality trade-off exists and whether income inequalities will gradually flatten-out as these economies mature. The fact that over the past few years China's Gini coefficient has seen a marginal decline (reaching 0.463 in 2015) has led some to suggest that China has reached the "Kuznets turning point" – when income inequality peaks and then starts to fall.

Not surprisingly, given the pervasive belief that there exists an explicit correlation between economic growth and inequality, policymakers often confidently assert that their central responsibility and duty is to promote national economic development by generating robust and sustained growth. This is because the problems of widening inequality and poverty are transitory and will inevitably ameliorate themselves as the economy expands and matures. However, as Ravallion (2016; 2013) and others have cautioned, evidence for such a correlation is weak. Specifically, this does not mean that the evidence suggests that there are no inevitable trade-offs between efficiency and equity. Rather, various cross-country studies have failed to produce conclusive evidence that supports the existence of an "equity-efficiency trade-off" – meaning that redistribution to make incomes more equal would inevitably lower economic growth. In fact, an exhaustive IMF study (see Ostry, Berg, and Tsangarides 2014) persuasively argues that societies with more unequal income distribution not only grow at a much slower pace, but also that a more equitable distribution of income does not have a negative effect on economic growth. Unlike Kuznets, who based his conclusions on the very limited survey data that was then available, recent research drawing on the World Bank's extensive PovcalNet database and the *World Development Indicators*, among other sources for national household surveys, finds that there is little or no correlation between rates of economic growth and changes in inequality. Indeed, even the existence of a trade-off between economic growth and inequality is far from obvious with regard to China – often used to support the growth-equity trade-off. To the contrary, evidence shows that periods of high economic growth in China did not translate into increases in higher levels of inequality, while the periods of falling inequality (1981–1985 and 1995–1998) experienced the highest average growth in average household income. And, second, Chinese provinces that experienced more rapid rural income growth did not see a concomitant sharp rise in income inequality (Ravallion 2011).

The policy implications of these findings are significant. It means that policy makers can no longer simply focus on generating aggregate economic growth and dismiss the problems of widening inequality (and in some cases worsening poverty) as an unfortunate and unavoidable by-product of economic growth and development that will automatically correct itself as the economy matures. In fact, high levels of inequality not only impose a direct (and significant) economic cost, they are also morally indefensible, with negative ramifications, as inequality is about more than just income and wealth. A society and citizenry starkly segregated into "haves" and "have-nots," in which the haves live in literally gated communities and hold divergent values, habits, and outlooks from the have-nots, who suffer from all manner of socioeconomic maladies – in particular, weak socioeconomic and cultural cohesion – will further undermine the political stability necessary for sustained economic development. Indeed, in the United States and other advanced economies, the rising income and wealth inequality has not only spawned what Fukuyama (2014) has called "political decay," and the resultant deep sense of disenfranchisement and hopelessness, it has also given rise to parochial nationalism and "anti-market populism" – which poses a challenge not only to free market economies and globalization, but also to political pluralism and democratic governance (also see Zingales 2012). Clearly, the cancer of rising economic inequality must be addressed head-on rather than being relegated to some opportune later date.

But how best to reconcile economic growth and rising prosperity with a more balanced and equitable distribution? There is a large and growing body of research on the subject of how to combat the problem of rising inequality that almost defies summary and makes it difficult to draw conclusions. Nevertheless, it is fair to say that possible solutions cover the gamut: from those ("conservatives") who support market-based solutions, those ("progressives") who call for greater government intervention, and those who advocate a blend of market and statist solutions. Yet, as illustrated in the preceding discussions, the reality is that markets and states are intrinsically interwoven and their impact (both intended and unintended) is more complex than is usually assumed. As such, and again as is explicit in the preceding case studies, in each of the three countries the sources of rising inequality are different, each country faces a very different set of challenges, and how best each can ameliorate the problem will vary, sometimes significantly. Given this, the ideologically motivated solutions to rising inequality proffered by Piketty and others, which arguably have great appeal for their seeming commitment to socioeconomic justice and fairness, turn out to be more problematic after careful review.

More specifically, to Piketty, the solution to rising economic inequality is straightforward. Namely, governments can reverse the advantages currently enjoyed by the rich or the owners of capital via imposition of a "progressive" (and punitive) income tax, with rates of 50 to 60 percent on high incomes and a top marginal rate of 80 percent on "very high incomes," including complete abolishment, if not drastic scaling back, of a wide range of tax deductions and exemptions enjoyed by high-income earners. *The Economist* (2014) presciently notes that when it comes to offering prescriptions on how best to ameliorate the inequality gap, "here 'Capital' drifts to the left and loses credibility. Mr. Piketty asserts rather than explains why tempering wealth concentration should be the priority (as opposed to, say, boosting growth). He barely acknowledges any trade-offs or costs to his redistributionist agenda … Mr. Piketty's focus on soaking the rich smacks of socialist ideology, not scholarship. That may explain why 'Capital' is a bestseller. But it is a poor blueprint for action."[1] Indeed, Piketty's remedy raises many troubling questions. For example, is it not unjust to punish high earners such as a Bill Gates, Warren Buffet, the late Steve Jobs, or Mark Zuckerman – individuals whose wealth is derived from their unique innovative abilities and entrepreneurial talents and who have provided valued goods and services, including creating good-paying jobs in the United States and elsewhere? After all, isn't it prudent to reward such creativity and entrepreneurial spirit, if for no other reason than to provide incentives to a future Steve Jobs? And what is so wrong with the premise that one's income should be proportional to effort and talent – an idea that is at the very core of liberalism? Certainly, it is far more difficult to justify punitive and confiscatory taxes for wealth redistribution if the income is earned from free and open market competition and not accumulated through predatory rent-seeking, ill-begotten from crony capitalism, or, as in the United States, due to "upward redistribution" – the result of perverse incentives and regulatory barriers to entry and competition that protect the outsized incomes of numerous services providers, including lawyers, doctors, dentists, and other so-called "licensed" professions (Baker 2016). Similarly, given the structural changes in the global economy – namely that the skill-biased technological changes disproportionately reward skilled labor in advanced economies (meaning the better educated) at the expense of the unskilled and poorly educated – is it just (and prudent) for governments to punish the skilled and better educated?

Also, there is Okun's (1975) apt caution that a "trade-off" exists between efficiency and equality, and that the pursuit of economic equality through non-market mechanisms can reduce efficiency and further exacerbate inequality and poverty. This is not only because a more equitable distribution of incomes reduces incentives to work and invest, but also because state intervention to redistribute wealth (via punitive taxation, welfare and entitlement payments, or arbitrary raising of minimum wages) are both ineffective and damaging; not to mention inequalities generated by public policies that distort market allocations of resources via perverse incentives and regulatory overreach that tend to undermine economic growth. Take the case for a higher minimum wage. On one hand, it seems like an immediate way to help lift families out of poverty and mitigate the problem of rising inequality. On the other, the minimum wage is about low-wage work, while poverty is based on the family income, and not all low-wage workers (for example, students and the retired) come from low-income families. Further, research shows that increases in minimum wage also result in declines in employment. This means that raising wages for some needs to be balanced against potential job losses for others (Neumark 2015; Neumark and Wascher 2008). Not surprisingly, the statistical relationship between raising the minimum wage and reducing inequality, especially poverty, is rather weak. As Okun (1975) warned, governmental efforts are as effective as a "leaky bucket," because much of the income meant to uplift the poor "will simply disappear in transit, so the poor will not receive all the money that is taken from the rich" (Okun 1975, 15). The whole exercise is a net "lose-lose" – creating disincentives to work by both donors (that is, taxpayers) and beneficiaries – the large and costly bureaucratic and administrative apparatus to support it notwithstanding.

Of course, Okun's conclusions are based on his implicit assumption that markets work with perfect efficiency, and that in a less-than-perfectly efficient market economy, policy interventions only tend to increase inefficiencies and distortions. Yet, in the real world evidence confirms that some policy interventions can be a "win-win," as they help reduce both inequality and inefficiency. For example, it is widely acknowledged that investments in early childhood education can yield significant dividends in building human capital as they disproportionately benefit talented children from low-income families. By lifting barriers to opportunity that disadvantaged children face, the programs can not only help them to more effectively navigate the labor market later in life, they can also prevent the perpetuation of inequality of economic outcomes across generations. As discussed in Chapter 2, Raj Chetty and his co-authors (2014; 2014a) find significant variation in intergenerational mobility in the United States across different metro and rural areas. Although some regions in the United States match the highest mobility levels among advanced countries, others offer less mobility than is available in some developing countries. What explains these variations? Are they the result of living in different neighborhoods, or due to differences in the attitudes of people and families who live in these neighborhoods? In an effort to shed light on these questions, the authors study children from families who changed their neighborhood during childhood. Their research shows that much of the variation in upward mobility reflects the experience of living in particular neighborhoods. In other words, upward mobility depends strongly on where one grows up as a child rather than the family the child comes from. This raises the next question – what types of neighborhoods are associated with greater upward mobility? The authors find that higher upward mobility is associated with neighborhoods that are less residentially segregated by race or income, have lower income inequality (that is, a larger middle class), higher community involvement, relatively stable family structures, and good quality schools. Therefore, if intergenerational mobility is primarily determined in the local neighborhoods, this suggests that public policies that can reform and change the socioeconomic environment may be effective in promoting economic mobility. Thus, it makes good sense for policy makers to improve conditions in such at-risk communities, including assisting families in relocating to areas with better childhood environments – such as good public schools and investment in high-quality education, especially since having the "college premium" (college graduates earn much more in their lifetime than high school graduates) is a key determinant of economic mobility. Similarly, even as an increase in minimum wage may have a potentially negative impact on employment, it also assists poor families, especially single mothers. In other words, the potential for a trade-off between efficiency and equity should not necessarily mean public policies should not play any role in mitigating the problem of rising economic inequality. Rather, the trade-off should carefully factor-in the relative size of the benefits and the costs – with support for intervention if its impact is outweighed by greater gains (that is, benefits for a relatively larger number of beneficiaries) and lower potential losses.

Moreover, economic theory (in particular, the Kaldor–Hicks criterion) has long informed that high levels of inequality ultimately lead to economic inefficiencies because over time they stifle growth, shrink the size of the overall economic pie, and lead to declines in the standard of living. This is because high levels of inequality exacerbate their own vicious cycle by further entrenching even more inequality. Over time, such inequality translates into reduced upward mobility. Also, as Roemer (1998) has pointed out, there is more to the idea of "equality of opportunity" than first meets the eye. That is, "fairness" is not only about ensuring that all individuals enjoy the same "outcomes" regardless of their ability or effort, but also, to the extent possible, that each person has the same chances or "opportunities." As Roemer notes, outcomes (for example, one's income) can be determined both by individual "effort" and by factors beyond one's control, or the so-called "circumstance variable." Thus, to Roemer, a level playing field is one where opportunities are equalized to the best extent that is possible. Only under such circumstances can differences in individual outcomes be deemed fair and acceptable. Finally, there are compelling moral and practical reasons for public authorities to meaningfully respond to the problem of rising inequality. First, it is hard to justify on moral and ethical grounds the currently high and growing levels of disparities in income and wealth, given the crushing societal hardship and need – especially in the aftermath of the global financial crisis. And, second, as noted earlier, pervasive and widening inequalities have corrosive societal consequences. Research shows that rising inequality not only undermines the sense of social and civic affinity between the various socioeconomic classes and groups, it also weakens support for redistribution, especially to the poor and the vulnerable (Cavaille and Trump 2015; Lupu and Pontusson 2011).

As the preceding chapters have shown, in none of the three countries does a Roemer style "level playing-field" of equality of opportunity actually exist – albeit, the field is more level in the United States than in China and India. In fact, in China and India, the playing field is highly truncated in favor of those blessed with initial advantageous circumstances (such as income, wealth, and education) and influential political and economic connections. This partly explains why even high (and sustained) economic growth in these countries (in particular, China) has not been effective in lifting all boats. It also means that concentrating exclusively on aggregate economic performance without due consideration to how to facilitate a more balanced and equitable income and wealth distribution is problematic – not only for China and India, but also for the United States.

Given this, what can these countries do to make economic growth more inclusive?

Certainly, the backlash against globalization epitomized by Brexit and Donald Trump's election victory in the advanced economies and the inability of China and India to reconcile their high economic growth rates with more equitable distribution underscore that deepening economic globalization, and preserving its economic gains will also require that economic globalization be made more fair. More specifically, the concerns of large constituencies that make up globalization "losers" must be addressed, not only via compensation programs, but also through the adoption of public policies that meaningfully address what Rodrik (2011) has called the faulty asymmetry upon which globalization has been built. For example, the assumption that free trade is a win-win for all stakeholders cannot be supported in light of the fact that exports from China have contributed to the loss of millions of US manufacturing jobs, and imports from China and other developing economies is an important factor for stagnating or declining wages for labor – especially for unskilled workers in the United States. This means that trade between countries at very different levels of development and with very large differences in wages, including the multilateral trade agreements and the global regulatory regimes that undergird them, must be better calibrated not only to protect the interests of capital but also those of labor, through fair wages, good working conditions, and reasonable employment security. After all, surveys of "measures of life satisfaction" apart from income and wealth confirm that the psychological effects of unemployment, such as feelings of diminished self-worth and mental stress, have a hugely corrosive impact on individuals, their families, and communities (Vance 2016). Similarly, the fact that labor faces numerous (and punitive) restrictions on mobility (unlike capital, which is free to move relatively unhindered across borders) means that the economic risks and uncertainties are borne disproportionately by labor. Not surprisingly, economic downturns and recessions can have a hugely negative impact on workers and their communities. Although owners of capital also suffer losses, they are partially shielded from negative effects by government bailouts and diversification of their capital and assets.

In the specific case of the United states, measures that provide long-term economic opportunity such labor market initiatives that encourage innovation and improvements in worker productivity through job training, reforming the tax code and campaign-finance laws, and broadening access to education – in particular, early childhood programs and better educational access to the least skilled – can help improve an individual's earning capacity and reduce the demographic and national income and wealth gap.

Indeed, targeted investments in education and health can help reduce income inequality as well as enhance social mobility – thereby mitigating the persistence of poverty across generations. Yet in each of the three countries, significant gaps remain in regard to accessibility to quality education and health services. However, access to quality and affordable education (at all levels) is fundamental, as education has long served as a reliable equalizer when it comes to socioeconomic mobility, and in particular, intergenerational mobility. Goldin and Katz (2008; 2007) have persuasively argued that the sharp rise in inequality in the United States has much to do with the skills gap (due to technological change) and "an educational slowdown," unable to fill this gap. Goldin and Katz (2007, 158) note that the "changes in the organization of work associated with computerization has led to changes in the organization of work which raise the demand for the cognitive and interpersonal skills (called 'abstract tasks') used by educated professional and mangers and reduce the demand for the clerical and routine analytical and mechanical skills (called 'routine tasks') that characterize many middle-educated white collar positions and manufacturing production jobs ... The indirect effects of computerization in reducing the communication and coordinating costs that facilitate international outsourcing are likely to have reinforced this pattern." Yet they also note that in the United States, between 1980 and 2005 the level of educational attainment has dramatically slowed. In 1980, Americans aged 30 years or older had 4.7 years more of schooling on average than did Americans in 1930. However, in 2005 Americans had only 0.8 years more schooling on average than Americans in 1980. This "education gap" has translated into reduced availability of educated and skilled workers in the labor market. With advanced digital technologies such as cloud computing, robotics, and analytics (including big data and artificial intelligence) dramatically transforming the workplace – indeed, the very way Americans live – correcting this education gap is urgent. Indeed, Autor et al. (2016) find that the demand for advanced high-level work requiring cognitive skills such as numeracy, literacy, and problem solving greatly increases with an economy's technological sophistication. In the United States, the surge in demand for such high-level or "non-routine" jobs between 1980 and 2000 has coincided with the decline in demand for routine and manual jobs – and that this trend will only accelerate, with significant implications for the labor market. Put bluntly, formal skill development through education is essential in a knowledge-based world economy. Without the necessary investments in education and skills enhancement, the labor market will become further stratified with negative consequences for upward mobility, besides threatening the United States' ability to remain economically competitive globally.

Moreover, if Robert Gordon's (2016) gloomy predictions come true, Americans will have to come to terms and live with much lower growth rates for the foreseeable future. In his provocative *The Rise and Fall of American Growth*, which provides a comprehensive analysis of the long-run trends in American living standards from 1870 to mid-2000, Gordon argues that the United States' usually high mid-twentieth century productivity growth rate (c. 1870–1970) was an anomaly, the result of the industrial revolution – and something that will not be repeated. Contrary to conventional wisdom, Gordon argues that this is because technological innovations since the 1940s have not been "revolutionary," but merely "evolutionary." Although the United States could very well continue to be the world's technological leader, it will occupy a position in a world in which technological innovations will not only be incremental, narrowly focused, and highly specialized, but unlike the sweeping revolutionary changes ushered in by the industrial revolution, the newer post-industrial evolutionary innovations coupled with outsized reliance on the service sector at the expense of manufacturing (Gordon rightly notes that, compared to manufacturing, the services sector has much lower productivity) will not have such transformational effects on living standards. The resultant new equilibrium will be characterized by much lower growth rates with limited impact on average well-being. Notwithstanding the flaws of expert predictions, Gordon's caution about the inherent limitations of the services sector and unduly blind faith of "technological-optimists" are certainly warranted – as is his recommendation that investment in education, and in particular, more government investment in research, will be essential to nurture and produce the creative and entrepreneurial talent who can develop innovations capable of making a meaningful impact on the living standards of large numbers of the world's people.

There is no disputing the fact that income inequality has been widening in the United States over the past few decades, with the US median household income remaining stagnant over the past four decades, while the incomes of high-earning households have doubled. As the gains have disproportionately gone to the high-income earners – in particular, the very rich – is it not reasonable (and only fair) to raise the taxes of the top 10 percent of the income earners to make the distribution more equitable? After all, this solution is recommended by Piketty and others. As noted earlier, for Piketty, the solution to rising inequality is straightforward: national governments can reverse the advantages currently enjoyed by the owners of capital via imposition of a "progressive" income tax, with rates of 50 to 60 percent on high incomes and a top marginal rate of 80 percent on very high incomes, including ending the various tax deductions and exemptions enjoyed by high-income earners. Similarly, the doyen of inequality studies, Tony Atkinson (2014, 188), has argued that "we should return to a more progressive rate structure for the personal income tax, with marginal rates of tax increasing by ranges of taxable income, up to a top rate of 65 percent, accompanied by a broadening of the tax base."

Certainly, fiscal policy can help reduce income inequality via progressive direct taxation and transfers, by reducing disposable income inequality (or inequality of income after taxes and transfers) so that it is less than market income inequality (or inequality of income before taxes and transfers). And, no doubt, even a small increase in the tax rates applied to the top 10 percent of income earners could significantly raise tax revenues, as the top 10 percent of income earners contribute disproportionately to total US output and total tax revenue. As discussed in Chapter 2, given the progressive structure of the US federal tax system, high income earners pay 39.6 percent on all their taxable income – which is also the highest marginal income tax rate in the United States applied to the amount of one's income that exceeds the highest income bracket in the tax code. In fact, according to the non-partisan Congressional Budget Office (CBO 2016; 2011), although the top 1 percent of income earners have seen a sharp rise in their incomes and wealth, they also pay an increasingly bigger share of the nation's taxes – about 40 percent of all federal taxes in 2007, compared to less than 20 percent in the 1970s. In addition, the owners of capital are taxed on the value of their assets, and sometimes taxed twice on capital gains income: once when earned as profits by a corporation and again as dividends earned as an individual. Yet, the United States' progressive income tax structure has proven not to be very effective in narrowing the gap in after-tax income between the high-income and the middle- and low-income earners or reducing inequality more broadly. Hence, the recommendation of Piketty and others to raise the tax rates for high-income earners to even much higher levels.

Not surprisingly, high-income earners are very sensitive to changes, especially increases (real and imagined) to the tax rates, and could "vote with their feet," and exit a country to escape unfavorable and punitive taxation. In this age of global mobility, the rich can with relative ease move, or move their income or income sources, to a country with lower tax rates. Indeed, in 2013, when France introduced a 75 percent "super-tax" on French citizens whose income was over 1 million euros (approximately US$1.4 million at that time), a number of wealthy French citizens threatened to renounce their citizenship, and the actor Gerald Depardieu moved to Russia (see Ales and Sleet 2016; Akcigit, Baslandze, and Stantcheva 2016; Diamond and Saez 2011; Kleven et al. 2014; 2013). This underscores that public policies have unintended consequences. Therefore, raising taxes, in particular on high income earners, means that policy makers need to be cognizant of Okun's warning – how to balance the complex trade-off between equity and efficiency. Moreover, imposing a higher marginal tax rate on high-income earners – who also include the economy's most productive members, such as inventors (like Bill Gates or the late Steve Jobs), entrepreneurs, and job creators, could reduce the incentives for such creative and productive individuals and discourage them from fully participating in the nation's economy. In fact, the problem is not so much the tax rates (after all, high-income earners pay the lion's share of taxes), but "tax expenditures," or more appropriately, deductions via numerous loopholes (under exemptions, deferrals, and credit) such as the deduction for mortgage interest on owner-occupied homes, capital-gains exclusion on home sales, and the taxation of capital gains and dividends at different rates, among others, some of which tend to disproportionately benefit higher income earners – hence, the oft-cited quip from Warren Buffet that he pays a lower effective tax rate than his secretary.

Finally, deepening global economic integration also has implications (both costs and benefits) for national taxation policy. On the cost side, it places limits on a country's ability to tax income earned by multinational corporations and businesses, as they can with relative ease shift production between countries in order to reduce their taxation burden via "profit-shifting" – that is, reducing their taxes by shifting their profits to lower-taxation jurisdictions. In the United States, some hold the view (including the congressional Republicans and the Trump administration) that because US corporate tax rates are among the highest among OECD countries, reduction in corporate tax rates is essential if US corporations and businesses are to remain globally competitive and not be forced to consider tax reduction strategies. Suffice it to note, Democrats generally disagree, noting that the revenue generated from corporate taxes in the United States is quite low (compared to other OECD countries) because corporations do not pay their fair share of taxes. Clearly, globalization places enormous constraints on a country's ability to deter profit-shifting and other tax avoidance, reduction, and evasion strategies by corporations, businesses, and wealthy individuals. To mitigate this problem, it will be essential for countries to work cooperatively to recalibrate and balance the international differences in corporate tax rates. Finally, meaningful reforms to the education and tax system will mean reforming the American political system, which (as discussed earlier) has been compromised by big money, pervasive conflicts-of-interests, opaque campaign contribution regulations, lobbying, and gerrymandered electoral districts, among others. Similarly, without fundamental reforms to the widening structural gaps between current federal and state revenue projections and huge future liabilities, the problem of widening economic inequality will not be resolved.

The Chinese and the Indian political systems' (for different reasons) more limited institutional and administrative capacity has prevented the creation a level playing field where everyone has an equal opportunity to become better off. The problem is particularly stark in China. In November 2013, following the Third Plenum of the Eighteenth National Congress, the Central Committee of the Chinese Communist Party announced that China's political system is officially "socialist consultative democracy." Of course, China lacks many of the essential institutions of a participatory democracy, such as independent political organizations, separation of powers, multiparty elections, popular representation, inclusive decision-making, and the rule of law, among others. Although Chinese citizens engage in numerous "everyday" forms of collective dissent and protest, and local governments are bombarded with petitions from angry citizens, this has hardly prevented privileged and well-connected insiders and their cronies from amassing huge fortunes at the expense of more inclusive growth. With much of the gains going to (or being captured by) connected vested interests, China and India have opted for "second-best" solutions, which ostensibly rely on various types of state intervention to mitigate inequalities. To this effect, Beijing has unveiled a series of policies and programs to reduce socioeconomic disparities – or in the official (and altruistic) sounding jargon, to "harmonize" economic development. These include a commitment to the gradual dismantling of the institutional foundations of the rural-urban divide – the *hukou* system – and expanding the scope and coverage of various social insurance programs.

For example, as discussed in Chapter 3, the Chinese state's flagship social assistance/safety-net program, the "Minimum Livelihood Guarantee Scheme" popularly known as *Dibao*, has been the main response to the growing income divide in China. Introduced in 1993, the *Dibao* was initially designed to provide assistance to urban workers laid-off by the closure and downsizing of state-owned enterprises. The *Dibao* is a classic "cash-transfer program" that has been progressively extended nationwide to all "urban areas" in 1999 and to the "rural areas" in 2007. By 2013, program had expanded greatly, covering more than 50 million individuals – making it "comparable in size to large-scale cash transfer programs like India's National Rural Employment Guarantee and Brazil's Bolsa Familia program" (Golan, Sicular, and Umapathi 2015, 2). Indeed, according to Gao (2017), the *Dibao* is currently the world's largest social assistance program. Although the central and provincial governments make fiscal transfers to fund the *Dibao* (albeit, local governments with resources and the necessary fiscal capacity are required to commit a budget), local governments (at the municipal level) are responsible for both the administration and the implementation of the program, including carrying out the means test (with eligibility determined in reference to a maximum income threshold) in order to identify individuals and families eligible for the benefits. The beneficiaries are "low-wage families" whose incomes fall below the local *Dibao* line. More specifically, the amount of assistance or benefit one receives under the program equals the household's size multiplied by the gap between per-capita household income and a locally determined minimum living standard.

Despite the significant expansion in coverage, the program nevertheless suffers from the usual problems associated with poor and haphazard targeting of recipients, including the exclusion of rural migrants living in urban areas who do not hold urban household registration (and are thus ineligible for the urban *Dibao*). Thus, the problem is not simply logistical, stemming both from not having access to accurate data on individual and family incomes, but also from government policies like the *hukou* system, which excludes a majority of poor rural migrant households and their families who reside in urban areas, because they do not have the urban *hukou*. Moreover, the actual transfer packet (albeit, it tops up a recipient's income to a basic level below the minimum wage) tends to be rather low relative to the average consumption costs – not to mention that, since implementation is decentralized, it gives local authorities tremendous discretion not only regarding who meets the eligibility criteria to receive the transfer payments, but also how to allocate and use the resources, especially if it is financed by local governments.

Golan, Sicular, and Umapathi's (2015) nuanced research on the question of who benefits from the rural *Dibao* program and whether the scheme has helped to reduce rural poverty further elaborates. Using nationwide household and village-level survey data complemented with county-level administrative data from China's Ministry of Civil Affairs covering the period 2007–2009, they found (a) the program suffers from many irregularities in implementation due to large exclusionary and inclusionary targeting errors and (b) although the program "provided sufficient income to poor beneficiaries, it does not substantially reduce the overall level of poverty, in part because the number of beneficiaries is small relative to the number of poor," and because the relatively low local *Dibao* thresholds usually fall far short of the national poverty line, thereby severely limiting the program's impact on poverty alleviation. Finally, the design of the *Dibao* scheme also creates a disincentive for the social assistance recipients to eventually move away from welfare dependence and into gainful employment. This is in part because, unlike many other conditional cash transfer programs, participation in the *Dibao* program does not require the transfer of benefits to be conditional upon the recipients' meeting officially prescribed rules such as making pre-specified investments in the human capital of their children (such as enrolling beneficiaries children into public schools with attendance on 80 to 85 percent of school days, making sure that the children receive periodic medical check-ups, including vaccinations, and making sure mothers attend perinatal care classes). To the contrary, the *Dibao* actually discourages recipients from seeking full-time employment because an increase in household wage income results in a proportionate decrease in the *Dibao* benefit a recipient receives.

To further assist rural residents, Beijing eliminated agricultural taxes nationwide in 2006; in 2008 the Rural Cooperative Medical Insurance was fully restored, and in 2009, a rural pensions program was introduced. Perhaps most significantly, in 2008 Beijing introduced the Labor Contract Law, which requires employers not only to sign legal labor contracts with migrant workers, but also to provide these workers with basic social insurance coverage. However, implementation has been incremental and spotty, and suffice it to note that, until the *hukou* is fully eliminated (thereby allowing rural labor and households to move freely between the countryside and cities), the source of China's growing inequality will not be resolved. More broadly, in the wake of the global financial crisis, China can longer depend on export-led growth to create jobs. That is, China can no longer rely purely on the high growth rates to ensure that incomes will continue to rise for millions of its workers. The key for China is to make a shift from an economy dominated by labor-intensive manufacturing, exports, large-scale infrastructure investment, and reliance on heavy industry, to a diverse service economy underpinned by domestic demand. How Beijing navigates through this period of slow (and uncertain) growth, and in particular, how well it makes this economic transition, will fundamentally determine the nature and extent of the inequality problem in the People's Republic.

India, too, has a long and troubled history of direct intervention by both the central and state governments, aimed ostensibly at *garibi hatao*, or "eradicating poverty and inequality." A variety of rural "uplift programs," ranging from food subsidy schemes and guaranteed work targeting the rural poor to farm-input subsidies such as fertilizers, pesticides, and irrigation (via loan waivers and underpricing of energy and water supplies), including cheap (subsidized) credit to farmers, have been provided over the years. However, the actual outcome of these programs has been mixed. Although there is acknowledgment that these complicit interventions have helped to alleviate poverty and deprivation (by how much is hotly debated), there is also recognition that a huge gulf exits between intentions and outcomes. The problem not only has to do with ineffective implementation and failure to properly target the needy, but also with pervasive corruption (in both the state and society) and the fraught calculations of democratic politics, where the exigencies of the electoral cycle makes ad-hoc populist programs attractive. The Indian government's recently announced massive "Food Security Program" is a case in point. Facing increasingly frustrated voters angry at fast-rising food prices and growing shortages of basic essentials, the incumbent government announced what seems to be a politically expedient (but economically imprudent) program to distribute an estimated 62 million metric tons of cereals (rice and wheat) to the "poor." Costing the exchequer an estimated US$20 billion every year (at a time when the government's fiscal deficit is already at an unsustainable 9 percent of GDP), the program inevitably has triggered inflationary pressures, with huge adverse consequences for the very groups the program is designed to help. The irony is that India already has a massive food distribution system – but, like the proverbial "leaky bucket," it is hugely wasteful and inefficient, "spilling" over 70 percent of the goods before it even reaches the intended beneficiaries. Even relatively successful programs such as the Mahatma Gandhi National Rural Employment Guarantee Scheme (MGNREGA), India's largest public works program, designed to guarantee to all rural households up to 100 days of unskilled manual wage employment per year at the minimum wage for agricultural workers, has limits. Specifically, even as the MGNREGA has helped to provide employment and income for the rural poor during lean times, the preponderance of evidence suggests it is hardly a long-term solution to rural poverty and inequality.

As noted in Chapter 4, despite the promises, the policy response of the administration of Prime Minister Narendra Modi to the problems associated with subsidized water, electricity, and agricultural inputs (such as fertilizers and pesticides) and "pro-poor" social welfare programs has been disappointing – with Modi seemingly succumbing to the imperatives of "competitive populism."

Nevertheless, the Modi administration has taken some important steps to address the problem of exclusion and rising inequality by combining what Kapur and Nangia (2015) refer to as "basic public goods" and "social protection."

For example, because millions of Indians – in particular, women – lack access to formal banking and credit markets (thereby making them vulnerable to predatory lending by informal moneylenders), Modi, who has long been a champion of "financial inclusion" and "financial empowerment," has introduced a number of programs to address this imbalance. Indeed, during his tenure as Chief Minister in his home state of Gujarat, Modi was responsible for providing access to formal credit and finance to the hitherto excluded (in particular, women), and was able to significantly expand female entrepreneurship. At the national level, the Modi administration has made significant progress in enhancing financial inclusion. Under the *Pradhan Mantri Jan Dhan Yojana* (launched in August 2014), an estimated that 240 million previously unbanked individuals (with the majority being rural residents) gained access to bank accounts. At this rate of progress, this initiative could most likely meet its stated aim to achieve universal access to basic banking services by 2018. Similarly, the *Pradhan Mantri MUDRA Yojana* (launched in January 2016) to provide micro, small and medium-sized businesses access to collateral-free loans, has made good progress. To date, roughly 1 percent of GDP in loans have been disbursed under this program.[2] Also, given the tragic reality that India has one of the worst child sex ratios in the world (that is, the number of girls per 1000 boys, which continues to decline), the *Beti Bachao Beti Padhao* (Celebrate Girl Child, Enable Her Education) scheme launched by Prime Minister Modi himself in January 2015 is most welcome. This scheme has already been implemented in 100 selected districts with low child sex ratio with the aim to prevent the practice of sex selection with better education and community involvement. Given the magnitude of the problem, much more needs to be done. Finally, the Prime Minister's much-publicized and favorite program, the *Swachh Bharat* (Clean India) program, launched in October 2014, according to government reports is off to a good start with some 31 million toilets built in the countryside. Of course, building latrines must go hand-in-hand with large-scale socio-cultural and behavioral change – something the Prime Minister is cognizant of.

Nevertheless, the two Asian giants can learn some valuable lessons on reducing inequality from their fellow Latin American giant: Brazil. Till recently, Brazil had the unflattering distinction for being a country with the worst income inequality in the world. However, since 2000, Brazil has made a significant dent in poverty and inequality, with the Gini coefficient falling sharply from a high of about 0.63 in 1990 to around 0.54 in 2009 (Barros, de Carvalho, Franco, and Mendoca 2010; Ferreira, Leite, and Ravallion 2010). In January 2012, the Gini had dropped to 0.52. If current trends continue, the Gini was projected to fall below the 0.5 line sometime in 2014 – or in 2015 at the latest. Brazil's remarkable achievement underscores that there is nothing inevitable about economic growth resulting in increased income inequality. Brazil's success in reducing income inequality is due to a combination of factors. First, an effectively reining-in of the pervasive problem of hyperinflation has meant that incomes are no longer being rapidly eroded through inflation tax. Second, there is the unwavering commitment of the Lula administration (which took office in 2003) to redistributive justice, and in particular to amelioration of Brazil's long and deep-rooted economic and social inequalities.

Targeted programs, namely the implementation of the minimum wage policy under the *Beneficio de Prestacao Continuada* (BPC) and the *"Bolsa Família"* or Family Grant program, have allowed for a simultaneous reduction in poverty levels and income inequalities. Like China's *Diabo*, the *Bolsa Família* is also a classic "conditional cash transfer" program. However, the difference is that the *Bolsa Família* not only provides extensive coverage, it is also better managed and implemented. The *Bolsa Família* provides regular payments to poor families either in the form of modest cash or electronic transfers into their bank accounts on the condition that they meet certain requirements such as making sure that their children attend school, get vaccinated, receive regular medical check-ups, and that mothers actively participate in educational programs. The program is well targeted – there are regular follow-ups, with each family's eligibility reassessed every two years through careful monitoring, including personal visits by social workers. A fortuitous outcome of such diligence is that it has enabled the program to establish an exhaustive register of poor families in the country called *Cadastro Único*. Under Lula's administration, *Bolsa Família's* coverage grew from some 4.9 million families in 2002 to over 12 million families (or 97.3 percent of the target population) by 2009. The IMF's (2017, 58) latest country report on Brazil notes that "beneficiary coverage has increased from about 6.5 million households in 2004, when it was founded, to over 14 million in 2014 (56 million people)." Although Brazil has been able to pay for the program because of windfall revenues from commodity exports, it is important to note that *Bolsa Família* is not only relatively inexpensive (that is, budgetary appropriations for the program have increased from about 0.3 percent of GDP in 2004 to 0.6 percent of GDP in 2014), it is already shown to have a positive impact on poverty alleviation (it is estimated "that 58 percent of the decline in extreme poverty in Brazil over 2004–14 was due to *Bolsa Família* transfers" (IMF 2017, 58)) as well as educational outcomes.[3] That is, by providing access to basic education (such as literacy and numeracy skills), *Bolsa Família* provides opportunities for the current generation to escape grinding poverty – with clear, long-term socioeconomic benefits (Lopez-Calva and Rocha 2012). The experience of *Bolsa Família* underscores that well-targeted and implemented programs can help to both significantly alleviate the immediate short-term inequality and poverty and break the cycle or transmission of intergenerational poverty. In fact, well-targeted social safety nets and transfer programs can actually contribute to growth itself – thereby reducing the overall cost of social safety nets and transfers over time. This is because beneficiaries of such programs not only use transfers to finance their immediate consumption needs, the cash also provides them with much-needed (and hard to get) credit.

This in turn allows poor households to overcome credit constraints and gives them some capital to invest. Gertler, Martinez, and Rubio-Codina (2012) show that many poor rural Mexican households invested part of the cash transfers they received from the *Oportunidades* program in productive assets, and some, after an 18-month period of diligent saving and investment, were able to increase their agricultural income by almost 10 percent.

The experience of Brazil underscores that targeted redistributive measures and the provision of a viable social safety net can go a long way towards alleviate the human suffering and income inequalities. Of course, continued spending on such programs requires sustained economic growth. For both China and India, promoting economic growth with redistribution will be essential to further improvement of the living standards of their citizens. The corrosive effects of rising socioeconomic disparities amid plenty is well known, and has triggered revolutionary upheavals throughout history – most recently in the "Arab Spring" (Wilkinson and Pickett 2009). The widening inequality, and in particular the popular perception (with much truth to it) that corruption and connections are what enabled the *nouveau-riche* in both countries to amass their fortunes, not to mention the hedonistic and vicarious lifestyle of the rich, lies at the heart of the growing resentment, civil unrest, and popular mobilization in both countries (Schortgen and Sharma 2012). Both the Indian and Chinese governments recognize the imperative to reduce inequalities and promote more inclusive growth. If India has its massive food subsidy program and other short-term populist programs to buy voters and time, China's influential State Council (China's cabinet) endorsed an ambitious program put together by three key ministries (the National Development and Reform Commission, the Ministry of Finance, and the Ministry of Human Resources and Social Security), unambiguously titled "On Deepening the Reform of the System of Income Distribution," to reduce income inequalities. Most importantly, the new program plans to simultaneously crack down on corruption and reduce income inequality. Of course, its effectiveness remains to be seen.

The historian Walter Scheidel (2017), in his provocative and deeply pessimistic book *The Great Leveler*, argues that "from the Stone Age to the Twenty-First Century," rising and high inequality has been the norm. The only time inequality is reduced or "leveled" is when traumatic and cataclysmic events (the "Four Horsemen" of leveling) such as major conflicts (wars), transformative revolutions, state collapse, or a devastating pandemic dramatically flattens income and wealth distribution. Yet, Scheidel notes that such reverses are temporary and incremental, with rising inequality returning with a vengeance once stability and order is restored. Rather, Scheidel claims, if history teaches us anything it is that absence violent and catastrophic upheaval it is impossible to meaningfully reduce economic inequality. However, this study shows that such pessimism is not entirely warranted. Global inequality has been greatly reduced since World War II (an era of the "long peace"), even as income and wealth inequality has risen within countries. In other words, these are times of relative prosperity because incomes have grown for most households, even as inequality has widened because the gains have been proportionally larger for those households in the higher income deciles. Nations around the world – in particular, China and India – have made unprecedented strides in reducing poverty and improving the lives of millions. With concerted efforts they (as well as other nations) can also mitigate and reconcile the capricious problem of rising economic inequalities. Nevertheless, *The Great Leveler* provides apt warning to global and national economic and political elites about the imperative of meaningfully addressing the growing economic divide.

Notes

1 INTRODUCTION: PROSPERITY WITH INEQUALITY IN THE AGE OF GLOBALIZATION

1. Income inequality refers to income earned in a given year, whereas wealth inequality refers to how the ownership of assets (minus liabilities) is distributed.

2. The Gini coefficient uses an algorithm to produce a numerical rating to show how far a society is from perfect income equality – denoted by a Gini of 0. A higher Gini coefficient means greater income inequality. A Gini coefficient of 1 means maximum or extreme inequality. Thus, in the Gini Index, 0 is perfect equality, while 1 can mean one individual gets all the income. A more practical way to understand the Gini Index is to see it as corresponding to the share of total income that would be needed for redistribution in order to achieve perfect income equality. For example, a Gini Index of 0.60 means that 60 percent of the income would need to be redistributed to achieve complete income equality.

3. Similarly, household wealth distribution can vary for many reasons. Households' savings behavior, marriage and divorce, and the type of assets held (for example, portfolios composed of more risky, but higher-expected-return assets (such as stocks) tend to move up and down (sometimes dramatically) in their wealth position more than less-risky assets such as savings bonds or just savings. Finally, building household wealth follows a "life cycle." Younger households tend to be more wealth-poor as they are starting out and have had less time to save. In fact, they tend to be in debt as they borrow (based of their future income) to make investments in real estate or education. On the other hand, older households, because they have had more time to save, pay down their debts and build up their retirement funds, tend to have more wealth.

4. Saez and Zucman (2014) aptly note that "unfortunately, there is much less data available on wealth in the US than there is on income. Income tax data exists since 1913 – the first year the country collected federal income tax – but there is no comparable tax on wealth to provide information on the distribution of assets. Currently available measures of wealth inequality rely either on surveys (the Survey of Consumer Finances of the Federal Reserve Board), on estate tax return data, or on lists of wealthy individuals, such as the Forbes 400 list of wealthiest Americans."

5. Of course, inequality in outcomes and inequality of opportunity are deeply interconnected. After all, inequality of opportunity today helps reduce inequality of outcomes tomorrow. Therefore, addressing the problem of inequality in outcomes today can reduce inequality of opportunity for the next generation.

6. There is no agreement about the optimal level of inequality – or the point when too little or too much inequality undermines economic growth.

7. See https://sustainabledevelopment.un.org/topics. As a recent article in *The Economist* (May 3, 2017) notes, "In the past few decades something amazing has happened. The share and the number of extremely poor people in the world (on the current definition, people who consume less than $1.90 a day at purchasing-power parity) has plunged. This is hugely welcome. People who live on less than $1.90 a day are very poor indeed – poor, in fact, even by the standards of the world's poorest countries ... The 1.9bn people were extremely poor in 1981. In that year, the poor accounted for 42% of the world's population. In 2013, by contrast, only 767m people were poor. Because the world's population has grown so much in the interim, the share of poor people in the population has fallen even faster, to just below 11%. The single biggest reason for this delightful trend is China. In 1981, almost unbelievably, 88% of Chinese (and 96% of rural Chinese) seem to have lived below the poverty line. In 2013 only 2% of Chinese were extremely poor." www .economist.com/blogs/economist-explains/2017/05/economist-explains-1 (accessed May 3, 2017).

8. However, Milanovic (2016) cautions that this trend may not continue once China's incomes per head rise above the global average. This means that further reductions in global inequality will then depend on growth rates in other large developing economies, namely, India.

9. That is, the proportion of the world's population living in "extreme poverty" or with an income below $1.25 a day at 2005 dollars adjusted for purchasing power.

10. It is important to not lose sight of Amartya Sen's (1999) caution that the quantitative estimates of poverty do not always factor in limitation of access to a wide range of resources such as education, health, and democratic freedoms.

11. In other words, an individual's demand for redistribution is a function of mean income minus his/her own income. As inequality increases and a larger percentage of the populace income falls below the mean, the demand for greater redistribution grows.

12. It should be noted that there is a body of research that has reported a negative relationship between democracy and inequality using specific historical periods or cross-national studies (Gradstein and Milanovic 2004; Scheve and Stasavage 2012).

13. Collier (1999, 24) notes that "Democracy, as a regime type, may be defined in terms of three components: constitutional, electoral, and legislative. As such it includes the following attributes: 1. Liberal constitutional rule, in which government leaders and state actors, including the military, are constrained from arbitrary action by the rule of law; 2. Classical elections; and 3. a legislative assembly that is popularly elected and has substantial autonomy from the executive power."

14. The World Trade Organization (and before it, the General Agreement on Tariffs and Trade (GATT)), coupled with a series of bilateral and regional trade

negotiations, has helped bring the average tariff on goods in most advanced nations down to under 5 percent. However, the average tariff on goods in emerging markets (albeit, much lower than in the past) still remain two to three times higher than in the advanced economies. The latest most round of WTO negotiations (or the Doha Development Round), which began in 2001, remains stalled in large part because large emerging market economies – in particular, China and India – resist removing tariff and non-tariff barriers (such as licensing rules, intellectual property protection, restrictions on foreign investment, domestic regulatory standards, among others) designed to circumvent multilateral rules and protect domestic industries. Although agreements on financial services and telecommunications have helped establish some basic rules for services, the use of both tariff and non-tariff barriers in services still remains high.

15. For example, according to the World Trade Organization, "between 1995 and 2011, most developed and developing countries significantly increased their contributions to global value chains (GVCs), resulting in a geographically more diverse manufacturing base. Lower trade costs and improved communication technology have fostered this development. In 2011, nearly half (49 percent) of world trade in goods and services took place within GVCs, up from 36 percent in 1995. The tendency of countries to specialize in particular stages of a good's production (known as vertical specialization), brought about by foreign direct investment, has created new trade opportunities ... As a result, world trade in intermediate goods has grown with the rise of vertical specialization" (WTO 2015, 18).

16. However, according to Goldin and Katz (2008), the problem is not technological change, but the "education gap" – or the reduced availability of educated and skilled workers in the labor market. They note that in the United States, between 1980 and 2005 the level of educational attainment has dramatically slowed. In 1980, Americans aged 30 years or older had 4.7 years more schooling on average than Americans in 1930. However, in 2005, Americans had only 0.8 years more schooling on average than Americans in 1980.

17. Of course, trade deficits alone are not a good indicator of US competitive strength because they are influenced by various factors, including the relative value of currencies and the level of national savings. In fact, US trade deficits usually rise when the economy is doing well and tend to fall when the economy is weak and not doing well. Therefore, a rising trade deficit normally signals US economic strength, not weakness.

18. Of course, political scientists have long argued that the sustained economic growth and prosperity during the period from 1945 up to the mid-1970s was the result of "embedded liberalism" – where advanced economies adopted free-market economic policies with a commitment to socioeconomic welfare and redistribution.

19. Judith Stein (2011) provides a more nuanced rendition of the US experience, noting that the era of postwar liberalism ushered in under the New Deal, which laid the foundations of "regulated capitalism" and produced both robust economic growth and greater income equality, came to an abrupt end in the 1970s. The combination of skyrocketing oil prices and intense economic competition from Japan and Germany severely battered the American economy. As US policies waged war

against inflation (rather than against unemployment) and government policies placed priority on achieving a balanced budget instead of growth, "it marked the beginning of the age of finance and subsequent deregulation, free trade, low taxation, and weak unions that has fostered inequality and now the worst recession in sixty years." In a similar vein, according to Lindert and Williamson (2016), beginning at the end of WWI and lasting to around 1973, the United States witnessed a dramatic reduction in inequality – with a decline not only in the top income deciles, but a leveling throughout the income distribution. However, from the mid-1970s, rising inequality occurred throughout the income distribution – albeit, it was more pronounced at the very top. Rapid expansion of the financial sector, coupled with the deregulation of financial markets, including lax regulation of investment banking, is the major factor why the top income shares have made significant gains (at least compared to middle and lower income deciles) – and in the process exacerbated income and wealth inequality.

20. Wang's (2016, 320) extensive study of China's "politically connected firms" (for which the author compiled "a database of all the publicly traded firms in China in 1993, 2002 and 2012, through coding the biographies of hundreds of thousands of board members" who had "connections with seven political organizations: the national government, local government, the national parliament, local parliament, the National Party Congress, local Party congress, and the People's Liberation Army (PLA). A firm is defined as being connected if at least one of its board members is formerly or currently an employee or a member of these organizations") finds "that, first, political connections are ubiquitous among listed firms in China: almost 90 percent of firms are connected. Second, firms are overwhelmingly connected with the government rather than the parliament, which is a more common form of connection in democracies. Third, while more firms are connected with local governments than with the national government, there has been a significant increase in the percentage of firms that are connected with the national government in the last 20 years. The proportion of firms connected with the national government has tripled between 1993 and 2012, whereas the proportion of firms connected with local governments has increased only by 30 percent."

21. The Economist, (January 21, 2012) www.economist.com/node/21543160/print.

22. Milhaupt and Zheng (2016, 10) note, "We studied the government or Party affiliations of the founders or de-facto controllers of China's 100 largest private firms (by revenue) as ranked by the China National Association of Industry and Commerce, as well as China's top ten private Internet firms (by revenue), as ranked by the China Internet Association. Based on publicly available information, we identified 95 out of the top 100 private firms and eight out of the top ten Internet firms whose founder or de-facto controller is currently or formerly a member of central or local political organizations such as People's Congresses and People's Political Consultative Conferences."

23. "Shiller tells Yahoo's Daily Ticker, a finance blog." http://finance.yahoo.com/blogs/da ily-ticker/robert-shiller-financial-capitalism-taking-over-world-good-130531139.html (accessed June 8, 2014).

24. Derivatives are used by financial institutions and corporations to adjust their exposure to particular financial risks, such as the default of a borrower or wild swings in interest rates.

25. In India, most welfare-enhancing programs are legislated and funded by the central government, but implementation remains the domain of state and local governments.

26. China's constitution divides the local administration into three tiers: province, county, and township. However, in practice, there are five levels of government: central, provincial, municipal (or prefectural), county, and township. China has thirty-four provincial-level administrative units.

2   WIDENING INCOME AND WEALTH GAP IN THE UNITED STATES

1. The CBO examined the years 1979 and 2007, as both years were before recessions.
2. As noted, the Gini coefficient uses an algorithm to produce a numerical rating to show how far a society is from perfect income equality – denoted by a Gini of 0. A higher Gini coefficient means greater income inequality. A Gini coefficient of 1 means maximum or extreme inequality. The Gini Index based on net after-tax income is lower than the same index based on before-tax income. In the United States, in 1979, the Gini Index based on after-tax income was 0.36, but by 2013 it had risen to 0.44.
3. The US Census Bureau ranks all households by "household income" and divides this distribution of households into "quintiles." The highest-ranked household in each quintile provides the upper income limit for each quintile. By comparing the changes in the upper income limits over time for different quintiles, the Census Bureau concludes that the income of highest-ranked households has been growing faster than the income of lower-ranked households. Although, the Census Bureau provides consistent time series data, it is also limited to pre-tax income and does not include noncash benefits, government transfers, and tax benefits or payments that can affect a household's disposable income.
4. Income tax data for the US goes back to 1913. However, it should be noted that although the IRS data does provide a more comprehensive coverage of the highest-income households, it also has limitations as it excludes government transfers and under-represents the lower end of the income distribution, as these groups are not required to file income tax returns.
5. Standard & Poor's Financial Services LLC, "How Increasing Income Inequality Is Dampening U.S. Economic Growth, and Possible Ways to Change the Tide," accessed at www.globalcreditportal.com on October 10, 2014.
6. Western and Rosenfeld (2011) point out that union density has been in steady decline in the United States since reaching its peak in the mid-1950s. For example, private-sector union density has declined from one-in-four union members among all wage and salary workers in the early 1970s to below one-in-thirteen by mid-2000.
7. According to Baker (2016), "the bulk of this upward redistribution [of income] comes from the growth of rents in the economy in four major areas: patent and copyright protection, the financial sector, the pay of CEOs and other top executives, and protectionist measures that have boosted the pay of doctors and other highly educated professionals."
8. Since for most American households, wages make-up the primary source of disposable income, the slow growth in disposable income has led many middle- and lower-income households to turn to debt to finance their consumption. The unsustainability of this was starkly revealed during the global financial crisis.

Notes to Pages 45–62 175

9. In 2017, there are seven IRS tax brackets: 10, 15, 25, 28, 33, 35, and 39.6 percent. The amount of income tax owed depends on taxable income and filing status. Income falling within a particular bracket is taxed at that tax rate. Additional income is taxed according to the rate in the next tax bracket.

10. Similar to a sales tax, the VAT is a tax on consumption. However, unlike a sales tax, which is charged only at the final point of sale, a VAT is levied on all sales of inputs throughout the chain of production. The European Union requires member countries to have a minimum 15 percent VAT – albeit, a number of countries have rates higher than 20 percent. Such high rates mean that the VATs can raise substantial revenues. The Congressional Budget Office estimates that a 5 percent broad-based VAT in the United States would raise over $2.7 trillion over 10 years.

11. A cursory look shows that individuals who were on the original "Forbes 400" list of richest Americans in 1982 were not on the list in 2013. They were replaced by new names.

12. During the golden years (1947 through 1973), economic growth per annum was slightly above 4 percent per year.

13. Data from the Bureau of Labor Statistics (BLS) show that for 12 of the 22 major occupation groups tracked by the BLS, average annual wages adjusted for inflation shrank from 2004 to 2014, two registered no wage change, while only two saw an increase of more than 5 percent in average annual wage.

14. A 2012 survey conducted by Chicago's Booth School found that about 80 percent of leading economic experts agreed that the major reason for rising US income inequality was that technological change has impacted workers with different skillsets differently. "Inequality and Skills," IGM Forum, Chicago Booth, January 24, 2012, www.igmchicago.org/igm-economic-experts-panel/poll-results?SurveyI D=SV_oIAlhdDH2FoRDrm (accessed October 1, 2015).

15. Barack Obama (2011), "Remarks by the President on the Economy in Osawatomie, Kansas," December 6, www.whitehouse.gov/the-press-office/2011/12/06/remarks-president-economy-osawatomie-kansas.

16. Paul Krugman (2011), "Oligarchy, American Style," *The New York Times*, November 3, www.nytimes.com/2011/11/04/opinion/oligarchy-american-style.html.

17. The bulk of the data are drawn from polls conducted between 1981 and 2002, with supplementary data from polls conducted from 1964 to 1969 and 2005 to 2006.

18. Gilens notes that the preferences of poor and middle-class Americans have a higher chance to be enacted into law (albeit, much watered-down versions) during the run-up to presidential elections, but not congressional elections. However, during periods of gridlock, Congress tends to be more responsive to popular preferences.

19. Cozzi and Impullitti (2016, 984) note that "The geography of technological leadership, measured as countries' share of innovation inputs and outputs, shows remarkable changes between the mid-1970s and the late 1980s. As the distribution of leadership moved from being drastically skewed towards the United States to a more equal global playing field, clear convergence patterns could be observed in the share of patents, patent citations, and R&D spending. The share of foreign patents in the US Patent Office was about one-third in 1977 and grew to about one-half 10 years later. The US share of global industrial R&D declined from about 50 percent in 1979 to 39 percent in 1995. Most of this technological catching up was due to a

massive acceleration in Japanese innovation activity, although some European countries, such as Germany and France, played a major role in some sectors . . . "

20. While Autor, Dorn, and Hanson (2016) see a clear linkage between China's export surge following its entrance into the WTO, Pierce and Schott (2016) attribute the sharp drop in US manufacturing employment after 2000 to changes in US trade policy that eliminated potential tariff increases on Chinese imports. In other words, to Pierce and Schott (2016), US job losses are mainly due to the change in US trade policy – namely, the United States granting permanent normal trade relations (PNTR) to China in October 2000 – which eliminated the threat of substantial tariff increases on Chinese imports. They find that "Industries more exposed to the change experience greater employment loss, increased imports from China, and higher entry by US importers and foreign-owned Chinese exporters."

21. The total US trade deficit in 2015 was $531.5 billion. Yet, it should be noted that the trade deficit is more a function of national saving and investment decisions than of the weakness of the United States in international trade.

22. General Motors (2017), "2016 Full-Year and Fourth-Quarter Earnings," February, http://media.gm.com/content/dam/Media/gmcom/investor/2017/feb/earnings/q4-doc uments/GeneralMotors-q4-2016-Earnings.pdf, and General Motors (2016), "Media, China, General Motors Announces Growth Strategy for China," March 21, http:// media.gm.com/media/cn/en/gm/news.detail.html/content/Pages/news/cn/en/2016/M ar/0321_annoucement.html.

23. For details, see Congressional Research Service (CRS) 2016, March 28, *Foreign Holdings of Federal Debt*, CRS Report RS22331, by Marc Labonte and Jared C. Nagel, and 2013, August 19, *China's Holdings of U.S. Securities: Implications for the U.S. Economy*. CRS Report RL34314, by Wayne M. Morrison and Marc Labonte.

24. The decline in manufacturing employment has led both Democratic and Republican senators to threaten the Chinese with substantial tariffs on Chinese imports to offset the Chinese currency advantage. For details, see Hufbauer and Wong (2004).

25. Some economists claim that the yuan is anywhere from 15 to 40 percent undervalued against the dollar, making Chinese exports to the United States cheaper and contributing to China's trade surplus with the United States. Of course, no one really knows the true extent of the undervaluation. This is because not letting the market decide a currency's value means that the nominal exchange rate – literally the number of units of one currency you can get for one unit of another – is essentially made up. It is whatever the government chooses it to be, so long as the regime can be feasibly maintained. For a good overview, see Lardy (2005), Subramanian (2010), and Makin (2007).

26. Indeed, following the Chinese revaluation, Malaysia responded by shifting its own currency regime from a dollar peg to a basket peg. However, given the very small initial change in the yuan's value, most countries in the region seem to be waiting for a more substantial yuan revaluation before taking action.

27. Revaluation is the resetting of the fixed value of a currency at a higher level.

28. Both flexible and floating exchange rates have distinct advantages – albeit, no single exchange rate regime is appropriate for all countries in all circumstances. A fixed exchange rate that pegs the value of a currency to a stronger foreign currency like the US dollar or the euro has advantages for developing countries seeking to build

confidence in their economic policies. On the other hand, countries with fixed exchange rates are seemingly more vulnerable to currency crises. As economies mature and become more closely aligned with the international financial markets, exchange rate flexibility seems more advantageous.

29. When a currency increases in value, it experiences appreciation. When it falls in value and is worth fewer US dollars, it undergoes depreciation. Thus, when a country's currency appreciates (rises in value relative to other currencies), the country's goods abroad become more expensive and foreign goods in that country become cheaper. Conversely, when a country's currency depreciates, its goods abroad become cheaper and foreign goods in that country become more expensive.

30. Both the central bank governor Zhou Xiaochuan and Premier Wen Jiabao noted that the revaluation should be viewed as the first in what is expected to be a series of steps over years to shift the yuan towards even greater flexibility as China increases its participation in the world trading system. See People's Bank of China (2005), "Public Announcement of the People's Bank of China on Reforming the RMB Exchange Rate Regime," July 21, www.pbc.gov.cn/english/detail.asp?col=6500&id=82.

31. Figure 2.9 downloaded from Humpage and Herrell (2009).

32. Between July 2005 and 2008, a managed currency float saw the yuan gradually gain 21 percent against the dollar.

33. According to the Bank for International Settlements, from July 2005 to February 2009 the yuan rose by 28 percent in real trade-weighted terms. However, the sharp export contraction forced Beijing to repeg the yuan to the dollar. Since February 2009, the yuan's real trade-weighted value has lost about 8 percent. Of course, disagreement persists regarding the extent to which the yuan is undervalued – with claims that the yuan is undervalued anywhere from 10 to 30 percent. For details, see Subramanian (2010).

34. Schumer made clear that he would push a bill to impose anti-dumping duties on some Chinese goods and countervailing tariffs on all of them if Beijing did not allow its currency to strengthen.

35. John Pomfret (2010), "China's Commerce Minister: U.S. Has the Most to Lose in a Trade War," *Washington Post*, Monday, March 22, A06, and Gillian Wong (2010), "China Warns US against Sanctions over Currency," *Associated Press*, Sunday, March 21, http://news.yahoo.com/s/ap/20100321/ap_on_bi_ge/as_china_trade/print. Striking a more conciliatory tone, Zhong Shan, Chinese vice-minister of commerce, in an op-ed in *The Wall Street Journal* argued that there is "little connection between the trade balance and the value of the renminbi." To the contrary, "China–U.S. trade and economic cooperation has generated huge and real benefits for the United States ... Since the outbreak of the international financial crisis, China has been supporting the efforts of the American people to tackle the crisis. On the one hand, China has increased imports from the U.S. While overall U.S. exports dropped 17.9% in 2009, exports to China hardly decreased. Many U.S. manufacturing firms have found comfort in the Chinese market as a shelter against the global financial storm. On the other hand, good value-for-money, labor-intensive goods imported from China have helped keep the cost of living down for Americans even when they become increasingly cash-strapped. Without consumer goods from China, the U.S. price index would go up an extra two percentage points every year ... As Wen Jiabao, the Chinese premier,

recently reiterated, it is always better to have a dialogue than a confrontation, cooperation than containment, and a partnership than a rivalry. As long as we approach the China–U.S. commercial relationship in a responsible manner we will definitely be able to make it more stable and sound." See, Zhong Shan (2010), "U.S.–China Trade Is Win-Win Game," *The Wall Street Journal*, March 26.

36. Kathy Wang (2008), "Protect China's assets, US Told," *The Standard: China's Business Newspaper*, Friday, 5 December, www.thestandard.com.hk/news_print .asp?art_id=75364&sid=21758213.

37. "Statement of Treasury Secretary Geithner on the Report to Congress on International Economic and Exchange Rate Policies," April 3, 2010, United States Department of the Treasury, no, TG-627, www.ustreas.gov/press/releases/tg627 .htm.

38. Bill Powell (2010), "Why Geithner Made a Surprise Stop in Beijing" *Time*, April 8, www.time.com/time/world/article/0,8599,1978666,00.html?xid=rss-fullworld-ya hoo; and Keith Bradsher (2010), "China Seems Set to Loosen Hold on Its Currency," April 8, *The New York Times*, www.nytimes.com/2010/04/09/busi ness/global/09yuan.html?ref=business&src=me&pagewanted=print.

39. In his written statement to the Senate panel, Geithner noted then Senator Obama's support for "tough legislation to overhaul the U.S. process for determining currency manipulation and authorizing new enforcement measures so countries like China cannot continue to get a free pass for undermining fair trade principles." However, the Obama administration quickly backtracked from Geithner's statement and declined to label China a "currency manipulator." Rather, the administration noted that while it still believes that the yuan is undervalued, it also recognizes that China has taken steps to rebalance its economy and enhance exchange-rate flexibility. See, Lori Montgomery and Anthony Faiola (January 23, 2009), "Geithner Says China Manipulates Its Currency," *The Washington Post*, January 23, p. A08, www.washingtonpost.com/wpdyn/content/article/2009/01/22/A R2009012203796.html. Also, "Statement by Treasury Secretary Timothy Geithner on Release of Semi-Annual Report to US Congress on International Economic and Exchange Rate Policies" (April 15, 2009), www.treas.gov/press/rel eases.tg90.htm.

40. Treasury securities are the debt financing instruments of the US Federal Government. They are often referred to as Treasuries. There are four types of marketable treasury securities: Treasury bills, Treasury notes, Treasury bonds, and Treasury Inflation Protected Securities (TIPS).

41. Ian Talley and Tom Barkley (2010), "US Lawmakers Press Geithner on China Currency, Trade Policies," *The Wall Street Journal*, June 10, http://online.wsj .com/article/BT-CO-20100610-711862.html?mod=WSJ_latestheadlines, Martin Crutsinger (2010), "Geithner pressed by Congress on China currency," Associated Press, June 10, http://finance.yahoo.com/news/Geithner-pressed-by -Congress-apf 2170249732.

42. The People's Bank of China (2010), "Further Reform the RMB Exchange Rate Regime and Enhance the RMB Exchange Rate Flexibility," June 19, www.pbc.gov .cn/english/detail; also see Cline (2010a).

43. Back and Browne argue that "the argument over whether China should allow its currency to appreciate was fierce and public: The Ministry of Commerce, a strong backer of Chinese exporters, was adamantly opposed to a stronger yuan. The

People's Bank of China which is responsible for the overall health of the economy took a different view: A stronger yuan helps China combat inflation by bringing down the cost of imports, including energy and raw materials . . . Beijing has always insisted that it will only carry out currency reform when its economic conditions permit. A raft of economic data out last week, including surging exports and rising inflation in May, likely convinced Chinese policy makers that the time had come. China's consumer price index rose 3.1% in May from a year earlier, above the psychologically significant 3% level, which is Beijing's official target for average inflation over all of 2010. A stronger yuan can help tame inflation by reducing the price of imports. In theory, a more flexible exchange rate should also strengthen the independence of China's monetary policy, allowing it to raise interest rates without fearing an influx of foreign money seeking high returns on yuan-denominated assets." Aaron Back and Andrew Browne (2010), "Pragmatism Drove Beijing's Decision to Drop Peg," *The Wall Street Journal*, June 20, http://onli ne.wsj.com/article/SB10001424052748704638504575318671733450594.html? mod=WSJ_hpp_LEFTTopStories.

44. MarketWatch and Ronald D. Orol (2010), "China to Ease Yuan-Dollar Peg," *MarketWatch*, June 20, www.marketwatch.com/story/story/print?guid=5D521 B66-AD70-4E0E-BA4B-275DE549D3FA.

45. Cara Anna (2010), "China to Allow More Exchange Rate Flexibility," June 19, http://news.yahoo.com/s/ap/20100619/ap_on_bi_ge/as_china_currency/print.

46. Rebecca Christie and Ian Katz (2010), "Geithner Calls for Follow-Up to China's Yuan Decision," June 19, *Bloomberg News* www.businessweek.com/news/2010-0 6-19/geithner-calls-for-follow-up-to-china-s-yuan-decision-update2-.html.

47. Between July 2014 and March 2015, the dollar index (which measures the value of the dollar against a basket of six major currencies) gained about 25 percent.

48. For details, see www.treasury.gov/resource-center/international/exchange-rate-poli cies/Documents/20161014%20%28Fall%202016%20FX%20Report%29%20FI NAL.PDF.

49. US Department of the Treasury (2017), Foreign Exchange Policies of Major Trading Partners of the United States. "Semiannual Report on International Economic and Exchange Rate Policies," April, Washington, DC: US Treasury, www.treasury.gov/ resource-center/international/exchange-rate-policies/Pages/index.aspx.

50. According to the Federal Reserve, since mid-2008 the dollar has risen by 13 percent against major foreign currencies after adjusting for inflation. Foreign holdings of Treasury bills rose by $456 billion in 2008.

51. International financial institutions and businesses need US dollars to fund their investments that are denominated in dollar assets such as retail and corporate loans, including holdings of structured finance products based on US mortgages and other underlying assets. Although the shocks to the US subprime and mortgage-based securities markets further weakened the dollar (by about 8.5 percent in real effective terms between June 2007 and July 2008), the dire predictions of a massive flight from US assets and a sudden drop in the value of the dollar failed to materialize. Indeed, the assumption that if the American economy went into a sharp downturn, foreign central banks would be reluctant to invest their national savings into the US dollar proved to be incorrect. Rather, the dollar was once again affirmed as the global reserve currency. The massive "flight to safety" by panicked

investors following the collapse of Lehman Brothers into US Treasuries only underscored that the US government is still the safest investment in the world.

52. Of course, large currency depreciation (usually the result of countries having few foreign assets but extensive liabilities denominated in a foreign currency like the US dollar) can severely undermine the real economy.

53. The current account measures the value of a country's net exchange of goods and services with other countries. Overall, the balance of trade makes up the bulk of the share of the current account. The attractiveness (and safety) of the United States as an investment destination therefore helps drive up its current account deficit. It is also important to note that by keeping interest rates too low for too long, the Fed triggered a "search for yield," with domestic investors looking abroad for better returns. This in turn can generate bubbles in emerging economies and appreciation in the foreign exchange value of their currencies.

54. The real conundrum is the so-called "trilemma," which explicitly states that a country can only have two out of the three things: a stable exchange rate, openness to global capital flows, and the ability to determine its own interest rates. Prior to the Asian crisis of 1997–1998, many countries chose fixed currencies and openness to capital inflows, but did not enjoy independent monetary policy. This resulted in the build-up of massive dollar-denominated debts. However, the sudden and sharp reversal of inflows caused these economies to collapse when the currency peg to the dollar broke following a sharp contraction in capital inflows. The value of several Asian currencies sharply dropped, dramatically pushing upward the cost of their dollar-denominated debts, including a painful recession.

55. China's fixed peg generate its own problems. Specifically, when US interest rates rise, the dollar appreciates as does the RMB, negatively impacting Chinese exports. However, a falling dollar results in the reserves losing value.

56. Nouriel Roubini (2009), "The Almighty Renminbi," *New York Times*, May 14; Wang (2007) and Setser (2008a).

57. Geoff Dyer (2009), "China's Dollar Dilemma," *Financial Times*, February 22; Paul Krugman (2009), "China's Dollar Trap," *New York Times*, April 3; David Leonhardt (2009), "The China Puzzle," *New York Times Magazine*, May 17.

58. Martin Feldstein (2010), "How Safe Are Your Dollars?" *Project Syndicate*, February 25, 2010, www.project-syndicate.org/commentary/feldstein20/English.

59. Wayne M. Morrison and Marc Labonte (2008), "China's Holdings of U.S. Securities: Implications for the U.S. Economy," Congressional Research Service, Order Code RL34314; May 19. See www.fas.org/sgp/crs/row/RL34314.pdf.

3   RISING PROSPERITY AND WIDENING INEQUALITY IN THE PEOPLE'S REPUBLIC OF CHINA

1. Over the past three decades, the Chinese economy grew at an unprecedented rate of just over 10 percent. However, in the post-global financial crisis era, such sustained and high growth rates will be hard to maintain. Although growth remains robust when compared to the OECD average, it is nevertheless slowing down. In 2013, China notched a 7.8 percent GDP growth.

2. Gross Domestic Product (GDP) represents the size of a country's economy. Purchasing Power Parity (PPP) GDP is gross domestic product converted to US dollars using purchasing power parity rates. The PPP is more useful when comparing broad differences in the living standards between countries because it factors the relative cost of living and the inflation rates rather than relying exclusively on exchange rates (World Bank 2012).

3. Till recently, China's official poverty line was derived from levels of food grain consumption that did not always reflect changes in consumption patterns, nor was it adjusted for inflation. In 2011, the central government adjusted the country's rural poverty line from 1,274 yuan per year in 2010 to 2,300 yuan (an increase of over 80 percent). When adjusted by the PPP of 2005, the new poverty line is equivalent to approximately US$1.80 per day – which is above the US$1.25 used by the World Bank for international poverty comparisons. Specifically, the World Bank has set $1.25 a day of consumption (rather than income) as the poverty rate. This rate is based on averaging the "poverty lines" in the world's 15 poorest countries. On the basis of this, the World Bank concludes that if, in 1981, roughly 52 percent of the global population lived in "absolute poverty" (meaning less than $1.25 a day), in 2012 the percentage had dropped to 20 percent. As a comparison, in the United States, the "poverty line" is set at around $11,500 per year for a one-person household. This translates into just over $30 a day.

4. Ding and He (2016, 9) note that the Urban Household Survey (UHS) is conducted by the National Bureau of Statistics (NBS) of China. The UHS is based on a multi-stage probabilistic sample and stratified design, similar to that used in the Current Population Surveys (CPS) in the US. The UHS provides detailed information about income, consumption expenditure, and the demographic characteristics of household members at the household and individual levels. In that sense, it can be viewed as the Chinese counterpart of a combination of CPS and Consumer Expenditure Survey (CEX) in the United States.

5. In the Asian region, the Asian Development Bank reports that "Inequality widened in 11 of the 28 economies with comparable data, including the three most populous countries and drivers of the region's rapid growth – the PRC, India, and Indonesia. From the early 1990s to the late 2000s, the Gini coefficient – a common measure of inequality – worsened from 32 to 43 in the PRC, from 33 to 37 in India, and from 29 to 39 in Indonesia. Treating developing Asia as a single unit, its Gini coefficient went from 39 to 46 in that period" (ADB 2012, xviii).

6. Ravallion (2011) has noted that the existence of a trade-off between growth and inequality is far from obvious with regard to China. First, the more rapid periods of economic growth in China did not translate into more rapid increases in inequality, while periods of falling inequality (1981–1985 and 1995–1998) came with the highest average growth in average household income. And second, provinces that experienced more rapid rural income growth did not see a concomitant sharp rise in income inequality.

7. It is estimated that during the height of SOE restructuring from 1997 to 2002, more than 35 million SOE workers were laid off.

8. Chinese trade unions have nominal authority and are hamstrung in their ability to fight for and defend workers' rights because they are subordinate to the Communist Party and the government.

9. "Local governments" is a broad term that includes the province, prefecture, county and township levels.

10. Song (2013, 295) notes that "as a result of the decentralized fiscal system, the share of central government revenues dropped sharply from the mid-1980s to 1993. Specifically, the central share of the government's budgetary revenues dropped from about 40 percent in the mid-1980s to only 22 percent in 1993, while the central share of expenditure decreased quickly from 55 percent in 1981 to 28 percent in 1993. In 1994, the central government implemented a *tax sharing reform* ... to give the central government a larger share of the total revenue ... However, the expenditure assignment did not recentralize accordingly ... that is, the expenditure decentralization continued even after the 1994 fiscal reform."

11. "As of 2010, there were 50 million mostly low-skilled, disabled or unwell people in China receiving the stipend at a cost equivalent to 0.14 per cent of GDP – tiny by any measure of global social welfare spending" (see David Green, 2017). "Getting Paid to Do Nothing: Why the Idea of China's Dibao Is Catching On," *South China Morning Post*, 14 April. www.scmp.com/week-asia/article/2087486/getting-paid -do-nothing-why-idea-chinas-dibao-catching.

12. According to a recent report, "Regional governments set up more than 10,000 local financing units to fund construction projects after they were barred from directly issuing bonds under a 1994 budget law. Local-government debt swelled to 17.9 trillion yuan ($2.96 trillion) as of June, compared with 10.7 trillion yuan at the end of 2010, according to data compiled by the National Audit Office." "China LGFV Sells First Dollar Bond as Yuan Borrowing Costs Rise," 2014, *Bloomberg News*, January 2. www.bloomberg.com/news/print/2014-01-02/china-lgfv-sells-first-dol lar-bond-as-yuan-borrowing-costs-rise.html.

13. This is in sharp contrast to the tax structure in OECD countries, which depends heavily on income and property tax as the sources of revenue. Lam and Wingender (2015, 4) note that "Indirect tax on goods and services, including the VAT and business operation tax, however, accounts for more than half of tax revenue ... Direct taxes such as personal income tax and corporate income tax account for a small fraction of tax revenue, much lower than the OECD average." For data on China, see "China's Tax Structure in 2012." http://szs.mof.gov.cn/zhengwuxinxi/ gongzuodongtai/201301/t20130123_729605.html.

14. Lardy notes that the amount of household deposits is around five times higher than the amount of their bank borrowing – hence, his argument about a de facto redistribution of income from households.

15. Furthermore, the absence of sophisticated financial intermediation contributes to high level of savings. For example, private companies are forced to save a significant proportion of their earnings to finance future investment, as access to bank lending can be unpredictable. Also, the relative lack of consumer credit fosters precautionary savings.

16. Russian President Dmitry Medvedev on several occasions has noted that the dollar system is "flawed" and that a new supranational currency should be created. Similarly, a senior economic adviser to Indian Prime Minister Manmohan Singh has urged the government to diversify its $264.6 billion foreign exchange reserves (2008 figures) and hold fewer dollars.

17. The Chiang Mai Initiative was initially set up as a set of bilateral currency swap lines in the wake of the Asian crisis. Specifically, the initiative was designed to prevent a sudden run on financial assets that wreaked havoc on Asian economies in the late 1990s.

18. Of course, China's contribution of $38.4 billion to the fund was made in US dollars, as its own currency is not fully convertible.

19. It is not the case that countries caught in a middle-income trap will not experience any growth. Rather, growth will continue, but at a pace that is much lower than if these countries had graduated to the high-income level.

20. Malkin and Spiegel's (2012, 2) predictions are based on broad statistical analysis. Namely, they divide China's provinces into high- and low-income, and then, using data from a group of selected high-growth Asian economies (Hong Kong, Japan, Korea, and Taiwan from 1950 to 2009), conduct statistical analysis to predict expansion rates for both the high- and low-income provinces based on their current income levels. The authors note that "our results indicate that growth of the wealthier portion of China is likely to slow, but substantial room remains for continued growth in China's interior. For example, among the advanced Chinese provinces, average growth is predicted to slow to 7 percent in the five years beginning in 2016. However, growth among China's emerging provinces is not expected to fall to that rate until sometime during the five years beginning in 2024. Thus, the emerging Chinese provinces are predicted to enjoy more than an additional decade of high growth before succumbing to the middle-income trap."

4 DEMOCRACY, PROSPERITY, AND INEQUALITY IN INDIA

1. In 2012, India's $4.7 trillion economy (in purchasing power terms) became the third-largest in the world after it surpassed Japan. The largest is the United States, followed by China. Arvind Subramanian (2013), "Deepening US-India Trade Relations," Congressional Testimony before the Ways and Means Committee of the United States Congress, hearing on "US-India Trade Relations," March 13 (available at Peterson Institute for International Economics, www.iie.org).

2. The government's countercyclical fiscal policy in response to the global financial crisis helped to reverse the decline in the central government's fiscal deficit, which had increased to 7 percent of GDP in 2008 (see Sharma, 2014a, chapter 7). By mid-2017, the deficit had declined to around 3.8 percent of GDP (due to the government's fiscal consolidation policies and lower global oil prices) – albeit, it is still above the 3 percent ceiling as stipulated by the Fiscal Responsibility and Budget Management Act of 2003.

3. However, growth declined to under 7 percent in 2016–2017 due to slower export growth, reduction in both public and private investment, and the demonetization of large rupee notes, which has adversely impacted economic activity.

4. It should be noted that, given the lack of reliable income, wage, and asset data in India, income and wealth inequality is extremely difficult to measure. Income tax data (which Piketty heavily relies on) cannot be relied on in the case of India. After all, in 2013, India's then finance minister Palaniappan Chidambaram famously stated that 2.89 percent of the population (about 36 million people) had filed their income taxes. Also, the more accessible household consumption expenditure data (collected by the National Sample Survey Organization (NSSO) every five years) can capture consumption inequality, but it is not always useful in measuring income levels because consumption expenditure (as a share of household income) tends to decline with increase in income.

5. Total household assets consist of "physical assets like land, buildings, livestock, agricultural machinery and implements, non-farm business equipment, all transport equipment, durable household goods and financial assets like dues receivable on loans advanced in cash or in kind, shares in companies and cooperative societies, banks, national saving certificates and the like, deposits in companies, banks, post offices and with individuals."

6. Net worth is defined as the total household assets net of the indebtedness of households.

7. Passed into law in 2005, the MGNREGA, for example, is designed to provide rural households with at least 100 days (out of a year) of guaranteed wage employment. MGNREGA's budget for 2012–2013 was US$5.28 billion, or 0.28 per cent of GDP. The central government covers 90 percent of program costs. Although the Act provides all rural households with a right to 100 days per year of unskilled employment, state governments have authority to set MGNREGA wages equal to or above the minimum wage for unskilled workers.

8. In fact, India's leap into services fundamentally challenges the long-held assumptions of economic theory that maintain that technology, capital, and labor are immobile and that low-wage countries receive more benefits by concentrating on labor-intensive production – leaving innovation and capital-intensive production to the advanced economies. Global economic integration has not only enabled India to defy earlier assumptions by making the once "non-tradable" service jobs in developed economies into tradable ones, it has also made possible the cross-border exchange of tradable manufactured goods.

9. It has long been recognized that manufacturing growth is a prerequisite for development, especially in labor-abundant economies (Kuznets 1966; Chenery and Syrquin 1975).

10. According to the Government of India's "National Industrial Classification of 2008," services include:

- Wholesale and retail trade; repair of motor vehicles and motorcycles
- Transportation and storage
- Accommodation and food service activities
- Information and communication
- Financial and insurance activities
- Real estate activities
- Professional, scientific, and technical activities
- Administrative and support services
- Public administration and defense; compulsory social security
- Education
- Human health and social work activities
- Arts, entertainment, and recreation
- Other service activities
    - Activities of households as employers; undifferentiated goods and services producing activities of households for own use
    - Activities of extraterritorial organizations and bodies

Original Source: National Industrial Classification 2008,
http://mospi.nic.in/Mospi_New/upload/nic_2008_17apr09.pdf
Cited in Mukherjee (2013, 2).

11. McKinsey Global Institute. 2014. *From Poverty to Empowerment: India's Imperative for Jobs, Growth, and Effective Basic Services*, McKinsey & Company. February, www.mckinsey.com/mgi.

12. International Labor Organization. 2012. Department of Statistics, "Statistical Update on Employment in the Informal Economy," June. http://laborsta.ilo.org/applv8/data/INFORMAL_ECONOMY/2012–06Statistical%20update%20-%20v2.pdf.

13. In fiscal year 2015 (ending 31 March 2016), FDI increased by 26 percent when compared to the previous year.

14. "Foreign direct investment, net inflows (BoP, current US$)," World Bank, accessed February 21, 2017, http://data.worldbank.org/indicator/BX.KLT.DINV.CD.WD.

15. Department of Industrial Policy and Promotion. 2016. "Fact Sheets on FDI from May 2014 to September 2016," New Delhi: Ministry of Commerce and Industry.

16. Article 19(c) of the Constitution of India guarantees the right to association to all citizens. However, given the central and state governments increasing involvement in industrial relations, most unions have been closely aligned with major political parties. In fact, every major political party in India has an affiliated trade union which is led by party members. The BJP's affiliated union is the Bharatiya Mazdoor Sangh (BMS), and the Indian National Trade Union Congress (INTUC) is affiliated with the Indian National Congress or the Congress Party. As a result unions have become relatively centralized and unrepresentative – guided more by the parties political agenda than the immediate and long-term interests of rank and file union members.

17. Modi's BJP has a majority in the lower house of parliament (the Lok Sabha), the bill cannot become law unless it also receives assent in the upper house, the Rajya Sabha, where the BJP does not have the majority to push it through.

18. A committee to review the GST was set-up in 2000 under Prime Minister A.B. Vajpayee of the BJP. The committee submitted its report in 2009 which was supported by the then Congress government and slated for implementation in April 2010. However, the BJP-led Opposition boycotted Parliament and the bill was never implemented. When the BJP came back to power, it proposed to enact the bill. However, the Congress party decided to boycott the bill in the Rajya Sabha.

19. The World Bank data is based on the period 2009–2013. See, The World Bank. 2013. "Ease of Doing Business." Also see, World Bank, *Doing Business Project*. http://www.doingbusiness.org/.

20. US trade preference programs such as the Generalized System of Preferences (GSP) established by the Trade Act of 1974, was designed to assist the world's poorest countries access to the US market. GSP assists by eliminating duties on up to 5,000 types of products when imported from one of 122 designated beneficiary countries. The GSP program expired on August 1, 2013 after Congress did not extend the program.

21. E. Ashley Wills, 2013. "India Undermines Its Own Economy," *U.S. News and World Report*, September 27.

22. It should be noted that India which is neither a signatory to the Nuclear Nonproliferation Treaty nor a member of the Nuclear Suppliers Group was fortunate to get this agreement – which was endorsed by the US Congress in 2008. Arguably, India's Civil Liability for Nuclear Damage Bill which makes reactor

suppliers and operators liable for damages caused by reactor accident or failure may not be consistent with the Convention on Supplementary Compensation for Nuclear Damage.

23. A large percentage of India's fresh food produce rots away because of poor transport and rat-infested storage facilities. Foreign super-stores such as Wal-Mart by providing good storage would have helped to reduce waste, and thereby price.

24. Unable to arrive at a consensus on how best to open India's huge retail market, New Delhi finally passed the buck to India's 28 state governments and union territories by giving them the power to either allow or prohibit FDI up to 51 percent in multi-brand retail stores. Moreover, foreign retailers are required to get 30 percent of their sourcing from small and mid-size domestic enterprises. The previous Congress government-led in New Delhi was among the first to give permission to foreign retailers to set-up shop in its territory. However, the AAP which sees the world as characterized by a Manichean struggle between the good (Indian) and the bad (foreign), overturned this.

25. www.waysandmeans.house.gov/ (United States House and Means Committee).

26. Although, both India and the United States adhere to the WTO Agreement on the "Trade-Related Aspects of Intellectual Property Rights (TRIPS) Agreement," India has been accused (again with some justification) for its inadequate intellectual property rights protection and enforcement.

27. Steve Minter, 2013. "India's Trade Practices 'Discriminatory and Unfair,' US Businesses Charge," *IndustryWeek*, June 18, www.industryweek.com/trade/indi as-trade-practices-discriminatory-and-unfair-us-businesses-charge (accessed January 15, 2014).

28. India has not only argued that its solar energy policies are legal because WTO "government procurement rules" permit countries to exempt certain projects from "non-discrimination obligations," it has also accused Washington of hypocrisy claiming that the US continues to provide numerous "incentives" and "subsidies" to its domestic companies involved in green technology.

29. The Indian government has (and continues to) complain about the restrictive US immigration policy regarding high skilled workers. No doubt, both sides will benefit from a more accommodative H-1B visa program (for professional specialty workers) and L visas for intra-company transferees. It is useful to keep in mind that the WTO views the employment of temporary foreign workers as "importation of services" and, therefore, a trade issue. However, the US Congress has tended to view the matter as an immigration issue. Also, India has raised objection regarding the deduction of social security taxes from the salary of Indian nationals temporarily working in the United States.

30. See, Sadanand Dhume, Julissa Milligan, Aparna Mathur, and Hemal Shah, 2013. "Falling short: How Bad Economic Choices threaten the US-India Relationship and India's Rise," American Enterprise Institute, October 8.

31. The USITC is an independent and nonpartisan federal agency whose major task is to engage in fact-finding. The USITC is tasked to enumerate all the restrictive trade and investment policies that the Indian government maintains or has recently erected, including its impact on the US economy. The USITC report will be available by 30 November 2014.

32. Under WTO rules, member states have 60 days to reach a resolution. However, if no resolution is reached, the US, in this case, can request the WTO to establish an independent panel to determine whether India has violated WTO trade rules.

33. The September 2012 program involved purchasing $40 billion in mortgage-backed securities (MBS) every month. It was expanded in December 2012 to include $45 billion in monthly Treasury security purchases.

34. However, China's robust current account surplus and huge foreign exchange reserves made the economy better weather the announcement.

35. Specifically, with the US dollar functioning as the global reserve currency means that shifts in the dollar's value directly affects expectations for borrowing costs globally. Thus, any rise in US interest rates means higher borrowing costs elsewhere in the world.

36. Dani Rodrik and Arvind Subramanian, 2014. "Emerging Markets' Victimhood Narrative," *Bloomberg*, January 31. www.iie.com/publications/opeds/oped.cfm? ResearchID=2561.

37. Reserve Bank of India. 2013. "India's External Debt end-March 2013," June 27. www.rbi.org.in; also see, Government of India. 2012. *India's External Debt: A Status Report, 2011–12*. New Delhi: Ministry of Finance, Department of Economic Affairs (External Debt Management Unit), August. www.finmin.nic.in.

38. As Subramanian (2013) aptly notes, "to hedge against inflation and general uncertainty, consumers have furiously acquired gold, rendering the country reliant on foreign capital to finance its trade deficit." Similarly, a recent IMF study notes that "of the several reasons cited for the increased demand for gold, there is strong evidence that gold is increasingly being used as a hedge against inflation. Gold imports are highly correlated with households' inflation expectations." IMF. 2014. "India: Selected Issues," IMF Country Report No. 14/58, Washington, DC: International Monetary Fund, p. 6.

39. India's current account deficit (or excess of imports over exports and remittances) in 2012/13 was 4.8 percent of GDP, or $87.8 billion. This is more than double the 2.5 percent the RBI considers sustainable.

40. India's total fiscal deficit (both the federal and state government) is among the highest in G-20 countries. In 2016, India's general government debt to GDP ratio stood at 68.5 percent – much higher than other emerging market economies such as China (46.3 percent) and Indonesia (27.5 percent).

41. For example, the BJP when in power championed major reforms to the retail sector, but strongly opposed it when they were in opposition and the reform measures were tabled by the Congress-led government.

42. The term *backward castes* (also referred to in the 1950 constitution as "Other Backward Classes") is used to refer to a broad range of subcastes of intermediate ritual status in the Hindu caste hierarchy. These castes fall between the elite upper castes (the forward castes) and the lower, Scheduled Castes (previously known as "untouchables," now often referred to as Dalits, or "oppressed ones") and Scheduled Tribes. The Indian Constitution recognizes the backward castes and the Scheduled Castes and Scheduled Tribes as "disadvantaged lower castes" or "weaker sections" and has allowed them remedial solutions, such as reserving legislative seats, government posts, and places in educational institutions for these groups. Yet it is important to note that the low castes are not a monolithic group. Divided into literally thousands of subcastes, they, like the upper castes, are governed by strict rules and ritual taboos.

43. The Dalits, or the former "untouchables" in the Hindu caste order, are referred to as Scheduled Castes. They represent the most exploited and the poorest sectors in society.

44. "Social capital" refers to the institutions, relationships, and standards that shape and determine a society's social interactions.
45. Chhibber (1999) has questioned the conventional wisdom by arguing that India's civil society is actually marginal. The dearth of civic associations has forced India's political parties to mobilize society on the basis of caste, language and other ascriptive identities.
46. Although the upper-caste Hindus were gradually eased out of political power in the major southern states in the 1960s and 1970s, this process did not take place in the Hindi-speaking heartland until the 1980s. Squeezed by the assertiveness of the lower castes, the upper castes, traditionally supporters of the Congress Party, have flocked to the BJP because it is widely perceived to be the true protector of their interests. It is important to note that the BJP is part of a larger "Hindu family." The parent organization, the Rashtriya Swayamsevak Sangh, founded in 1925, stands for the consolidation of all Hindus into a united community. The BJP's main goal is to unite Hindus politically to achieve national power and to transform India into a Hindu nation-state. The Vishwa Hindu Parishad (VHP) is involved in mass-mobilization activities, while the Bajrang Dal serves as the armed wing, often using violence and intimidation against opponents.
47. For example, making-up around 20 percent of the population (and it some states as high as 30 percent), dalits comprise a potent political force with their political party, the Bahujan Samaj Party (BSP, Majority People's Party) controlling the government of Uttar Pradesh (India's most populous state), on four different occasions in recent years. Yet, maintaining "dalit unity" has not been easy. Caste, as Ambedkar once observed is structured along an "ascending scale of reverence and a descending scale of contempt." Thus, despite the rhetorical commitment to "dalit unity," in practice this means that castes within the broader Dalit caste-system look down upon and discriminate against members they perceive to be beneath them (Gundimeda 2016).
48. Comparable reservations for the Scheduled Castes and Scheduled Tribes were also made by state governments.
49. Although Singh declared that the reservations were being implemented to correct social injustices, his political opponents saw it as a cynical move to shore up his support among the backward castes.
50. Of course, everything is politically expedient in the name of competitive populism – from costly loan waiver for farmers (including India's agriculture minister even urging farmers to stop repayments to "unauthorized" lenders and ordering the police to protect defaulting farmers from debt-collectors), subsidies for energy and fertilizer, promise of free water and electricity; reservations for the low-caste employees for promotions in government jobs.
51. India's food security program includes public procurement, storage and distribution of wheat and rice – which are procured from farmers at a guaranteed Minimum Support Price (MSP). Public stocks are classified into "strategic" and "operational stocks." A strategic stock is a buffer designed to stabilize grain supply and prices and operational stock feeds the Public Distribution System (PDS) which provides grain to the poor at subsidized prices. In 2014–15, the food subsidy bill totaled 0.8 percent of GDP.
52. The National Food Security Bill was first proposed by the National Advisory Council headed by Congress President Sonia Gandhi. In October 2010, the basic framework of the Bill which envisaged providing food security to 75 percent of the

country's population (90 percent in rural areas and 50 percent in urban areas) via subsidized food under Targeted Public Distribution System (TPDS) was handed to Prime Minister Manmohan Singh. In turn, the prime minister set up an expert panel to study the proposal. Among other things, the panel recommended coverage to 67 percent of India's population. In September 2013, India's Parliament unanimously passed the National Food Security Act (NFSA) with the stated goal to provide a legal right to food at subsidized prices to 67 percent of India's population. Indeed, given NFSA's avowed aim to "provide for food and nutritional security ... by ensuring access to adequate quantity of quality food at affordable prices" so that people can "live a life with dignity," NFSA is committed to providing staple foodgrains (rice, wheat, and coarse cereals) at highly subsidized prices, including maternity benefits of Rs. 6,000 to pregnant and lactating mothers.

53. The Food Security Bill is an extension of the Targeted Public Distribution System (PDS), via which the Indian government (including many state governments) have been providing subsidized food. In fact, PDS is India's largest food subsidy program which provides households subsidized food (wheat, rice, cooking oils, sugar), including cooking fuel such as kerosene. The PDS also functions as a minimum support price mechanism for farmers.

5 PROSPERITY WITH EQUALITY: FUTURE DIRECTIONS

1. *The Economist* (2014), "Capitalism and Its Critics: A Modern Marx," May 3, www .economist.com/node/21601512/print (accessed July 7, 2015).
2. For details, see, www.pmjdy.gov.in/scheme, and http://pmjandhanyojana.co.in/prad han-mantri-mudra-yojana-bank.
3. *Bolsa Família* is not the only such cash transfer program. Mexico's *Oportunidades* covers about a quarter of the population and provides a 20 percent increment over pre-transfer income on average at a cost of 0.5 percent of GNP in 2006 (Fiszbein et al. 2009).

Bibliography

Abdelal, Rawi. 2007. *Capital Rules: The Construction of Global Finance*. Cambridge, MA: Harvard University Press.

Abramowitz, Alan. 2011. *The Disappearing Center: Engaged Citizens, Polarization and American Democracy*. New Haven, CT: Yale University Press.

Acemoglu, Daron. 2009. *Modern Economic Growth*. Princeton, NJ: Princeton University Press.

2008. "Oligarchic vs. Democratic Societies," *Journal of the European Economic Association*, vol. 6, no. 1, pp. 1–44.

Acemoglu, Daron and David Autor. 2011. "Skills, Tasks and Technologies: Implications for Employment and Earnings," NBER Working Paper No. 16082. Cambridge, MA: National Bureau of Economic Research.

Acemoglu, Daron and Pascual Restrepo. 2016. "The Race between Machine and Man: Implications of Technology for Growth, Factor Shares and Employment," NBER Working Paper No. 22252, May. Cambridge, MA: National Bureau of Economic Research.

Acemoglu, Daron and James Robinson. 2012. *Why Nations Fail: The Origins of Power, Prosperity and Poverty*. New York, NY: Crown Business.

2006. *Economic Origins of Dictatorship and Democracy*. New York, NY: Cambridge University Press.

Achen, Christopher and Larry Bartels. 2016. *Democracy for Realists: Why Elections Do Not Produce Responsive Government*. Princeton, NJ: Princeton University Press.

ADB (Asian Development Bank). 2012a. *Asian Development Outlook, 2012: Confronting Rising Inequality in Asia*. Manila: Asian Development Bank.

2012b. *Framework of Inclusive Growth Indicators 2012: Key Indicators for Asia and the Pacific Special Supplement*. Manila: Asian Development Bank.

Ahuja, Ashvin, Nigel Chalk, Malhar Nabar, Papa N'Diaye, and Nathan Porter. 2012. "An End to China's Imbalances?" IMF Working Paper, WP/12/100. Asia and Pacific Department. Washington, DC: International Monetary Fund.

Akcigit, Ufuk, Salome Baslandze, and Stefanie Stantcheva. 2016. "Taxation and the International Mobility of Inventors," *American Economic Review*, vol. 106, no. 10, pp. 2930–2981.

Akerlof, George and Robert Shiller. 2010. *Animal Spirits: How Human Psychology Drives the Economy, and Why It Matters for Global Capitalism*. Princeton, NJ: Princeton University Press.

Ales, Laurence and Christopher Sleet. 2016. "Taxing Top CEO Incomes," *American Economic Review*, vol. 106, no. 11, pp. 3331–3366.

Alesina, Alberto and Edward Glaeser. 2004. *Fighting Poverty in the US and Europe: A World of Difference*. New York, NY: Oxford University Press.

Alesina, Alberto and Howard Rosenthal. 1995. *Partisan Politics, Divided Government, and the Economy*. New York, NY: Cambridge University Press.

Alichi, Ali, Kory Kantenga, and Juan Sole. 2016. "Income Polarization in the United States," IMF Working Paper, WP/16/21, June. Washington, DC: International Monetary Fund.

Alon, Titan, Galina Hale, and Joao Santos. 2010. "What Is China's Capital Seeking in a Global Environment?," FRBSF Economic Letter, March 22, San Francisco, CA: Federal Reserve Bank of San Francisco.

Amable, Bruno. 2003. *The Diversity of Modern Capitalism*. Oxford: Oxford University Press.

Anand, Rahul, Volodymyr Tulin, and Naresh Kumar. 2014. "India: Defining and Explaining Inclusive Growth and Poverty Reduction," IMF Working Paper, WP/14/63, April. Washington, DC: International Monetary Fund.

Anderson, Benedict. 1983. *Imagined Communities: Reflections on the Origin and Spread of Nationalism*. London: Verso.

Andrews, David. 2008. *Orderly Change: International Monetary Relations since Bretton Woods*. Ithaca, NY: Cornell University Press.

Aslund, Anders. 2007. *Russia's Capitalist Revolution*. Washington, DC: Peterson Institute for International Economics.

Athreya, Kartik. 2016. "The Payoff from the Earned Income Tax Credit," *Econ Focus*, Second Quarter, Federal Reserve Bank of Richmond, p. 40.

Atkinson, Anthony. 2014. *Inequality: What Can Be Done?* Cambridge, MA: Harvard University Press.

Atkinson, Anthony, Thomas Piketty, and Emmanuel Saez. 2011. "Top Incomes in the Long Run of History," *Journal of Economic Literature*, vol. 49, no. 1, pp. 3–71.

Auten, Gerald, Geoffrey Gee, and Nicholas Turner. 2013. "New Perspectives on Income Mobility and Inequality," *National Tax Journal*, vol. 66, no. 4, December, pp. 893–912.

Autor, David. 2010. "The Polarization of Job Opportunities in the U.S. Labor Market." The Hamilton Project and The Center for American Progress, April, pp. 1–40.

Autor, David, David Dorn, and Gordon Hanson. 2016. "The China Shock: Learning from Labor Market Adjustment to Large Changes in Trade," NBER Working Paper, no. 21906, Cambridge, MA: National Bureau of Economic Research. www.nber.org/papers/w21906.

Bajpai, Nirupam, Anjali Chowfla, and Srilekha Jayanthi. 2013. "Inequality: A China and India Perspective," Working Paper No. 7, February. Ithaca, NY: Columbia Global Centers: Columbia University.

Baker, Dean. 2016. "The Upward Redistribution of Income: Are Rents the Story?," *Review of Radical Political Economics*, vol. 48, no. 4, pp. 529–543.

Balakrishnan, Ravi, Chad Steinberg, and Murtaza Syed. 2013. "The Elusive Quest for Inclusive Growth: Growth, Poverty, and Inequality," IMF Working Paper, WP/13/152, June, Washington DC: International Monetary Fund.

Baldwin, Peter. 1990. *The Politics of Social Solidarity: Class Bases of the European Welfare State, 1875–1975*. New York, NY: Cambridge University Press.

Baldwin, Richard. 2016. *The Great Convergence: Information Technology and the New Globalization*. Cambridge, MA: Harvard University Press.

Bardhan, Pranab. 2009a. "How Unequal a Country Is India?" *Business Standard*, September 5. www.business-standard.com/article/printer-friendly-version?article_id=109090500021_1.

2009b. "India and China: Governance Issues and Development," *The Journal of Asian Studies*, vol. 68, no. 2, May, pp. 347–357.

Barro, Robert. 2015. "Convergence and Modernization," *The Economic Journal*, vol. 125, no. 585, June, pp. 911–942.

Barros, Ricardo Paes de, M. de Carvalho, S. Franco, and R. Mendoca. 2010. "Markets, the State, and the Dynamics of Inequality in Brazil." In L. F. Lopez-Calva and Nora Lustig, eds., *Declining Inequality in Latin America: A Decade of Progress?* Washington, DC: The Brookings Institution Press.

Bartels, Larry. 2008. *Unequal Democracy: The Political Economy of the New Gilded Age*. Princeton, NJ: Princeton University Press.

Bartlett, Donald and James Steele. 2012. *The Betrayal of the American Dream*. New York, NY: PublicAffairs.

Basole, Amit. 2017. "What Does the Rural Economy Need?," *Economic and Political Weekly*, vol. 52, no. 9, March 4, pp. 40–43.

2014. "Dynamics of Income Inequality in India: Insights from Top World Incomes Database," *Economic and Political Weekly*, vol. 49, no. 40, October 4, pp. 14–17.

Basu, Kaushik. 2008. "India's Dilemmas: The Political Economy of Policymaking in a Globalized World," *The Economic and Political Weekly*, vol. 43, no. 5, February 2–8, pp. 53–62.

Baumol, William, Robert Litan, and Carl Schramm. 2007. *Good Capitalism, Bad Capitalism, and the Economics of Growth and Prosperity*. New Haven, CT: Yale University Press.

Bems, Rudolfs, Robert C. Johnson, and Kei-Mu Yi. 2010. "Demand Spillovers and the Collapse of Trade in the Global Recession," *IMF Economic Review*, vol. 58, no. 2, December, pp. 295–326.

Bergsten, Fred. 2016. "China Is No Longer Manipulating Its Currency," November 18. Washington, DC: Peterson Institute for International Economics. https://piie.com/blogs/trade-investment-policy-watch/china-no-longer-manipulating-its-currency (accessed November 22, 2016).

Berman, Sheri. 2006. *The Primacy of Politics: Social Democracy and the Making of Europe's Twentieth Century*. New York, NY: Cambridge University Press.

Bernanke, Benjamin. 2012. "U.S. Monetary Policy and International Implications," Speech delivered at the "Challenges of the Global Financial System: Risks and Governance under Evolving Globalization," a High-Level Seminar sponsored by Bank of Japan–International Monetary Fund, Tokyo, October 14. www.federalreserve.gov/newsevents/speech/bernanke20121014a.htm.

2005. "The Global Saving Glut and the U.S. Current Account Deficit," speech given on March 10, at the Sandridge Lecture, Virginia Association of Economists, Richmond, VA. www.federalreserve.gov/boarddocs/speeches/2005/20050414/default.htm.

Bhagwati, Jagdish. 2004. *In Defense of Globalization*. New York, NY: Oxford University Press.

Bhagwati, Jagdish and Arvind Panagariya. 2014. *Why Growth Matters: How Economic Growth in India Reduced Poverty and the Lessons for Other Developing Countries.* New York, NY: Public Affairs.

2012. *India's Reforms: How They Produced Inclusive Growth.* New York, NY: Oxford University Press.

Bivens, Josh. 2011. *Failure by Design: The Story behind America's Broken Economy.* Ithaca: NY: Cornell University Press.

Bonica, Adam. 2013. "Ideology and Interests in the Political Marketplace." *American Journal of Political Science*, vol. 57, no. 2, pp. 294–311.

Bonica, Adam, Nolan McCarty, Keith Poole, and Howard Rosenthal. 2013. "Why Hasn't Democracy Slowed Rising Inequality?" *Journal of Economic Perspectives*, vol. 27, no. 3, pp. 103–124.

Bosworth, Barry. 2012. "The Coming Demographic Impact on China's Growth: The Age Factor in the Middle-Income Trap," *Asian Economic Papers*, vol. 11, no. 1, Winter/Spring, pp. 114–117.

Bourguignon, Francois. 2015. *The Globalization of Inequality.* Princeton, NJ: Princeton University Press.

Bremmer, Ian. 2014. "The New Rules of Globalization," *Harvard Business Review*, January-February, pp. 103–107.

2012. *Every Nation for Itself: Winners and Losers in a G-Zero World.* New York, NY: Portfolio.

2010. *The End of the Free Market: Who Wins the War between States and Corporations.* New York: Portfolio.

2009. "State Capitalism Comes of Age: The End of the Free Market," *Foreign Affairs*, vol. 88, no. 3, May–June, pp. 40–55.

Bremmer, Ian and Nouriel Roubini. 2011. "A G-Zero World," *Foreign Affairs*, March/ April. vol. 90, no. 2, pp. 2–7.

Bricker, Jesse, Lisa J. Dettling, Alice Henriques, Joanne W. Hsu, Kevin B. Moore, John Sabelhaus, Jeffrey Thompson, and Richard A. Windle. 2014. "Changes in U.S. Family Finances from 2010 to 2013: Evidence from the Survey of Consumer Finances." *Federal Reserve Bulletin*, 100 September, pp. 1–41. www .federalreserve.gov/pubs/bulletin/2014/articles/scf/scf.htm.

Bricker, Jesse, Jacob Krimmel, Alice Henriques and John Sabelhaus, 2016. "Measuring Income and Wealth at the Top Using Administrative and Survey Data," *Brookings Papers on Economic Activity*, Spring, pp. 261–331.

Brynjolfsson, Erik and Andrew McAfee. 2014. *The Second Machine Age: Work, Progress, and Prosperity in a Time of Brilliant Technologies.* New York, NY: W. W. Norton.

Burrows, Matthew and Jennifer Harris, 2009. "Revisiting the Future: Geopolitical Effects of the Financial Crisis," *Washington Quarterly*, vol. 32, no. 2, April, pp. 27–38.

Burtless, Gary. "Income Growth and Income Inequality: The Facts May Surprise You," January 6, (2014). www.brookings.edu/research/opinions/2014/01/06-income-gains -and-inequality-burtless.

Cai, Fang. 2012. "Is There a Middle-Income Trap?: Theories, Experiences and Relevance to China," *China and World Economy*, vol. 20, no. 1, January–February, pp. 49–61.

Campbell, John. 2004. *Institutional Change and Globalization.* Princeton, NJ: Princeton University Press.

Carnes, Nicholas. 2013. *White Collar Government: The Hidden Role of Class in Economic Policy Making*. Chicago, IL: University of Chicago Press.

Cashin, Paul, Kamiar Mohaddes, and Mehdi Raissi. 2016. "China's Slowdown and Global Financial Market Volatility: Is World Growth Losing Out?" IMF Working Paper, WP/16/63. Asia and Pacific Department, Washington, DC: International Monetary Fund.

Cassidy, John. 2009. *How Markets Fail: The Logic of Economic Calamities*. New York, NY: Farrar, Straus and Giroux.

Cavaille, Charlotte and Kris-Stella Trump. 2015. "Support for the Welfare State in Western Democracies: The Two Dimensions of Redistributive Attitudes," *Journal of Politics*, vol. 77, no. 1, pp. 146–160.

Chen, Shaohua and Martin Ravallion. 2010. "The Developing World Is Poorer than We Thought, but No Less Successful in the Fight against Poverty," *Quarterly Journal of Economics*, vol. 125, no. 4, pp. 1577–1625.

Chenery, Hollis and Moshe Syrquin. 1975. *Patterns of Development, 1950–1970*. London: Oxford University Press.

Chetty, Raj, Nathaniel Hendren, Patrick Kline, and Emmanuel Saez. 2014a. "Where Is the Land of Opportunity: The Geography of Intergenerational Mobility in the United States," *Quarterly Journal of Economics*, vol. 129, no. 4, pp. 1553–1623.

Chetty, Raj, Nathaniel Hendren, Patrick Kline, Emmanuel Saez, and Nicholas Turner. 2014b. "Is The United States Still a Land of Opportunity: Recent Trends in Intergenerational Mobility." *American Economic Review: Papers & Proceedings*, vol. 104, no. 5, pp. 141–147.

Chhibber, Pradeep. 1999. *Democracy without Associations: Transformation of the Party System and Social Cleavages in India*. Ann Arbor, MI: The University of Michigan Press.

Chwieroth, Jeffrey. 2009. *Capital Ideas: The IMF and the Rise of Financial Liberalization*. Princeton, NJ: Princeton University Press.

Cline, William. 2010a. *Financial Globalization, Economic Growth and the Crisis of 2007–09*. Washington, DC: Peterson Institute for International Economics.

2010b. "Renminbi Undervaluation, China's Surplus and the US Trade Deficit," Policy Brief, no. PB10-20, August, Washington, DC: Institute for International Economics.

Collier, Ruth Berins. 1999. *Paths toward Democracy*. New York, NY: Cambridge University Press.

Congressional Budget Office. 2016. *The Distribution of Household Income and Federal Taxes, 2013*. June. Washington, DC: The Congress of the United States. www.cbo.gov/publication/51361.

2011. *Trends in the Distribution of Household Income between 1979 and 2007*. October, Washington, DC: The Congress of the United States. http://cbo.gov/sites/default/files/cbofiles/attachments/10-25-HouseholdIncome.pdf.

Congressional Research Service (CRS). 2016. "Foreign Holdings of Federal Debt," by Marc Labonte and Jared C. Nagel, CRS Report RS22331, March 28.

2013. "China's Holdings of U.S. Securities: Implications for the U.S. Economy," by Wayne Morrison and Marc Labonte, CRS Report RL34314, August 19.

Cook, Phillip and Robert H. Frank. 1995. *The Winner-Take-All Society*. New York, NY: Free Press.

Corak, Miles. 2013. "Income Inequality, Equality of Opportunity, and Intergenerational Mobility," *Journal of Economic Perspectives*, vol. 27, no. 3, Summer, pp. 79–102.

Cowen, Tyler. 2014. "All in All, a More Egalitarian World," The New York Times, July 20, p. BU6.
2011. "The Inequality That Matters," *The American Interest*, vol. 6, no. 3, January/February (internet edition). www.the-american-interest.com/2011/1/1/the-inequality-that-matters/.
Cozzi, Guido and Giammario Impullitti. 2016. "Globalization and Wage Polarization," *The Review of Economics and Statistics*, vol. 98, no. 5, December, pp. 984–1000.
Cramer-Walsh, Katherine. 2012. "Putting Inequality in Its Place: Rural Consciousness and the Power of Perspective," *American Political Science Review*, vol. 106, no. 3, pp. 517–532.
Credit Suisse. 2015a. Global Wealth Report 2015. October, Credit Suisse.
2015b. Global Wealth Databook 2015. October, Credit Suisse.
Crouch, Colin. 2005. *Capitalist Diversity and Change*. New York, NY: Oxford University Press.
Dabla-Norris, Era and Kalpana Kochhar. 2015. "India: In Search of the Drivers of the Next Wave of Growth," *India Review*, vol. 14, no. 1, pp. 153–173.
Dahl, Robert A. 1961. *Who Governs? Democracy and Power in an American City*. New Haven, CT: Yale University Press.
Danninger, Stephan. 2016, "What's Up with U.S. Wage Growth and Job Mobility?" IMF Working Paper, 16/122, Washington, DC: International Monetary Fund.
Datt, Gaurav and Martin Ravallion. 2002. "Is India's Economic Growth Leaving the Poor Behind?," *Journal of Economic Perspectives*, vol. 16, pp. 89–108.
Davis, Jonathan and Bhashkar Mazumder, 2017. "The Decline in Intergenerational Mobility After 1980," Opportunity and Inclusive Growth Institute at the Federal Reserve Bank of Minneapolis, Working Paper 17–21. www.chicagofed.org/~/media/publications/working-papers/2017/wp2017-05-pdf.pdf.
De Haan, Arjan. 2010. "A Defining Moment? China's Social Policy Response to the Financial Crisis," *Journal of International Development*, vol. 22, no. 6, August, pp. 758–771.
De Roy, Shantanu. 2017. "Economic Reforms and Agricultural Growth in India," *Economic and Political Weekly*, vol. LII, no. 9, March 7, pp. 67–72.
Deaton, Angus. 2013. *The Great Escape: Health, Wealth, and the Origins of Inequality*. Princeton, NJ: Princeton University Press.
Debacker, Jason, Bradley Heim, Vasia Panousi, Shanthi Ramnath, and Ivan Vidangos. 2013. "Rising Inequality: Transitory or Persistent? New Evidence from a Panel of U.S. Tax Returns, *Brookings Papers on Economic Activity*, Spring, pp. 67–142.
DeNavas-Walt, Carmen and Bernadette D. Proctor. 2015. *Income and Poverty in the United States: 2014*. US Census Bureau, Current Population Reports, P60-252, September, Washington, DC: US Government Printing Office.
Deng, Q. and S. Li. 2009. "What Lies behind Rising Earnings Inequality in Urban China? Regression-Based Decompositions," *CESifo Economic Studies*, vol. 55, nos. 3–4, pp. 598–623.
Deshpande, Ashwini and Rajesh Ramachandran. 2017. "Dominant or Backward? Political Economy of Demand for Quotas by Jats, Patels, and Marathas," *Economic and Political Weekly*, vol. LII, no. 19, May 18, pp. 81–92.
Diamond, Peter and Emmanuel Saez. 2011. "The Case for a Progressive Tax: From Basic Research to Policy Recommendations," *Journal of Economic Perspectives*, vol. 25, no. 4, pp. 165–190.

Dickson, Bruce. 2016. *Dictator's Dilemma: The Chinese Communist Party's Strategy for Survival.* New York, NY: Oxford University Press.

Ding, Haiyan and Hui He. 2016. "A Tale of Transition: An Empirical Analysis of Economic Inequality in Urban China, 1986–2009," IMF Working Paper, WP/16/239, August. Washington, DC: International Monetary Fund.

Dobson, Wendy. 2017. "China's State-Owned Enterprises and Canada's Foreign Direct Investment Policy," *Canadian Public Policy*, vol. 43, Supplement 2, April, pp. S29–S44.

Dollar, David. 2007. "Poverty, Inequality and Social Disparities during China's Economic Reform." World Bank Policy Research Working Paper, no. 4253, Washington, DC: The World Bank.

Domhoff, G. William. 2013. *Who Rules America: The Triumph of the Corporate Rich.* 7th ed. New York, NY: McGraw-Hill.

Dreze, Jean and Amartya Sen. 2013. *An Uncertain Glory: India and Its Contradictions.* Princeton, NJ: Princeton University Press.

Druck, Pablo, Nicolas E. Magud, and Rodrigo Mariscal. 2015. "Collateral Damage: Dollar Strength and Emerging Markets' Growth," IMF Working Paper, WP/15/17, July. Washington, DC: International Monetary Fund. www.imf.org/external/pubs/ft/wp/2015/wp15179.pdf.

Du, Ming. 2014. "China's State Capitalism and World Trade Law," *International and Comparative Law Quarterly*, vol. 63, no. 2, April, pp. 409–448.

Dunn, John. 2014. *Breaking Democracy's Spell.* New Haven, CT: Yale University Press.

Easterly, William. 2013. *The Tyranny of Experts: Economists, Dictators, and the Forgotten Rights of the Poor.* New York, NY: Basic Books.

The Economist. 2012. The Rise of State Capitalism (January 21, 2012). www.economist.com/node/21543160/print.

Eichengreen, Barry. 2015. *Hall of Mirrors: The Great Depression, the Great Recession, and the Uses – and Misuses – of History.* New York, NY: Oxford University Press.

2006. *The European Economy since 1945: Coordinated Capitalism and Beyond.* Princeton, NJ: Princeton University Press.

Eichengreen, Barry, Donghyun Park, and Kwanho Shin. 2013. "Growth Slowdowns Redux: New Evidence on the Middle-Income Trap," NBER Working Paper No. 18673, January.

2011. "When Fast Growing Economies Slow Down: International Evidence and Implications for China," NBER Working Paper No. 16919, March.

1996. *Globalizing Capital.* Princeton, NJ: Princeton University Press.

Esping-Andersen, Gosta. 1990. *The Three Worlds of Welfare Capitalism.* Princeton, NJ: Princeton University Press.

Fajgelbaum, Pablo and Amit Khandelwal. 2016. "Measuring the Unequal Gains from Trade," *Quarterly Journal of Economics*, vol. 131, no. 3, pp. 1113–1188.

Fei, John and Gustav Ranis. 1964. *Development of the Labor Surplus Economy.* New Haven, CT: Yale University Press.

Feldstein, Martin. 2008. "Resolving the Global Imbalance: Dollar and U.S. Savings Rate," *The Journal of Economic Perspectives*, vol. 22, no. 3, Summer, pp. 113–126.

Ferguson, Niall. 2008. *The Ascent of Money: A Financial History of the World.* New York, NY: Penguin Press.

Ferreira, F. H. G., P. Leite and M. Ravallion. 2010. "Poverty Reduction without Economic Growth? Explaining Brazil's Poverty Dynamics, 1985–2004," *Journal of Development Economics*, vol. 93, no. 1, pp. 20–36.

Fewsmith, Joseph. 2013. *The Logic and Limits of Political Reform in China*. New York, NY: Cambridge University Press.

Fewsmith, Joseph and Xiang Gao. 2014. "Local Governance in China: Incentives and Tensions." *Daedalus*, vol. 143, no. 2, Spring, pp. 170–183.

Fiszbein, Ariel, Norbert Schady, Francisco H. G. Ferreira, Margaret Grosh, Niall Keleher, Pedro Olinto, and Emmanuel Skoufias. 2009. *Conditional Cash Transfers: Reducing Present and Future Poverty*. Washington, DC: World Bank.

Ford, Martin. 2016. *The Rise of the Robots: Technology and the Threat of Mass Unemployment*. London: Oneworld Publications.

Formisano, Ronald. 2015. *Plutocracy in America: How Increasing Inequality Destroys the Middle Class and Exploits the Poor*. Baltimore, MD: John Hopkins University Press.

Frankfurt, Harry. 2015. *On Inequality*. Princeton, NJ: Princeton University Press.

Freeland, Chrystia. 2012. *Plutocrats: The Rise of the New Global Super-Rich and the Fall of Everyone Else*. New York, NY: Penguin Press.

Freeman, Richard. 2010. "It's Financialization," *International Labour Review*, vol. 149, no. 2, pp. 165–183.

Freund, Caroline. 2016. *Rich People, Poor Countries: The Rise of Emerging-Market Tycoons and Their Mega Firms*. Washington, DC: Peterson Institute for International Economics.

Frieden, Jeffry. 2006. *Global Capitalism: Its Fall and Rise in the Twentieth Century*. New York, NY: W. W. Norton.

Friedman, Thomas. 2005. *The World Is Flat: A Brief History of the Twenty-First Century*. New York, NY: Farrar, Straus and Giroux.

Fukuyama, Francis. 2014. *Political Order and Political Decay: From the Industrial Revolution to the Globalization of Democracy*. New York, NY: Farrar, Straus and Giroux.

2012. "The Future of History: Can Liberal Democracy Survive and Decline of the Middle Class?" *Foreign Affairs*, vol. 91, no. 1, January–February, pp. 53–61.

2011. "Left Out," *The American Interest*, vol. 6, no. 3. www.the-american-interest .com/article-bd.cfm?piece=906.

Furman, Jason. 2016. "Norms and Sources of Inequality in the United States," March 17, http://voxeu.org/article/forms-and-sources-inequality-united-states (accessed November 30, 2016).

Galbraith, James. 2012. *Inequality and Instability: A Study of the World Economy Just before the Great Crisis*. New York, NY: Oxford University Press.

Gao, Qin. 2017. *Welfare, Work and Poverty: Social Assistance in China*. New York, NY: Oxford University Press.

Garon, Sheldon. 2011. *Beyond Our Means: Why America Spends While the World Saves*. Princeton, NJ: Princeton University Press.

Gertler, Paul, Sebastian Martinez, and Marta Rubio-Codina. 2012. "Investing Cash Transfers to Raise Long-Term Living Standards," *American Economic Journal: Applied Economics*, vol. 4, no. 1, pp. 164–192.

Ghemawat, Pankaj and Thomas Hout. 2016. "Can China's Companies Conquer the World?," *Foreign Affairs*, vol. 95, no. 2, March/April, pp. 86–98.

Gilens, Martin. 2014. *Affluence and Influence: Economic Inequality and Political Power in America*. Princeton, NJ: Princeton University Press.

1999. *Why Americans Hate Welfare: Race, Media, and the Politics of Antipoverty Policy*. Chicago, IL: University of Chicago Press.

Gilens, Martin and Benjamin Page, 2014. "Testing Theories of American Politics: Elites, Interest Groups, and Average Citizens," *Perspectives on Politics*, vol. 12, September, pp. 564–581.

Gilpin, Robert. 2000. *The Challenge of Global Capitalism: The World Economy in the 21st Century*. Princeton, NJ: Princeton University Press.

Goel, Manisha and Paulina Restrepo-Echavarria. 2015. "India's Atypical Structural Transformation," *Economic Synopses*, no. 23. October, Federal Reserve Bank of St. Louis.

Goetzmann, William N. 2016. *Money Changes Everything: How Finance Made Civilization Possible*. Princeton, NJ: Princeton University Press.

Golan, Jennifer, Terry Sicular, and Nithin Umapathi. 2015. "Unconditional Cash Transfers in China: An Analysis of the Rural Minimum Living Standard Guarantee Program," Policy Research Working Paper, WPS7374, World Bank: Social Protection and Labor Global Practice Group.

Goldin, Claudia and Lawrence Katz. 2008. *The Race between Education and Technology*. Cambridge, MA: Harvard University Press.

2007. "Long-Run Changes in the Wage Structure: Narrowing, Widening, Polarizing," *Brookings Papers on Economic Activity*, vol. 38, no. 2, pp. 135–168, Brookings Institution: Economic Studies Program.

Goldstein, Morris and Nicholas Lardy. 2005. "China's Role in the Revived Bretton Woods System: A Case of Mistaken Identity," Working Paper, 05-2, Washington, DC: Peterson Institute for International Economics.

Gordon, Robert. 2016. *The Rise and Fall of American Growth: The U.S. Standard of Living since the Civil War*. Princeton, NJ: Princeton University Press.

Gourevitch, Peter. 1986. *Politics in Hard Times: Comparative Responses to International Economic Crises*. Ithaca, NY: Cornell University Press.

Government of India. 2014. "Employment and Unemployment Situation in India 2011–2012, Report 554, NSS 68th Round." New Delhi: Government of India, National Sample Survey Office, Ministry of Statistics and Programme Implementation.

2013. "Press Note on Poverty Estimates, 2011–12." New Delhi: Planning Commission, July.

2011. *Economic Survey* (various years). New Delhi: Ministry of Finance, Government of India.

Gradstein, Mark and Branko Milanovic. 2004. "Does Liberté = Égalité? A Survey of the Empirical Evidence on the Links between Political Democracy and Income Inequality," *Journal of Economic Surveys*, vol. 18, no. 4, pp. 515–537.

Gray, John. 1999. *False Dawn: The Delusions of Global Capitalism*. New York, NY: New Press.

Green, Russell and Thomas McAuley. 2014. "Four Tough Reforms to Revive the Manufacturing Sector in India," Issue Brief no. 06.25.14. Houston, TX: Rice University: Baker Institute for Public Policy.

Greenspan, Alan. 1998. "The Globalization of Finance," *Cato Journal*, vol. 17, no. 3, Winter, pp. 243–250.

Greenwood, Jeremy. 2014. "Marry Your Like: Assortative Mating and Income Inequality." Working Paper, National Bureau of Economic Research.

Greenwood, Robin and David Scharfstein. 2013. "The Growth of Finance," *Journal of Economic Perspectives*, vol. 27, no. 2, Spring, pp. 3–28.

Gundimeda, Sambaiah. 2016. *Dalit Politics in Contemporary India*. Abingdon: Routledge.

Guo, Kai and Papa N'Diaye. 2009. "Employment Effects of Growth Rebalancing in China," IMF Working Paper, no. 09/169, Washington DC: International Monetary Fund.

Gustafsson, Björn, Li Shi, and Terry Sicular, eds. 2008. *Income Inequality and Public Policy in China*. New York, NY: Cambridge University Press.

Hacker, Jacob and Paul Pierson. 2010. *Winner-Take-All Politics: How Washington Made the Rich Richer – and Turned Its Back on the Middle Class*. New York, NY: Simon and Schuster.

Hall, Peter. 1989. *The Political Power of Economic Ideas: Keynesianism across Nations*. Princeton, NJ: Princeton University Press.

Hall, Peter and David Soskice, eds. 2001. *Varieties of Capitalism: The Institutional Foundations of Comparative Advantage*. New York, NY: Oxford University Press.

Han, Jun, Runjuan Liu and Junsen Zhang. 2012. "Globalization and Wage Inequality: Evidence from Urban China," *Journal of International Economics*, vol. 87, no. 2, July, pp. 288–297.

Hasan, Rana, Nidhi Kapoor, Aashish Mehta, and Asha Sundaram. 2017. "Labor Regulations, Employment and Wages: Evidence from India's Apparel Sector," *Asian Economic Policy Review*, vol. 12, pp. 70–90.

Helleiner, Eric. 1994. *States and the Reemergence of Global Finance*. Ithaca, NY: Cornell University Press.

Hetherington, Marc J. and Jonathan D. Weiler. 2009. *Authoritarianism and Polarization in American Politics*. New York, NY: Cambridge University Press.

Huang, Yasheng. 2008. *Capitalism with Chinese Characteristics: Entrepreneurship and the State*. New York, NY: Cambridge University Press.

Hufbauer, Gary Clyde and Kati Suominen. 2010. *Globalization at Risk: Challenges to Finance and Trade*. New Haven, CT: Yale University Press.

Hufbauer, Gary Clyde and Yee Wong. 2004. "China Bashing" International Economics Policy Briefs, no. PB04-5. Washington, DC: Institute for International Economics.

Humpage, Owen F. and Caroline Herrell. 2009. "Renminbi-Dollar Peg Once Again," *Economic Trends*, Federal Reserve Bank of Cleveland, November 25.

Hung, Ho-fung and Jaime Kucinskas. 2011. "Globalization and Global Inequality: Assessing the Impact of the Rise of China and India, 1980–2005," *American Journal of Sociology*, vol. 116, no. 5, March, pp. 1478–1513.

Huntington, Samuel. 1968. *Political Order in Changing Societies*. New Haven, CT: Yale University Press.

International Monetary Fund (IMF). 2017. *Brazil: Selected Issues*, IMF Country Report No. 17/216, July. Washington, DC: International Monetary Fund.

2016. *Regional Economic Outlook: Asia and Pacific – Building on Asia's Strengths during Turbulent Times*. Washington, DC: International Monetary Fund.

2015. *World Economic Outlook*. Washington, DC: International Monetary Fund.

2014. "Fiscal Policy and Income Inequality," IMF Policy Paper, January 23, Washington, DC: International Monetary Fund. www.imf.org/external/pp/ppindex.aspx.

2013. "People's Republic of China: Staff Report for the 2013 Article IV Consultation," *Country Report No. 13/211*, July. Washington, DC: International Monetary Fund. www.imf.org/external/np/sec/pr/2013/pdf/pr13192an.pdf.

Iversen, Torben. 2005. *Capitalism, Democracy, and Welfare.* New York, NY: Cambridge University Press.

1999. *Contested Economic Institutions: The Politics of Macroeconomics and Wage Bargaining in Advanced Democracies.* New York, NY: Cambridge University Press.

Jaimovich, Nir and Henry Siu, 2012. "The Trend Is the Cycle: Job Polarization and Jobless Recoveries," NBER Working Paper No. 18334. National Bureau of Economic Research, August, pp. 1–36.

Janeway, William. 2012. *Doing Capitalism in the Innovation Economy.* New York, NY: Cambridge University Press.

Jaumotte, Florence, Subir Lall, and Chris Papageorgiou. 2013. "Rising Income Inequality: Technology, or Trade and Financial Globalization?," *IMF Economic Review,* vol. 61, no. 2, pp. 271–309.

Jayadev, Arjun, Sripad Motiram, and Vamsi Vakulabharanam, 2007. "Patterns of Wealth Disparities in India during the Liberalisation Era," *Economic and Political Weekly,* vol. 42, no. 38, September 22, pp. 3853–3863.

Johnson, Simon and James Kwak. 2010. *13 Bankers: The Wall Street Takeover and the Next Financial Meltdown.* New York, NY: Vintage.

Jones, Daniel Stedman. 2012. *Masters of the Universe: Hayek, Friedman and the Birth of Neoliberal Politics.* Princeton, NJ: Princeton University Press.

Joumard, Isabelle, Urban Sila, and Hermes Morgavi. 2015. "Challenges and Opportunities of India's Manufacturing Sector," OECD Economics Department Working Papers, no. 1183, Paris: OECD Publishing. http://dx.doi.org/10.1787/5js7t9q14moq-en

Kalleberg, Arne. 2011. *Good Jobs, Bad Jobs: The Rise of Polarized and Precarious Employment Systems in the United States, 1970s to 2000s.* New York, NY: Russel Sage Foundation.

Kanbur, Ravi and Zhang Xiaobo. 2005. "Fifty Years of Regional Inequality in China: A Journey through Central Planning, Reform and Openness." *Review of Development Economics,* vol. 9, no. 1, pp. 87–106.

Kapur, Devesh and Prakirti Nangia. 2015. "Social Protection in India: A Welfare State Sans Public Goods?," *India Review,* vol. 14, no. 1, pp. 73–90.

Kay, John. 2015. *Other People's Money: The Real Business of Finance.* New York, NY: PublicAffairs.

Keister, Lisa. 2014. "The One Percent," *Annual Review of Sociology,* vol. 40, pp. 347–367, 10.1146/annurev-soc-070513-075314.

Kelly, Nathan. 2009. *The Politics of Income Inequality in the United States.* New York, NY: Cambridge University Press.

Kenny, Charles. 2011. *Getting Better: Why Global Development Is Succeeding – and How We Can Improve the World Even More.* New York, NY: Basic Books.

Keohane, Robert. 1984. *After Hegemony: Cooperation and Discord in the World Political Economy.* Princeton, NJ: Princeton University Press.

Khanna, Parag. 2008. *The Second World: How Emerging Powers Are Redefining Global Competition in the 21st Century.* New York, NY: Random House.

Kirshner, Jonathan. 1995. *Currency and Coercion: The Political Economy of International Monetary Power.* Princeton, NJ: Princeton University Press.

Kleven, Henrik Jacobsen, Camille Landais, and Emmanuel Saez. 2013. "Taxation and International Migration of Superstars: Evidence from the European Football Market," *American Economic Review,* vol. 103, no. 5, pp. 1892–1924.

Kleven, Henrik Jacobsen, Camille Landais, Emmanuel Saez, and Esben Schultz. 2014. "Migration and Wage Effects of Taxing Top Earners: Evidence from the Foreigners' Tax Scheme in Denmark," *Quarterly Journal of Economics*, vol. 129, no. 1, pp. 333–378.

Knight, John. 2016. "The Societal Cost of China's Rapid Economic Growth," *Asian Economic Papers*, vol. 15, no. 2, Summer, pp. 138–159.

2013. "Inequality in China: An Overview," *The World Bank Research Observer*, vol. 29, no. 1, pp. 1–19.

Knight, John and Ramani Gunatilaka. 2010. "The Rural–Urban Divide in China: Income but Not Happiness?" *Journal of Development Studies*, vol. 46, no. 3, pp. 506–534.

Knight, John and Lina Song. 2005. *Towards a Labour Market in China*. Oxford: London: Oxford University Press.

2003. "Increasing Urban Wage Inequality in China," *Economics of Transition*, vol. 11, no. 4, pp. 597–619.

1999. *The Rural-Urban Divide: Economic Disparities and Interactions in China*. New York, NY: Oxford University Press.

Kocka, Jurgen. 2016. *Capitalism: A Short History*. Princeton, NJ: Princeton University Press.

Kohli, Atul. 2012. *Poverty Amid Plenty in New India*. New York, NY: Cambridge University Press.

Kotz, David. 2015. *The Rise and Fall of Neoliberal Capitalism*. Cambridge, MA: Harvard University Press.

Krippner, Greta. 2011. *Capitalizing on Crisis: The Political Origins of the Rise of Finance*. Cambridge, MA: Harvard University Press.

2005. "The Financialization of the American Economy," *Socio-Economic Review*, vol. 3, no. 2, pp. 173–208.

Krueger, Alan. 2012. "The Rise and Consequences of Inequality in the United States," speech presented at the Center for American Progress (January 12). www.whitehouse.gov/sites/default/files/krueger_cap_speech_final_remarks.pdf.

Krugman, Paul. 2012. *End This Depression Now*. New York, NY: W. W. Norton.

2009. *The Return of Depression Economics and the Crisis of 2008*. New York, NY: W. W. Norton.

2008. *The Return of Depression Economics and the Crisis of 2008*. New York, NY: W. W. Norton.

2007. *The Conscience of a Liberal*. New York, NY: W. W. Norton.

1994. *Peddling Prosperity: Economic Sense and Nonsense in the Age of Diminished Expectations*. New York, NY: W. W. Norton.

Kurlantzick, Joshua. 2016. *State Capitalism: How the Return of Statism Is Transforming the World*. New York, NY: Oxford University Press.

Kuttner, Robert. 2007. *The Squandering of America: How the Failure of Our Politics Undermines Our Prosperity*. New York, NY: Knopf.

Kuznets, Simon. 1955. "Economic Growth and Income Inequality," *American Economic Review*, vol. XLV, no. 1, March, pp. 1–30.

1966. *Modern Economic Growth: Rate, Structure and Spread*. New Haven, CT: Yale University Press.

Kvist, Jon, Johan Fritzell, Bjørn Hvinden and Olli Kangas, eds. 2012. *Changing Social Equality: The Nordic Welfare Model in the 21st Century*. Bristol: Policy Press.

Lam, Raphael and Philippe Wingender. 2015. "China: How Can Revenue Reforms Contribute to Inclusive and Sustainable Growth?" IMF Working Paper, WP/15/66, March, Asia Pacific Department and Fiscal Affairs Department. Washington, DC: International Monetary Fund.

Lapavitsas, Costas. 2014. *Profiting without Producing: How Finance Exploits Us All.* London: Verso.

Lardy, Nicholas. 2015. "False Alarm on a Crisis in China," New York Times, August 26.

2014. *Markets over Mao: The Rise of Private Business in China.* New York, NY: Columbia University Press.

2012. *Sustaining China's Economic Growth after the Global Financial Crisis.* Washington, DC: Peterson Institute for International Economics.

2010. "The Sustainability of China's Recovery from the Global Recession," Policy Brief, no. PB10-7. Washington, DC: Peterson Institute for International Economics.

2008. "Financial Repression in China," Policy Brief, no. PB08-8. Washington, DC: Peterson Institute for International Economics.

2006. China: Toward a Consumption-Driven Growth Path, Policy Briefs in International Economics, no. PB06-6, October, Washington, DC: Institute for International Economics Policy.

2005. "China: The Great New Economic Challenge," in C. Fred Bergsten, ed., *The United States and the World Economy: Foreign Economic Policy for the Next Decade.* Washington, DC: Institute for International Economics.

Lenz, Gabriel S. 2012. *Follow the Leader? How Voters Respond to Politicians' Performance and Policies.* Chicago, IL: University of Chicago Press.

Lewis, Arthur. 1955. *The Theory of Economic Growth.* London: Allen and Unwin.

1954. "Economic Development with Unlimited Supplies of Labour," *The Manchester School,* vol. 22, no. 2, pp. 139–191.

Lee, Chul-In and Gary Solon. 2009. "Trends in Intergenerational Income Mobility." *The Review of Economics and Statistics,* vol. 91, no. 4, pp. 766–772.

Lee, Il Houng, Murtaza Syed, and Xin Wang. 2013. "Two Sides of the Same Coin? Rebalancing and Inclusive Growth in China," IMF Working Paper, 13/185, Washington, DC: International Monetary Fund.

Leutert, Wendy. 2016. "Challenges Ahead in China's Reform of State-Owned Enterprises," *Asia Policy,* no. 21, January, pp. 83–99.

Li, Shi, Chuliang Luo, and Terry Sicular. 2013a. "Overview: Income Inequality and Poverty in China, 2002–2007," in Li Shi, Hiroshi Sato, and Terry Sicular, eds. *Rising Inequality in China: Challenge to a Harmonious Society.* New York, NY: Cambridge University Press.

Li, Shi, Hiroshi Sato, and Terry Sicular, eds. 2013b. *Rising Inequality in China: Challenges to a Harmonious Society.* New York, NY: Cambridge University Press.

Li, Shi and Haiyuan Wan. 2015. "Evolution of Wealth Inequality in China," *China Economic Journal,* vol. 8, no. 3, pp. 264–287.

Liebman, Benjamin and Curtis Milhaupt, eds. 2015. *Regulating the Invisible Hand? The Institutional Implications of Chinese State Capitalism.* New York, NY: Oxford University Press.

Lin, Justin Yifu. 2012a. *The Quest for Prosperity: How Developing Economies Can Take Off.* Princeton, NJ: Princeton University Press.

2012b. *Demystifying the Chinese Economy*. New York, NY: Cambridge University Press.

1992. "Rural Reform and Agricultural Productivity in China," *The American Economic Review*, vol. 82, no. 1, pp. 34–51.

1987. "The Household Responsibility System Reform in China: A Peasant's Institutional Choice," *American Journal of Agricultural Economics*, vol. 69, no. 2, pp. 410–415.

Lin, Ken-Hou and Donald Tomaskovic-Devey. 2013. "Financialization and US Income Inequality, 1970–2008," *American Journal of Sociology*, vol. 118, no. 5, March, pp. 1284–1329.

Lindert, Peter and Jeffrey Williamson. 2016. *Unequal Gains: American Growth and Inequality since 1700*. Princeton, NJ: Princeton University Press.

Ljungqvist, Alexander, Donghua Chen, Dequan Jiang, Haitian Lu, and Mingming Zhou. 2015. "State Capitalism vs. Private Enterprise," NBER Working Paper Series No. 20930, February, www.nber.org/papers/w20930, Cambridge, MA: National Bureau of Economic Research.

Lopez-Calva L. F. and S. Rocha. 2012. *Exiting Belindia? Lessons from the Recent Decline in Income Inequality in Brazil*. Washington, DC: The World Bank (Poverty, Equity and Gender Unit, Latin America and the Caribbean).

Lupu, Noam and Jonas Pontusson. 2011. "The Structure of Inequality and the Politics of Redistribution," *American Political Science Review*, vol. 105, no. 2, pp. 316–336.

Ma, Guonan and Wang Yi. 2011. "Why is the Chinese Saving Rate so High?" *World Economics*, vol. 12, no. 1, January–March, pp. 1–26.

Makin, Anthony J. 2007. "Does China's Huge External Surplus Imply an Undervalued Renminbi?," *China and the World Economy*, vol. 15, no. 3, pp. 89–102.

Malkin, Israel and Mark Spiegel. 2012. "Is China Due for a Slowdown?" FRBSF Economic Letter, October 15, San Francisco, CA: Federal Reserve Bank of San Francisco.

Mankiw, Gregory. 2013. "Defending the One Percent," *Journal of Economic Perspectives*, vol. 27, no. 3, pp. 21–34.

Martin, Fernando. 2016. "A Closer Look at Federal Income Taxes," Economic Synopses, no. 23, November, Federal Reserve Bank of St. Louis.

Martin, Michael. 2015. "What's the Difference? Comparing US and China Trade Data," Washington, DC: Congressional Research Service, May 4, no. RS22640.

Maskin, Eric. 2015. "Why Haven't Global Markets Reduced Inequality in Emerging Economies?" *The World Bank Economic Review*, vol. 29, (supplement), pp. S48–S52.

Mazumdar, Dipak and Sandip Sarkar. 2008. *Globalization, Labor Markets and Inequality in India*. New York, NY: Routledge.

McGregor, James. 2012. *No Ancient Wisdom, No Followers: The Challenges of Chinese Authoritarian Capitalism*. Westport, CT: Prospecta Press.

McKinnon, Ronald. 2005. *Exchange Rates under the East Asian Dollar Standard: Living with Conflicted Virtue*. Cambridge, MA: The MIT Press.

McKissack, Adam and Jessica Xu. 2011. "Chinese Macroeconomic Management through the Crisis and Beyond," *Asian-Pacific Economic Literature*, pp. 43–55.

McNally, Christopher. 2012. "Sino-Capitalism: China's Reemergence and the International Political Economy," *World Politics*, vol. 64, no. 4, pp. 741–776.

Meltzer, Allan and Scott Richard. 1981. "A Rational Theory of the Size of Government," *Journal of Political Economy*, vol. 89, no. 5, pp. 914–927.

Mettler, Susanne. 2014. *Degrees of Inequality: How Higher Education Politics Sabotaged the American Dream.* New York, NY: Basic Books.

Milanovic, Branko. 2016. *Global Inequality: A New Approach for the Age of Globalization.* Cambridge, MA: Harvard University Press.

2011. *The Haves and the Have-Nots: A Brief and Idiosyncratic History of Inequality around the Globe.* New York, NY: Basic Books.

2007. *Worlds Apart: Measuring International and Global Inequality.* Princeton, NJ: Princeton University Press.

Milhaupt, Curtis and Wentong Zheng. 2016. "Why Mixed-Ownership Reforms Cannot Fix China's State Sector," Paulson Policy Memorandum, January. Paulson Institute.

Mishkin, Frederic. 2011. *Macroeconomics: Policy and Practice.* Englewood Cliffs, NJ: Prentice-Hall.

2006. *The Next Great Globalization: How Disadvantaged Nations Can Harness Their Financial Systems to Get Rich.* Princeton, NJ: Princeton University Press.

Montinola, Gabriella, Yingyi Qian, and Barry R. Weingast. 1995. "Federalism, Chinese Style: The Political Basis for Economic Success in China." *World Politics,* vol. 48, no. 1, October, pp. 50–81.

Morrison, Wayne M. and Marc Labonte. 2009. *China's Currency: A Summary of the Economic Issues.* Washington, DC: Congressional Research Service, April 13, no. RS21625.

Motiram, Sripad and Karthikeya Naraparaju. 2015. "Growth and Deprivation in India: What Does Recent Evidence Suggest on "Inclusiveness?," *Oxford Development Studies,* vol. 43, no. 2, pp. 145–164.

Nau, Michael. 2013. "Economic Elites, Investments and Income Inequality," *Social Forces,* vol. 92, no. 2, December, pp. 437–461.

Naughton, Barry. 2009. "In China's Economy, the State's Hand Grows Heavier," *Current History,* vol. 108, no. 719, September, pp. 277–283.

2007. *The Chinese Economy: Transitions and Growth.* Cambridge, MA: MIT Press.

Neumark, David. 2015. "The Effects of Minimum Wages on Employment." FRBSF Economic Letter 2015–37, December 21, San Francisco, CA: Federal Reserve Bank of San Francisco. www.frbsf.org/economic-research/publications/economic-letter/2015/december/effectsof-minimum-wage-on-employment/.

Neumark, David and William L. Wascher. 2008. *Minimum Wages.* Cambridge, MA: Massachusetts Institute of Technology Press.

Noah, Timothy. 2012. *The Great Divergence: America's Growing Inequality Crisis and What We Can Do about It.* New York, NY: Bloomsbury.

OECD. 2011. *Divided We Stand: Why Inequality Keeps Rising,* Paris: OECD Publishing.

Ogle, Vanessa. 2015. *The Global Transformation of Time, 1970–1950.* Cambridge, MA: Harvard University Press.

Okun, Arthur. 1975. *Equality and Efficiency: The Big Tradeoff.* Washington, DC: Brookings Institution Press

Olson, Mancur. 1982. *The Rise and Decline of Nations: Economic Growth, Stagnation and Social Rigidities.* New Haven, CT: Yale University Press.

Ostry, Jonathan, Andrew Berg, and Charalambos Tsangarides. 2014. "Redistribution, Inequality and Growth," IMF Staff Discussion Note, no. SDN/14/02, February, Washington, DC: International Monetary Fund.

OXFAM. 2013. *Working for the Few: Political Capture and Economic Inequality.* Oxford: OXFAM Great Britain.

Page, Benjamin, Larry M. Bartels, and Jason Seawright. 2013. "Democracy and the Policy Preferences of Wealthy Americans," *Perspectives on Politics*, vol. 11, no. 1, pp. 51–73.

Palmer, Andrew. 2015. *Smart Money: How High-Stakes Financial Innovation Is Reshaping Our World – for the Better*. New York, NY: Basic Books.

Panagariya, Arvind. 2013. "Indian Economy: Retrospect and Prospect," Richard Snape Lecture, Melbourne, 6 November, Canberra: Productivity Commission.

 2010. "Growing out of Poverty," *Finance and Development*, September, vol. 47, no. 3, pp. 22–23.

Panitch, Leo and Sam Gindin. 2012. *The Making of Global Capitalism: The Political Economy of American Empire*. London: Verso.

Park, Albert and Dewen Wang. 2010, "Migration and Urban Poverty and Inequality in China," *China Economic Journal*, vol. 3, no. 1, pp. 49–67.

Pei, Minxin. 2016. *China's Crony Capitalism: The Dynamics of Regime Decay*. Cambridge, MA: Harvard University Press.

Philipsen, Dirk. 2015. *The Little Big Number: How GDP Came to Rule the World and What to Do about It*. Princeton, NJ: Princeton University Press.

Pierce, Justin R. and Peter K. Schott. 2016. "The Surprisingly Swift Decline of US Manufacturing Employment." *American Economic Review*, vol. 106, no. 7, pp. 1632–1662.

Piereson, James. 2015. "Background Facts," in Tom Church, Chris Miller and John B. Taylor, eds., *Inequality and Economic Policy: Essays in the Memory of Gary Becker*. Stanford, CA: Hoover Institution Press, pp. 1–16.

Pierson, Paul. 1994. *Dismantling the Welfare State? Reagan, Thatcher, and the Politics of Retrenchment*. New York, NY: Cambridge University Press.

Piketty, Thomas. 2014. *Capital in the Twentieth-First Century*, translated from the French by Arthur Goldhammer. Cambridge, MA: Belknap Press/Harvard University Press.

Piketty, Thomas and Emmanuel Saez. 2003. "Income Inequality in the United States, 1913–1998." *Quarterly Journal of Economics*, vol. 118, no. 1, pp. 1–39 (for data updated to 2011, see Saez, http://elsa.berkeley.edu/~saez).

Polanyi, Karl. 1944. *The Great Transformation*. New York, NY: Farrar and Rinehart.

Pontusson, Jonas. 2005. *Inequality and Prosperity: Social Europe versus Liberal America*. Ithaca, NY: Cornell University Press.

Posner, Richard. 2010. *The Crisis of Capitalist Democracy*. Cambridge, MA: Harvard University Press.

 2009. *A Failure of Capitalism: The Crisis of '08 and the Descent into Depression*. Cambridge, MA: Harvard University Press.

Prasad, Eswar. 2014. *The Dollar Trap: How the U.S. Dollar Tightened its Grip on Global Finance*. Princeton, NJ: Princeton University Press.

Prasad, Monica. 2012. *The Land of Too Much: American Abundance and the Paradox of Poverty*. Cambridge, MA: Harvard University Press.

Putnam, Robert. 1993. *Making Democracies Work: Civic Traditions in Modern Italy*. Princeton, NJ: Princeton University Press.

Qian, Yingyi and Barry Weingast. 1997. "Federalism as a Commitment to Preserving Market Incentives," *The Journal of Economic Perspectives*, vol. 11, no. 4, pp. 83–92.

Radelet, Steven. 2016. "Prosperity Rising: The Success of Global Development – and How to Keep It Going," *Foreign Affairs*, vol. 95, no. 1, January–February, pp. 85–95.

2015. *The Great Surge: The Ascent of the Developing World.* New York, NY: Simon and Schuster.

Rajan, Raghuram. 2010. *Fault Lines: How Hidden Fractures Still Threaten the World Economy*, Princeton, NJ: Princeton University Press.

2005. "Has Financial Development Made the World Riskier?," *The Greenspan Era: Lessons for the Future.* Kansas City, MO: Federal Reserve Bank of Kansas, pp. 313–369.

Rajan, Raghuram and Luigi Zingales. 2003. *Saving Capitalism from the Capitalists: Unleashing the Power of Financial Markets to Create Wealth and Spread Opportunity.* New York, NY: Crown Publishing Group.

Rao, Govinda M. 2015. "Economic reform needed to achieve Modi's 'Make in India' Slogan," East Asia Forum, Economics, Politics and Public Policy in East Asia and the Pacific, September 10. www.eastasiaforum.org.

Ravallion, Martin. 2016. *The Economics of Poverty: History, Measurement and Policy.* New York, NY: Oxford University Press.

2013. "How Long Will It Take to Lift One Billion People Out of Poverty?" *The World Bank Research Observer*, vol. 28, no. 2, August 2013, pp. 139–158.

2011. "A Comparative Perspective on Poverty Reduction in Brazil, China and India," *World Bank Research Observer*, vol. 26, no. 1, pp. 71–104.

2009. "Bailing out the World's Poorest," *Challenge*, vol. 52, no. 2, March/April, pp. 55–80.

Ravallion, Martin and Shaohua Chen. 2007. "China's (Uneven) Progress against Poverty," *Journal of Development Economics*, vol. 82, no. 1, pp. 1–42.

Reeves, Richard. 2017. *Dream Hoarders: How the American Upper Middle Class Is Leaving Everyone Else in the Dust, Why This Is a Problem, and What to Do about It.* Washington, DC: Brookings Institution Press.

Reinhart, Carmen and Kenneth Rogoff. 2009. *This Time Is Different: Eight Centuries of Financial Folly.* Princeton, NJ: Princeton University Press.

Riskin, Carl. 2014. "Trends in Income Inequality in China since the 1950s," in G. C. Chow and D. H. Perkins, eds., *Routledge Handbook of the Chinese Economy*, Abingdon: Routledge.

Roberts, Kevin. 1977. "Voting over Income Tax Schedules," *Journal of Public Economics*, vol. 8, pp. 329–340.

Rodrik, Dani. 2011. *The Globalization Paradox: Why Global Markets, States, and Democracy Can't Coexist.* New York, NY: Oxford University Press.

2007. *One Economics, Many Recipes: Globalization, Institutions and Economic Growth*, Princeton, NJ: Princeton University Press.

1999. "Democracies Pay Higher Wages," *Quarterly Journal of Economics*, vol. 114, no. 3, pp. 707–738.

Roemer, John. 1998. *Equality of Opportunity.* Cambridge, MA: Harvard University Press.

Romer, Thomas. 1975. "Individual Welfare, Majority Voting and the Properties of the Linear Income Tax," *Journal of Public Economics*, vol. 7, pp. 163–168.

Rostow, Walt W. 1960. *The Stages of Economic Growth: A Non-Communist Manifesto.* New York, NY: Cambridge University Press.

Rudolph, Lloyd and Susanne Rudolph. 1987. *In Pursuit of Lakshmi: The Political Economy of the Indian State.* Chicago, IL: Chicago University Press.

Rui, Huaichuan and George S. Yip. 2008. "Foreign Acquisitions by Chinese Firms: A Strategic Intent Perspective," *Journal of World Business*, vol. 43, pp. 213–226.

Sachs, Jeffrey. 2009. "Achieving Global Cooperation on Economic Recovery and Long-Term Sustainable Development," *Asian Development Review*, vol. 26, no. 1, pp. 3–15.

2005. *The End of Poverty: Economic Possibilities of Our Time.* New York, NY: Penguin.

Saez, Emmanuel and Gabriel Zucman, 2014. "Wealth Inequality in the United States since 1913: Evidence from Capitalized Income Tax Data," NBER Working Paper No. 20625, October. Cambridge, MA: National Bureau of Economics Research. www.nber.org/papers/w 1920625 (accessed September 29, 2015).

Sahoo, Pravakar, Niloptal Goswami, and Rahul Mazumdar. 2017. "Trade Facilitation: Must for India's Trade Competitiveness," *Journal of World Trade*, vol. 51, no. 2, pp. 285–307.

Schattschneider, E. E. 1960. *The Semi-Sovereign People: A Realist's View of Democracy in America.* Chicago, IL: Holt, Reinhardt, and Winston.

Scheidel, Walter. 2017. *The Great Leveler: Violence and the History of Inequality from the Stone Age to the Twenty-First Century.* Princeton, NJ: Princeton University Press.

Scheve, Kenneth and David Stasavage. 2012. "Democracy, War, and Wealth: Lessons from Two Centuries of Inheritance Taxation," *American Political Science Review*, vol. 106, no. 1, pp. 82–102.

Schlozman, Kay Lehman, Sidney Verba, and Henry Brady. 2012. *The Unheavenly Chorus: Unequal Political Voice and the Broken Promise of American Democracy.* Princeton, NJ: Princeton University Press.

Schortgen, Francis and Shalendra Sharma. 2012. "Manufacturing Dissent: Domestic and International Ramifications of China's Summer of Labor Unrest," *ProtoSociology: A journal of Interdisciplinary Project*, vol. 29, pp. 77–98.

Schumpeter, Joseph. 1942. *Capitalism, Socialism and Democracy.* New York, NY: Harper.

Scott, Robert. 2014. "Hearing on U.S.-China Economic Challenges: The Impact of U.S.-China Trade," Washington, DC: Economic Policy Institute, February 21.

Sen, Amartya. 2015. *The Country of First Boys.* New York, NY: Oxford University Press.

2013. "Why India Trails China," The New York Times, June 20, p. A27.

2011. "Putting Growth in Its Place," *Outlook India*, November 14, p. 7.

1999. *Development as Freedom.* New York, NY: Oxford University Press.

Setser, Brad. 2008a. *Sovereign Wealth and Sovereign Power: The Strategic Consequences of American Indebtedness.* New York, NY: Council on Foreign Relations Press.

2008b. "China: Creditor to the Rich," *China Security*, vol. 14, no. 4, Autumn.

Shiller, Robert. 2012. *Finance and the Good Society.* Princeton, NJ: Princeton University Press.

2008. *The Subprime Solution: How Today's Global Financial Crisis Happened, and What to Do about It.* Princeton, NJ: Princeton University Press.

Sharma, Shalendra. 2014a. *Global Financial Contagion: Building a Resilient World Economy after the Subprime Crisis.* New York, NY: Cambridge University Press.

2014b. "Shadow Banking: Chinese Style," *Economic Affairs: A Journal of Liberal Political Economy*, vol. 34, no. 3, October, pp. 340–352.

Sharma, Vivek. 2015. "The Myth of a Liberal India," *National Interest*, November–December. http://nationalinterest.org/feature/the-myth-liberal-india-14103 (accessed November 15, 2015).

Shonfield, Andrew. 1965. *Modern Capitalism: The Changing Balance of Public and Private Power*. New York, NY: Oxford University Press.

Solow, Robert. 1956. "A Contribution to the Theory of Economic Growth," *Quarterly Journal of Economics*, vol. 70, no. 1, February, pp. 65–94.

Son, Hyun. 2013. "Inequality of Human Opportunities in Developing Asia," *Asian Development Review*, vol. 30, no. 2, pp. 110–130.

Song, Yang. 2013. "Rising Chinese Regional Income Inequality: The Role of Fiscal Decentralization," *China Economic Review*, vol. 27, pp. 294–309.

Song, Zheng, Kjetil Storesletten, and Fabrizio Zilibotti. 2011. "Growing Like China," *American Economic Review*, 101, February, pp. 202–241.

Spiegel, Mark. 2015. "Global Fallout from China's Industrial Slowdown," FRBSF Economic Letter, Pacific Basin Note, November 23. San Francisco, CA: Federal Reserve Bank of San Francisco. www.frbsf.org/economic-research/files/el2015-35.pdf.

Stein, Judith. 2011. *Pivotal Decade: How the United States Traded Factories for Finance in the Seventies*. New Haven, CT: Yale University Press.

Stiglitz, Joseph. 2012. *The Price of Inequality: How Today's Divided Society Endangers Our Future*. New York, NY: W. W. Norton.

　　2010. *Freefall: America, Free Markets, and the Sinking of the World Economy*. New York, NY: W. W. Norton.

　　2008. "China: Towards a New Model of Development," *China Economic Journal*, vol. 1, no. 1, February, pp. 33–52.

　　2002. *Globalization and Its Discontents*. New York, NY: W.W. Norton.

Stigler, George. 1970. "Director's Law of Public Income Redistribution," *Journal of Law and Economics*, no. 13, pp. 1–10.

Streeck, Wolfgang. 2014. *Buying Time: The Delayed Crisis of Democratic Capitalism*. London: Verso.

Subramanian, Arvind. 2013. "Why India's Economy Is Stumbling," The New York Times, August 31, p. A19.

　　2011. *Eclipse: Living in the Shadow of China's Economic Dominance*. Washington, DC: Peterson Institute for International Economics.

　　2010. "New PPP-Based Estimates of Renminbi Undervaluation and Policy Implications," Policy Brief, no. PB10-8, April. Washington, DC: Peterson Institute for International Economics.

Susskind, Richard and Daniel Susskind. 2015. *The Future of the Professions: How Technology Will Transform the Work of Human Experts*. London: Oxford University Press.

Thomas, Jayan Jose. 2013. "Explaining the 'Jobless' Growth in Indian Manufacturing," *Journal of the Asia Pacific Economy*, vol. 18, no. 4, pp. 673–692.

Thorat, Sukhadeo and Amaresh Dubey. 2012. "Has Growth Been Socially Inclusive during 1993–94 – 2009–10?," *Economic and Political Weekly*, vol. XLVII, no. 10, March, pp. 43–54.

Tian, Wei, Liugang Sheng, and Hongyan Zhao. 2015. "State Capitalism: A New Perspective on Land Sale in China," *Pacific Economic Review*, vol. 21, no. 1, pp. 84–101.

Tomaskovic-Devey, Donald and Ken-Hou Lin. 2011. "Income Dynamics, Economic Rents, and the Financialization of the US Economy," *American Sociological Review*, vol. 76, no. 4, pp. 538–559.

Tsai, Kellie. 2007. *Capitalism without Democracy: The Private Sector in Contemporary China*. Ithaca, NY: Cornell University Press.

Tyson, Laura and Anu Madgavkar. 2016. "The Great Income Stagnation," Project Syndicate, September 7. www.project-syndicate.org/commentary/stagnating-wages-advanced-economies-by-laura-tyson-and-anu-madgavkar-2016–09 (accessed October 28, 2016).

United Nations. 2015. *Millennium Development Goals Report 2015*. New York, NY: United Nations.

Vance, J. D. 2016. *Hillbilly Elegy: A Memoir of a Family and Culture in Crisis*. New York, NY: Harper.

Wan, Guanghua. 2008. *Understanding Inequality and Poverty in China*. Tokyo: United Nations University.

2007. "Understanding Regional Poverty and Inequality Trends in China: Methodological Issues and Empirical Findings," *Review of Income and Wealth*, vol. 53, no. 1, pp. 25–34.

Wan, Guanghua, Lu, Ming, and Chen, Zhao. 2007. "Globalization and Regional Income Inequality: Empirical Evidence from within China," *Review of Income and Wealth*, vol. 53, no. 1, pp. 35–59.

Wang, Xiaobing and Jenifer Piesse. 2010. "Inequality and the Urban–rural Divide in China: Effects of Regressive Taxation." *China and the World Economy*, vol. 18, no. 6, November–December, pp. 36–55.

Wang, Xin. 2007. "China as s Net Creditor: An Indication of Strength or Weaknesses?" *China and World Economy*, vol. 15, no. 6, December, pp. 22–36.

Wang, Yuhua. 2016. "Beyond Local Protectionism: China's State–Business Relations in the Last Two Decades," *The China Quarterly*, vol. 226, June, pp. 319–341.

WEF (World Economic Forum). 2014. *Global Risks 2014, Ninth Edition*, World Economic Forum. Geneva, Switzerland.

Wen, Yi and Jing Wu. 2014. "Withstanding Great Recession Like China," Working Paper 2014-007A. St. Louis, MO: Federal Reserve Bank of St. Louis.

Western, Bruce and Jake Rosenfeld. 2011. "Unions, Norms, and the Rise in US Wage Inequality," *American Sociological Review*, vol. 76, no. 4, pp. 513–537.

Whyte, Martin. 2010. *Myth of a Social Volcano: Perceptions of Inequality and Distributive Injustice in Contemporary China*. Stanford, CA: Stanford University Press.

Wilkinson, Richard and Kate Pickett. 2009. *The Spirit Level: Why More Equal Societies Almost Always Do Better*. London: Allen Lane.

Winters, Alan and Shahid Yusuf, eds. 2007. *Dancing with Giants: China, India, and the Global Economy*. Washington, DC: The World Bank.

Wolf, Martin. 2008. *Fixing Global Finance*. Baltimore, MD: John Hopkins University Press.

World Bank. 2015. *Our World in Data, 2015*. New York, NY: World Bank.

2013. "Time to Export (days)," *Doing Business Project* (various years). Washington, DC: The World. https://data.worldbank.org/indicator/IC.EXP.DURS.

2012. *China 2030: Building a Modern, Harmonious, and Creative High-Income Society*, Washington, DC: The World Bank.

2009. *From Poor Areas to Poor People: China's Evolving Poverty Reduction Agenda, an Assessment of Poverty and Inequality in China.* Washington, DC: World Bank.

WTO (World Trade Organization). 2015. *International Trade Statistics 2015.* Geneva: World Trade Organization.

Wu, Xun. 2016. "China's Growing Local Government Debt Levels," *Policy Brief,* January, MIT Center for Finance and Policy. Cambridge, MA: Massachusetts Institute of Technology, pp. 1–10.

Xie, Yu and Yongai Jin. 2015. "Household Wealth in China," *Chinese Sociological Review,* vol. 47, no. 3, pp. 203–229.

Xing, Yuqing. 2016. "Global Value Chains and China's Exports to High-income Countries," *International Economic Journal,* vol. 30, no. 2, pp. 191–203.

Yang, Dennis Tao. 1999. "Urban-Biased Policies and Rising Income Inequality in China," *The American Economic Review,* vol. 89, no. 2, pp. 306–310.

Yu, Luo and Frank Zhu, 2014. "Financialization of the Economy and Income Inequality in China," *Economic and Political Studies,* vol. 2, no. 2.

Yu, Yongding. 2010. "Asia: China's Policy Response to the Global Financial Crisis," *Journal of Globalization and Development,* vol. 1, no. 1, pp. 1–10.

Zagha, Roberto. 2013. "India's Inequality: An Uneasy Reconciliation with Economic Growth," *Current History,* April, pp. 137–145.

Zakaria, Fareed. 2008. *The Post-American World.* New York, NY: W. W. Norton.

2003. *The Future of Freedom: Illiberal Democracy at Home and Abroad.* New York, NY: W. W. Norton.

Zhang, Yuanyan Sophia and Steven Barnett. 2014. "Fiscal Vulnerabilities and Risks from Local Government Finance in China," IMF Working Paper, WP/14/4, January. Fiscal Affairs Department and Asia and Pacific Department, Washington, DC: International Monetary Fund.

Zhou, Yixiao and Ligang Song. 2016. "Income Inequality in China: Causes and Policy Responses," *China Economic Journal,* vol. 9, no. 2, pp. 186–208.

Zhuang, Juzhong. 2012. "How China can avoid the middle income trap." *South China Morning Post,* 12 November. www.scmp.com/comment/insight-opinion/article/1080040/how-china-can-avoid-middle-income-trap (accessed April 4, 2013).

Zhuang, Juzhong and Li Shi. 2016. "Understanding Recent Trends in Income Inequality in the People's Republic of China," no. 489, July, ADB Economics Working Paper Series, Manila: Asian Development Bank.

Zingales, Luigi. 2012. *A Capitalism for the People: Recapturing the Lost Genius of American Prosperity.* New York, NY: Basic Books.

2009. "Capitalism after the Crisis," *National Affairs,* vol. 1, Fall, pp. 22–35.

Index

majoritarian democracy, 143
male labor earnings, 37
manufacturing sector
    China, 128–129, 164
    employment in, 128
    India, 123, 124–133, 125*t*, 126–127*f*
marginal income tax rate, 161
market-oriented exchange rate, 71
Marx, Karl, 3–4
Maskin, Eric, 62
McKinsey Global Institute report, 128
median household incomes, 48, 160
median voter, 52
Medicare, 58
mergers and acquisitions (M&A), 109
middle class
    adjusted income of, 16
    adverse consequences to, 17
    in China, 32
    easy credit and, 56
    economic losses of, 61, 62
    global middle class, 15–16
    political power to, 12, 52
    rapid expansion of, 9
    reduction in, 51–52
    in US, 36, 51
middle-income country, 111–112
middle-income trap, 111
middle-skilled occupations, 51
migrant rural labor, 89, 92, 164
minimum wage
    in Brazil, 167
    case for raising, 155, 156
    declines in employment and, 155
    decrease in, 40, 43
    in India, 165
    taxation and, 12
minority discrimination, 31
Minxin Pei, 90
mixed ownership, 112
Modi, Narendra, 131–132, 144, 165–166
*Money Changes Everything: How Finance
    Made Civilization Possible* report, 27
mortgage debt, 110
mortgage interest deductions, 161
municipal governments, 23
Muslim community, 147

Narasimbha Rao, P.V., 148
National Association of Manufacturers, 136
National Food Security Act (NFSA),
    122, 150

National Institution for Transforming India
    (NITI), 131
National Manufacturing Policy (NMP), 131
National Rural Livelihood Mission, 122
National Sample Survey Office (NSSO), 118
neighborhood inequality, 156
neo-corporatism, 22
neo-mercantilist economic policies, 102
neoclassical convergence growth theory, 8
neoliberal capitalism, 10, 21
New Deal era, 55
non-performing loans (NPLs), 91
non-salaried compensation, 5
non-standard employment practices, 40
nonagricultural employment, 86
Nunes, Devin, 136

Obama, Barack, 1–2, 43, 53, 70, 71, 72, 137
Occupy Wall Street movement, 1, 27
off-budget revenue sources, 95
Okun, Arthur, 6, 155
Olson, Mancur, 53
"One Belt, One Road," initiative, 110
one-percenters, defined, 46
open markets, 19, 23, 26, 65, 140, 142,
    150, 155
Oportunidades program, 168
Other Backward Castes (OBCs), 144, 148. *See
    also* backward castes
*Other People's Money: The Real Business of
    Finance* (Kay), 27

Pareto criterion, 6
participatory democracy, 162
particularism, 32, 55, 144, 146
People's Bank of China (PBC), 68, 98
People's Republic of China (PRC). *See* China
Pierson, Paul, 56–57
Piketty, Thomas, 3, 4, 10, 21–22, 154, 160
Plaza Accords (1985), 78
pluralism, 147, 154
political decay, 154
political economy theory, 12
political institutionalization, 145
*Political Order and Political Decay: From the
    Industrial Revolution to the Globalization
    of Democracy* (Fukuyama), 54–55
politics
    of China, 89–98, 162–164
    citizen political participation, 59–60
    democratic politics, 141–148
    economic globalization and, 120